Frederick Warren Grover

A practical Treatise on modern gas and oil Engines

Frederick Warren Grover

A practical Treatise on modern gas and oil Engines

ISBN/EAN: 9783743332300

Manufactured in Europe, USA, Canada, Australia, Japa

Cover: Foto ©ninafisch / pixelio.de

Manufactured and distributed by brebook publishing software (www.brebook.com)

Frederick Warren Grover

A practical Treatise on modern gas and oil Engines

A PRACTICAL TREATISE

ON

MODERN GAS AND OIL ENGINES

BY

FREDERICK GROVER, A.M.Inst.C.E., M.I.Mech.E.,

Consulting Engineer, Leeds.

(SECOND EDITION.)

PRICE FOUR SHILLINGS AND SIXPENCE NET.

1897.
THE TECHNICAL PUBLISHING CO. LIMITED,
31, WHITWORTH STREET, MANCHESTER.
JOHN HEYWOOD,
29 AND 30, SHOE LANE, LONDON; AND RIDGEFIELD, MANCHESTER;
And all Booksellers.

PREFACE.

In writing these pages I have endeavoured to supply to the average mechanical draughtsman the information necessary to enable him to apply his art to the design of gas engines. A real knowledge of the elements of machines can only be acquired in the fitting and erecting shops. There the eye is trained and a sense of proportion developed which is always helpful in the design of new patterns. Unless, however, a draughtsman thoroughly understands the principles which underlie his art, he is liable to errors which prove themselves as costly as those made by the mere theorist.

In developing the conception of the work before me, I have first described the general arrangement of a gas-engine plant, then the types of modern gas engines, and have afterwards attempted to explain how their leading dimensions may be calculated.

The importance of systematic testing is now felt by many engineers. I have therefore described in detail the apparatus required and the calculations necessary to make a complete gas-engine trial. In connection with this subject a chapter is added on the practical analysis of gases.

The first part of the book concludes with a description of a series of experiments made to determine the effects of products of combustion when present in explosive mixtures of coal gas and air. Some doubt has been expressed as to the accuracy of the conclusions drawn from these experiments, on the ground that the mixing of the gases was imperfect. Having regard to the fact that at least one minute of time elapsed between filling the vessel and igniting the charge, whereas in a gas engine running at 180 revolutions per minute only one-third of a second elapses, I think it improbable that the diffusion of products of combustion in a gas-engine cylinder is more perfect than in my experimental apparatus, notwithstanding the wide difference between the conditions.

In the second part of the book a brief description is given of the physical properties of oils, of oil-engine vaporisers, and a few special points in connection with oil-engine testing.

In conclusion, I desire to express my thanks to the following firms for their kindness in assisting me: Messrs. Crossley; Andrews; Dick, Kerr, and Co.; Tangye, Fielding, Wells Brothers, Barker, Dougill, Crosby, Globe Engineering Co., Priestman, and Elliott Brothers. I also desire to acknowledge the assistance I have derived from the works of Professor William Robinson, Professor Unwin, Mr. Bryan Donkin, Mr. Dugald Clerk, and from Professor Capper's report on the Royal Agricultural Society's Trials, held at Cambridge.

F. G.

Leeds,
July, 1897.

CONTENTS.

Chapter I.
Introduction 1

Chapter II.
Arrangement of Engine-room 7

Chapter III.
Types of Gas Engines: Atkinson's "Differential" and "Cycle" Engines — Comparative Cycles of Gas Engines — The Crossley Engine — The "Stockport" Gas Engines 19

Chapter IV.
The "Griffin" Engine 46

Chapter V.
The Tangye Engine — The Fielding Gas Engine — The "Premier" Gas Engine 53

Chapter VI.
Self-starters 71

Chapter VII.
Two-cycle and other Engines 77

Chapter VIII.
French Engines: Simplex Gas Engines — Lenoir Engine — Charon Engine — Niel Engine — Lalbin Engine. German Engines: Benz Engine — Koerting-Lieckfeldt Engine — The Daimler Gas Engine — The Capitaine Gas Engine 86

Chapter IX.
Testing Gas Engines: Indicating 92

Chapter X.
Indicators for Gas Engines: Crosby Indicator — The Tabor Indicator — The Wayne Indicator — The Simplex Indicator 99

Chapter XI.
Reducing Gear for Gas Engines 109

Chapter XII.
Gas-engine Trials 114

CONTENTS.

Chapter XIII.
The Practical Analysis of Coal Gas 126

Chapter XIV.
Calculations Required in Working Out Results of Engine Trials 139

Chapter XV.
Calculations on the Indicator Diagram 144

Chapter XVI.
Gas-engine Trial, Otto Cycle: Coal Gas Used 154

Chapter XVII.
Gas-engine Design 159

Chapter XVIII.
Producer Gas, and its Application to Gas Engines 176

Chapter XIX.
The Effects of the Products of Combustion upon Explosive Mixtures of Coal Gas and Air 183

Appendices to Part I. 200

PART II.—PETROLEUM ENGINES.

Chapter XX.
Petroleum 205

Chapter XXI.
Oil Engines: Priestman's, Griffin's, Hornsby-Akroyd, Crossley's, Wells', Trusty 215

Chapter XXII.
Oil Engines: Campbell's, Britannia, Capitaine, Fielding, The Daimler Motor. 231

Chapter XXIII.
Oil Engine Testing 241

MODERN GAS ENGINES.

CHAPTER I.

INTRODUCTION.

In writing upon the subject of modern gas engines, it may at first be thought that an historical preface is out of place; but in glancing through the records of progress made during the last 35 years, it is remarkable how many of the improvements we are apt to regard as new are merely the embodiment of suggestions made by those engaged in bringing the gas engine into practical use. In more than one instance has an important advance been entirely lost sight of until, by more recent investigation, it has been again introduced and submitted to practical tests. These remarks indicate the importance of a concise knowledge of the failures and successes of early inventors, and, if need be, justify the introduction of historical matter.

It is probable that ever since gunpowder has existed inventors have sought to utilise its potential energy for the use as well as for the destruction of their fellow-men. In support of this assumption, we find records of attempts to explode gunpowder in a cylinder as early as 1678. A practical form of engine might have been evolved had it not been for the mechanical difficulties to be overcome in obtaining continuous and regular explosions with such a substance as gunpowder. It is not surprising, therefore, that at a time when the steam engine was beginning to occupy men's minds, the combustion engine was entirely neglected; nor is it surprising that so long as an explosive substance could only readily be obtained in the form of solid matter, mechanical difficulties impeded all progress. When, however, Dr. Watson discovered that gas could be distilled from coal, and when, in the year 1792, Murdoch, a Cornish engineer, demonstrated the practical application of coal gas for lighting purposes, then we find the internal combustion engine again the subject of experiment. About this time, it will be remembered, the steam engine had become a powerful assistant in the mining industry, and was undergoing important development, brought about by the world-famed Watt. Naturally the majority of mechanicians were absorbed in furthering its possibilities. Nevertheless, from the year 1791 to 1801 three patents are on record setting forth the use of explosive mixtures of coal gas and air in motors. The first, by John Barber, explains how a wheel, with vanes upon its circumference, may be driven by releasing the pressure of an explosion through an orifice placed in proximity to the vanes. The second patent, taken out by Street in 1794, mentions the use of cylinder and piston, the latter being driven outwards by the pressure of the explosion. Flame ignition is first made use of in this engine. In 1801 another patent appeared under the name of Lebon, setting forth the advantages of compressing the gas and air before entering the explosion cylinder. Thus we see that as early as 1801 two of the principles had been explained, upon the merits of which later engines became a practical success. It appears curious that so much time should elapse between the publication of these specifications and the production of a really useful gas motor; but it is highly probable that the two factors contributing to this end were, firstly, the crude mechanical appliances for manufacturing purposes; and secondly, the tendency to follow the details of small steam-engine design, which in the matter of valves, glands, and pistons are entirely unsuitable for the peculiar conditions of gas engine work.

It is curious to note how the phases of construction of the steam engine, during a period extending over nearly 200 years, have been practically repeated in the case of the gas engine in about half the time. Just as in the steam engine, when low-pressure steam was condensed in the cylinder so that unbalanced atmospheric pressure could be utilised, so in the gas engine many attempts were made—and these were not without a measure of success—to utilise the unbalanced atmospheric pressure due to the contraction in volume of an explosive mixture, rather than the pressure produced during the explosion. In 1823 an English patent was taken out by Brown, giving the details of such an atmospheric engine. The pressure of the explosion was permitted to escape through valves in the piston, which, however, closed when the pressure of the atmosphere exceeded that of the gas. A little water injected into the cylinder assisted in cooling the products of combustion, and so reduced the pressure rapidly below that of the atmosphere. A few of these engines were constructed for commercial purposes, but owing to the difficulty in keeping them going, and to the expense in gas, they were finally abandoned. From 1823 to 1838 but little was done to popularise the gas motor, although during that lapse of time the water jacket was added to the cylinder for cooling purposes, and some attempts were made to govern the speed of an engine by controlling the admission of gas.

In 1838 Barnett made practical use of the principle of compression by constructing a single-acting motor cylinder, at each side of which was placed a gas and air pump. The three pistons moved simultaneously in the same directions; the gas and air pumps delivered into a receiver, from which communication was made to the motor cylinder as the charge was ignited. Barnett afterwards constructed double-acting engines, but with less success.

Between the years 1838 and 1860 nothing of much practical value was added to the gas motor. There were a considerable number of patents registered during this period, describing engines working with oxygen and hydrogen gases, but no real progress was made until 1860. About this time it became recognised that double-acting cylinders were not suitable for gas engines, on account of the necessary absence of compression, the intensity of heat, the difficulties of packing and keeping a narrow piston in order. All these points were fully exemplified by the working of the Lenoir engine, which made its appearance about 1860. Although exhibiting those weak points of design, the Lenoir engine, owing to commercial agencies, became popular. The details of construction resemble somewhat those of an ordinary steam engine: a slide valve, S ports for admission and escape of the gases, electric ignition, water-jacketed cylinder and covers, were amongst the special features of the engine, Notwithstanding the consumption of gas amounted to about 100 cubic feet per horse power per hour (a fact probably not known to purchasers), this engine had a large sale. The defects of working ruined the future of the engine; and although it was subject to alteration in the hands of Hugon by the introduction of flame instead of electric ignition, it never recovered the reaction of opinion set up by public disappointment.

In 1843 Joule determined the mechanical equivalent of heat, and from that time attention was drawn to the question of thermal efficiency of motors, although it was some years before this treatment of the subject was thoroughly understood. In 1860 Barsanti and Matteucci, appreciating the convertibility of heat into motion, pointed out the necessity of rapid expansion after explosion, in order that the heat might be utilised in doing work, instead of the greater part being transmitted through the walls of the cylinder to waste itself in heating the jacket water. The engine constructed by Barsanti and Matteucci never got beyond the experimental stage, in spite of the correct principle upon which it was worked. In 1863 Otto and Langen, having also conceived the necessity for rapid expansion, devised a motor somewhat similar to Barsanti's, making use of a free piston, which was shot upwards in a vertical cylinder by the force of the explosion. In its upward passage the weight of the piston only was overcome, but on its downward stroke the piston rod, made in the form of a rack, and geared to a pinion on the flywheel axle, caused the latter to rotate. A special ratchet gear was fitted to the pinion, so that it could revolve freely upon the flywheel axle during the upstroke of the rack. A few engines of this type are working at the present time, though they are regarded as curiosities amongst gas motors. The consumption of gas was only about 40 cubic feet per brake horse power per hour, but the noise and vibration were sufficiently objectionable features to prevent its gaining great popularity.

About this period (1861) it was again pointed out by Gustave Schmidt and Million that economy would be effected by compression before explosion. Million attempted the practical illustration of the principle of compression first upon lines similar to those of Barnard in 1838, but afterwards he introduced the compressed gas into the cylinder at the dead point, providing for that purpose an equivalent to the clearance space of a gas engine cylinder of the present day.

In 1862, a French engineer, Beau de Rochas stated definitely the conditions necessary for maximum efficiency, and formulated the well-known cycle, now termed the Otto cycle because carried into practical effect by one of that name. In the wording of the French patent taken out in 1862, Beau de Rochas manifests a clear and advanced knowledge of his subject. He says (translated): There are four conditions for perfectly utilising the force of expansion of gas in an engine:—

I. The largest possible cylinder volume contained by a minimum of surface.

II. The highest possible speed of working.

III. Maximum expansion.

IV. Maximum pressure at the beginning of expansion.

In connection with his first-stated condition, he goes on to say that a cylinder of the largest possible diameter for a given expenditure of gas should prove the most economical, and he deduces from this that only one explosion cylinder should be used in each engine. Following this significant conclusion, he touches upon the effect of time of expansion in causing the transmission of heat to the jacket water, and states definitely that the more rapid the piston speed, and consequently the expansion, the less will be the loss of heat to the jacket water. Speaking of maximum expansion, he points out that the lowest limit of pressure is soon attained, because of the rapid condensation of the gases. To obtain a maximum expansion, therefore, the gases should be compressed when cool to raise the initial pressure of explosion. In connection with this he also points out that the obvious limit to compression must occur when spontaneous combustion takes place.

Steam-engine makers, in taking up the manufacture of gas engines, have a tendency to think that the best results are only possible by a system of compounding gas engines. It is, indeed, natural that such should be the case. It should be remembered, however, that the best modern engines are working upon the precise principles laid down in 1862 by Beau de Rochas, and that their success testifies to the soundness of his views. Economy cannot be obtained by compounding, inasmuch as a great increase in compression is limited by spontaneous combustion, and expansion in two cylinders necessitates an increase in surface. Beau de Rochas anticipated in his specification still more, for he advocated combustion by compression, instead of by the electric spark, and finally gives a hint as to the value of a timing valve.

At this juncture, perhaps, the author may be permitted a digression, to arrest the attention of those apt to scoff at the value of scientific work in connection with the advancement of practical engineering. The position of science in relation to the development of the steam engine has been ably defended from the attacks of practical men by Prof. Unwin in his "James Forrest" lecture, published in volume cxxii. of the Proceedings of the Institution of Civil Engineers. What stronger evidence than the history of the gas engine could be adduced to prove that its ultimate success depended upon the scientific principles laid down by Beau de Rochas, who, although not concerning himself with the practical details of a gas engine, so thoroughly understood the scientific side of the question. Is it not rather a reflection upon the so-called practical engineer that it took fifteen years to bring about anything like a practical development of the principles enumerated in 1862?

The Otto and Langen engine was the most practical form of gas motor in the market from 1863 to 1876. Many attempts were made to improve it, but none were effectual until Otto himself, in 1876, brought out an entirely new design of the type now familiarly associated with his name. This was the first successful engine—designed by one of high scientific attainments—in which compression took place in the explosion cylinder; and its production marks the period at which the gas motor became a serious competitor against small steam engines.

CHAPTER II.

Arrangement of Engine-room.

THE reader being now acquainted with the main points in connection with the historical side of the subject, we may proceed at once to a description of the details of an Otto gas engine of the type brought out in 1876, many of which are working at the present time. Although Otto engines of later design exhibit many important improvements in the details—which will be described on another page — we shall not get far astray in accepting the arrangement of gas connections, jacket water circulation tanks, &c., as applicable to any gas engine at present on the market. On account of the unique position of the Otto engine as the pioneer of all practical gas motors, and because nearly all more modern engines work upon the Otto cycle, it is necessary for the sake of completeness to treat of it here.

The general outside appearance of the engine is somewhat similar to that of a small horizontal steam engine with overhanging cylinder, and a trunk piston, instead of piston rod and guides. Fig. 1 is a sectional plan. The piston B is shown at the back of its stroke; the space C is the clearance, provided in all gas engines, in which the charge is compressed before ignition takes place. In this engine the clearance volume is about 50 per cent of the volume swept out by the piston. The passage I is for the admission of air and gas, and also serves for the passage of flame in igniting the charge.

The burnt gases are discharged through the valve D, lifted by means of a lever worked by a cam on the lay shaft P. The slide M works to and fro between the fixed part N and the back of the cylinder, and effects both the admission of air and gas and the igniting of the charge. The slide M in moving upwards causes communication between the air passage F, the gas port G, and the entrance to the cylinder I. Air and gas are thus drawn into the cylinder upon the outstroke of the piston. The spacing of the port edges is so arranged as to allow the gas to enter the cylinder just after the air port is shut. In this position the port L is filled with gas at atmospheric pressure, which is ignited by momentary contact with flame. The slide M then moves rapidly downwards; meanwhile the piston B is returning to the back of the cylinder and compressing the charge to about 40 lb. per square inch ready for explosion. It is evident that the burning gas entrapped in the port L would be extinguished by the pressure of gas in C the moment L communicates with I, and ignition would not occur. In order to raise the pressure in the port L on its way to the inlet I, there is a very small passage provided from the clearance space communicating with the port L before it reaches I. Through this passage the compressed gas finds its way in very small quantities into L, raises the pressure in L, and maintains the combustion by the additional supply of air and gas. The passage through which this communication is made is too small to permit the firing of the charge in the cylinder, and this does not take place until the port L—carrying its burning gas now at the same pressure as that in C—reaches I and ignites the charge.

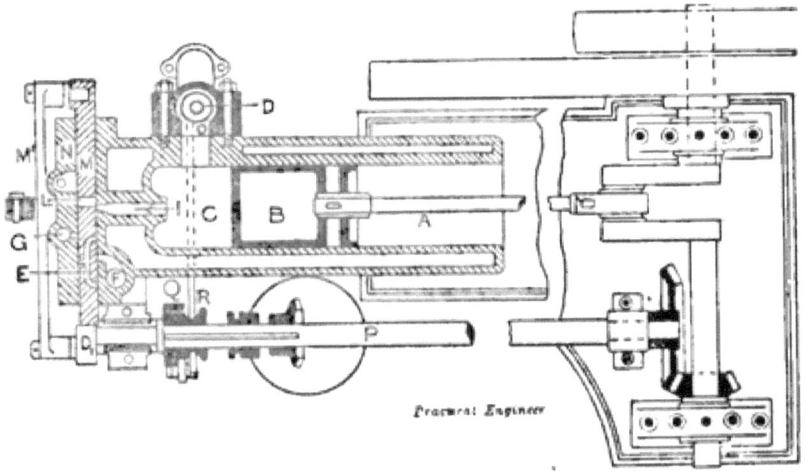

Fig. 1.—Sectional plan of Otto gas engine.

The piston is now driven forward by the explosion. The flywheels carry the piston back, driving the burnt gases out through D. It will be observed that an impulse is only given every two revolutions of the engine; hence the necessity for exceedingly heavy flywheels to maintain a constant speed. The Otto cycle, upon which nearly all modern engines work, may be summed up as follows:—

First revolution... { Outstroke draws in air and gas.
{ Instroke compresses charge.

Second revolution { Outstroke caused by the explosion.
{ Instroke discharges burnt products.

In the description of various designs of gas engines, we shall afterwards see that the mechanism for effecting this cycle of operations has undergone many changes. For the present we may turn our attention to the arrangement of the engine-room best suited for the working of a gas engine, and to those fittings external to the engine itself. When possible, the room in which a *large* gas engine is placed should be quite separated from any building in which vibration is likely to cause annoyance. If, however, it is not possible to provide a separate engine-house, two precautions may be taken to prevent unpleasant results. There should be no communication between the main building and the engine-room, excepting by means of well-fitting doors, which should be made to close automatically. This caution is not necessary in the case of small engines, but large engines of from 40 to 60 I.H.P., running at a speed of from 150 to 200 revolutions per minute, cause a rapid pulsation of air owing to the displacement of the large trunk piston; this pulsation may be transmitted through the passages and corridor to almost every room in the building, causing even the windows to vibrate to every revolution of the engine. For the same reason the engine-room should not be ventilated by connection with the air shafts of the building. Artificial ventilation is absolutely necessary, as the engine-room otherwise becomes unbearable. A small air propeller driven from the engine will answer this purpose admirably.

Another fruitful source of annoyance is the vibration of the engine transmitted through its foundations to the walls of the building. In some instances it has been found that an increase in the speed has checked the vibration of the foundations and walls. It is quite probable that every building has a period of vibration peculiar to itself, and if, therefore, a machine is running so as to have the same period of vibration, the results may be very noticeable. Increase the speed of the machine, alter its period of vibration until it no longer synchronises with that of the building, and the latter will not respond; thus the effect will be minimised to an inappreciable extent.

ARRANGEMENT OF ENGINE-ROOM.

Another method by which vibration of the engine itself may be prevented from transmission to the building is to bolt the engine bed down upon a somewhat soft and springy material. Let some timber baulks be placed longitudinally with the engine bed. Over these put a layer of iron plate, say $\frac{3}{8}$ in. thick, then put over the plate a layer of cocoanut matting. It is well to have these mats specially made. They should be manufactured after the manner of a thick pile cocoanut door mat; two should be made of the required area; the pile faces should be put together, and the two bound at the edges into one thick mat. By putting them together in this way a thickness of 4 in. or 5 in. may be obtained of springy texture, and presenting an exterior of comparatively tough material. Another plate over the mat serves to distribute the weight of the engine over the entire area, and then the whole may be loosely held together by means of the foundation bolts. If this method is adopted, the engine will no doubt rock considerably, and extra large bolts may be necessary for holding down. The rock of the engine will cause considerable oscillation of the belt, and for this reason a rather short drive is to be preferred. These objections are, however, entirely outweighed by the satisfactory prevention of the transmission of vibration throughout the building.

The next point to be considered in the arrangement of the engine-room is the position and size of the gas meter required. All engines should be provided with a separate gas meter, so that the consumption of the engine may be checked independently. The meter should be placed outside the engine-room in an atmosphere of normal temperature, for it must not be forgotten that an increase of temperature results in an increase in the volume of gas. If, therefore, the meter is kept at a high temperature, the cubic feet registered by it will be greater for the same weight of gas than if kept at normal atmospheric temperature. No injustice is done to the producers of the gas by taking this precaution, because the temperature of the supply is itself normal.

The size of a gas meter is usually gauged by the maximum number of lights for which it is designed. Thus, small houses are fitted with a 5-light meter, others a 10-light meter, according to the requirements, and this indication of the size is usually printed upon the index of the meter. A useful rule for determining the size of a dry meter required for a gas engine, the brake horse power of which is known, is as follows : $3.4 \times$ brake horse power $+ 5 =$ size of meter required (measured as above stated).

Thus, suppose an engine of 30 brake horse power is being erected, the meter required will be $3.4 \times 30 + 5 = 107$-light meter. In this instance a 100-light meter would suffice.

Gas and oil engine makers are now quoting in their catalogues the brake or effective horse power, instead of indicated and nominal horse powers. The relation between these will be dealt with upon following pages, devoted to gas-engine testing ; but it may here be said that this innovation is a great improvement, inasmuch as the purchaser knows exactly the capacity of an engine for doing useful work.

Having determined the size of meter suitable for measuring the gas supplied to an engine, we must next consider the size of pipe from the meter to the engine. The following rule gives the correct size of pipe for a given size of meter :

Meter size (measured in lights) $\times 0.008 + 0.75 =$ bore of pipe in inches. In the example previously worked it was calculated that a 100-light meter is suitable for a 30 brake horse power engine. The size of gas pipe for this meter will be equal to $100 \times 0.008 + 0.75 = 0.8 + 0.75 = 1.55$ in. Putting in a size of pipe to the nearest $\frac{1}{8}$ in., we should, in this instance, couple the gas supply to the engine by means of a $1\frac{1}{2}$ in. diameter pipe.

Another rule may be used for obtaining the diameter of gas pipe when only the brake horse power is known. If $D =$ inside diameter of pipe in inches, then we have—

$$D = 0.027 \times \text{brake horse power} + 0.75.$$

Working out the diameter suitable for a 30 brake horse power engine, we have—

$$D = 0\cdot027 \times 30 + 0\cdot75$$
$$= 0\cdot81 + 0\cdot75$$
$$= 1\cdot56 \text{ in. ;}$$

and putting in a size to the nearest $\frac{1}{8}$ in., we obtain $1\frac{1}{2}$ in. diameter, as before calculated from the other data.

Between the gas meter and the engine there should be fitted a flexible bag through which the gas passes. The bag may be made by clamping two sheets of indiarubber about $\frac{1}{8}$ in. thick to each side of a cast-iron ring, the diameter of which may be from 1 ft. 6 in. to 2 ft. 6 in., or more, according to circumstances. By this arrangement rapid fluctuation of pressure in the gas mains is prevented, thereby maintaining a steady light given by the burners in proximity to the engine. To contribute to this end, two bags are sometimes fitted in the following way: The bags, each composed of a cast-iron dish to form one side, and sheet rubber the other, are connected together, so that the gas enters and fills one, then passes on to the next. Between the entrance to the first gas bag and its pipe flange is fitted a cast-iron box containing a plain slide valve. This valve is moved by a lever attached to the centre of the rubber side of the bag in such a way as to close the entrance to the bag when the latter is full of gas. A similar valve is fitted between the two consecutive bags, and the whole forms a very efficient means of governing the pressure in the mains. In putting up the gas piping and bags, the rubber sides should be placed next the wall, and the bags should be as near the engine as possible. It is advisable to leave sufficient room between the wall and rubber to enable the attendant at any time to place his hand upon the rubber to flatten it. It is often necessary to do this in starting an engine, to get rid of an accumulation of poor gas in the bags when the machinery has been standing several days. It is also a useful precaution to have a small gas cock fitted to the mains near the meter, to which a ∪ glass tube may be attached by an indiarubber pipe

By partially filling the tube with water and opening the cock the fluctuation of pressure in the mains may be observed, and the efficiency of the gas bags tested when the engine is running. The rubber side of the bags must be kept perfectly clean and free from oil, or its corrosive effect will soon be evident, and, further, the rubber must not be subject to excessive temperatures.

The diameter of the engine exhaust pipe may be found from the following rule for any engine larger than 5 brake horse power: If D_e = diameter of exhaust pipe,

then we have $D_e = 0.528$ horse power $^{0.57}$

Taking the brake horse power at 30, as in the previous example, and applying the rule given to find the exhaust diameter, we have—

$$0.528 \times 30^{0.57} = D_e$$
$$\log 30 = 1.477 \; ;^*$$

and $1.477 \times 0.57 = 0.838$ (nearly) = the log of $(30^{0.57})$.

Finding the number corresponding to 0.838, we obtain 6.89 and $0.528 \times 6.89 = 3.64$ diameter of exhaust pipe in *inches*.

We should here adopt a $3\frac{5}{8}$ in. or $3\frac{3}{4}$ in. diameter pipe. Engines of from 1 to 5 brake horse power may have the exhaust pipes from 1 in. diameter to $1\frac{3}{4}$ in.

It is very important that the exhaust pipe should be free from bends, but where necessary they should be of large radius, say 6 in. Owing to the high temperature of the exhaust gases, the pipe should be isolated from inflammable material. When the mouth of the pipe discharges into the open air it should point downwards, to prevent the collection of rain water. When it is desirable to deaden the noise of the exhaust, it may be discharged into a cast-iron chamber partially filled with flint pebbles, or into the bottom of a trench filled with pebbles. Whatever form of

---

* All calculations will be worked out upon a 10 in. slide rule, and the results will be accurate to about one-half per cent.

exhaust chamber is made use of, it should always be placed in an accessible place, and provision made for efficiently draining water which may collect.

The next subject for consideration in the arrangement of gas-engine plant is the delivery of water to the jacket surrounding the working cylinder of the engine. The jacket water circulates round the cylinder in an annular space, formed by the outer wall of the explosion cylinder and the inner wall of a concentric casing. This casing is cast with the cylinder, and the space allowed for the water is from $\frac{3}{4}$ in. to 2 in. A flange is provided at the under side of the jacket for the inlet of the water, and another at the top and front end for the outlet. For small engines the inlet and outlet pipes may be the same size, but when circulation tanks are used, and the engine is over 20 horse power, it is better to have the outlet pipe from $\frac{1}{2}$ in. to $\frac{3}{4}$ in. larger in diameter.

The function of the jacket water is to carry away the excess of heat due to combustion in the cylinder, which, under the present conditions, cannot be converted into work. It is found in practice that the quantity of heat accounted for by the jacket water amounts to from 30 to 50 per cent of the total heat derived from the combustion of the gases in the cylinder, and that under these conditions lubrication is possible. In estimating, therefore, the quantity of jacket water required, it is necessary to bear in mind that it must absorb not less than 30 per cent of the heat of combustion, and that its maximum temperature should not exceed 150 deg. Fah. for continuous running. When the cooling water runs to waste, the maximum temperature may be somewhat higher, but when circulating tanks are used it is better not to exceed 150 deg. Fah. If we assume an average gas consumption of 22 cubic feet per indicated horse power per hour, we may estimate the heat units generated in the cylinder for each H.P. to be $22 \times 620 = 13,640$ units per hour, because 1 cubic foot of coal gas develops on an average 620 British thermal units. At our lowest estimate, 30 per cent of this must be taken up by the jacket water; this amounts to 4,092 units. We have said that the jacket water should not exceed 150 deg. Its inlet temperature may be taken at 60 deg. Fah., thus allowing a rise of temperature of $150 - 60 = 90$ deg. Fah. per pound of water, the pounds per I.H.P. required $= \frac{4092}{90} = 45 \cdot 5$ (nearly) per hour. This is equivalent to $4\frac{1}{2}$ gallons of water per I.H.P. per hour, and it approaches the minimum quantity allowable for continuous working. Thus we find that if the water supply is continuous, and passes through the jacket, afterwards running to waste, at the rate of $4\frac{1}{2}$ gallons per I.H.P. per hour, efficient lubrication may be maintained. With such an arrangement, the size of the jacket inlet and outlet pipes will depend entirely upon the head of water in the source of supply, but as the arrangement described is only suitable for experimental engines and other special cases, the jacket pipes are put in from 1 in. to 2 in. diameter up to engines of 20 I.H.P. Above 20 H.P. the diameters range from 2 in. to 3 in. for the inlet, and from $2\frac{1}{2}$ in. to $3\frac{3}{4}$ in. for the outlet.

The most usual method of supplying the jacket is to place it in communication with a set of tanks, through which there is a free circulation of water. The diagram (fig. 2) shows an arrangement of circulation tanks. The tank A is coupled to the jacket inlet, and receives the feed necessary to make up the loss from evaporation. The outlet pipe is taken to the normal water level of the tanks. This pipe should have a minimum rise of 2 in. per foot where it leads into the tank, in order to secure an easy circulation. The tank B communicates with A through a pipe starting from the bottom of B, passing out at the normal water level across to A. A drain pipe, slightly above the normal water level, serves to take away any excess of feed water. For clearness in the drawing the engine is shown between the tanks, but it is usual to have the tanks side by side, outside the engine-room, in as cool a place as possible. They should, however, not be placed in the open air, as, in the event of severe frost, much inconvenience may be occasioned. In this connection it may be well to mention, that when an engine is subject to frost, and is not running continuously, it is a wise precaution to have two valves fitted to the inlet jacket pipe, the one near the tank A to shut off the supply from A; the other at the bend of the pipe as it enters the jacket, and communicating with the atmosphere. Thus the jacket only may be drained, and be secured from bursting if the frost gets to the engine. The circulation tanks should have a capacity of from 20 gallons to 30 gallons per I.H.P.,

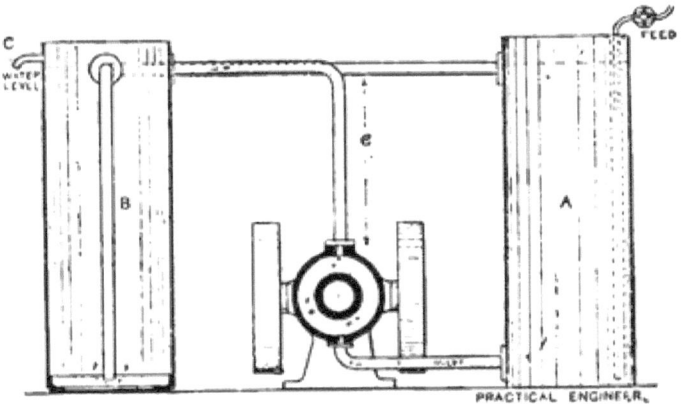

FIG. 2.—Arrangement of water tanks.

so as to allow a sufficient time for cooling. The form of tanks is usually cylindrical, though need not be. It is, however, necessary that the effective height should be from two and a half to three times the diameter or breadth, otherwise a good circulation will not be induced.

The circulation is induced by the expansion of the column of water in the pipe e leading from the jacket to the tank. When the engine is started the jacket temperature may reach about 160 deg. Fah., and the volume of the water will increase about $\frac{1}{25}$th. Thus, a column of water 8 ft. high will increase when heated nearly to 8 ft. 3½ in. There will then be an equivalent head of water in the cold tank A of $3\frac{1}{2}$ in., which, neglecting friction in the pipes, will cause the cold water to enter the jacket at the rate of 4·4 ft. per second. Thus, immediately upon starting the engine, a very brisk circulation of the water is induced. After some time has elapsed, the water in A rises nearly to the same temperature as at the bottom of B, so that the equivalent head, which afterwards maintains the circulation, may be calculated from the difference in temperature between a stratum of water at the bottom and that at the top of the tank B.

We have now dealt with the chief external fittings of a gas engine worked by town's gas. The economy to be gained by putting down plant for the production of Dowson gas depends upon many conditions which may or may not exist in any particular instance. Undoubtedly, for the constant running of large engines, producer gas is by far the most economical. This important subject will be more fully discussed later.

Before concluding these remarks upon the arrangement of an engine-room the following points may be noted: When possible, arrange for the tight side of the belt to run from the bottom of the driving-wheel. This is not always convenient when driving a dynamo, for the dynamo pulley must run in the same direction as the hands of a watch when viewed from a position facing the pulley end of the dynamo. When cramped for room, it is necessary that the gas-engine cylinder should lie between the dynamo and the engine crank shaft; thus, with an engine receiving its impulse on the top throw of the crank, the tight side will be at the top. With a fair width of belt no serious amount of slip will take place in transmitting, say, 40 horse power, even though the driving pulley be 7 ft. diameter, the driven pulley 18 in., and the shaft centres only 15 ft. apart. Gas engines have in some instances been coupled directly to the dynamo shaft, thus effecting a great saving of space. At Sunderland a gas-engine plant has recently been put down driving the centrifugal pumps at the docks without the use of either belts or gearing.

CHAPTER III.

Types of Gas Engines.

Atkinson's "Differential" and "Cycle" Engines.

Since the Otto patent expired, the commercial value of other engines has much depreciated, and in many cases makers have abandoned their own patents in favour of the Otto principle. In 1885, Mr. J. Atkinson, M.I.M.E., patented a motor known as the Differential engine. This engine was constructed upon different lines to any other gas engine that has been made, and from a theoretical point of view is the most perfect engine yet invented. Regarded however as a mechanical contrivance, Mr. Atkinson himself says it is not good, though it may be considered an ingenious combination of link motion. Although not now manufactured, no work upon the gas engine would be complete without a description of this machine. Figs. 3, 4, 5, and 6 show the engine diagrammatically in four positions of the crank pin. The cylinder is open at both ends, and water jacketed on the top only. Two pistons work in the cylinder, and are each connected with the crank pin P by means of a freely jointed connecting rod c, attached to the bent lever L. This lever oscillates upon the fixed pin D, which is attached to the framing of the engine. The upper end of the lever L drives the crank pin by means of the short connecting rod R. Fig. 3 shows the engine with the charge compressed between the two pistons. The left-hand piston is just uncovering the entrance to the ignition tube I. It will be observed that as the crank pin follows the direction indicated by the arrow, the rod R_1 merely revolves about the upper end of the lever L_1 until P arrives at position shown in fig. 5. The left-hand piston has therefore remained almost stationary, whilst the right-hand piston has moved very rapidly to the right

20   TYPES OF GAS ENGINES.

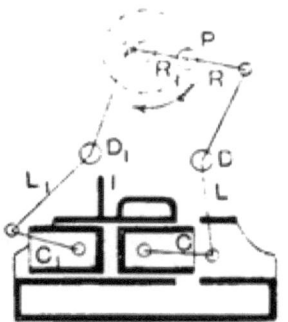 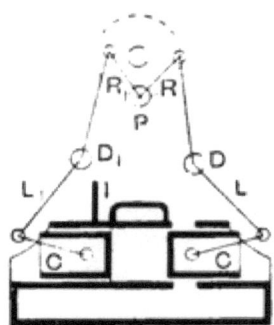

ATKINSON'S DIFFERENTIAL GAS ENGINE.

FIG. 3. Volume before explosion.   FIG. 4.—Volume when expanded.

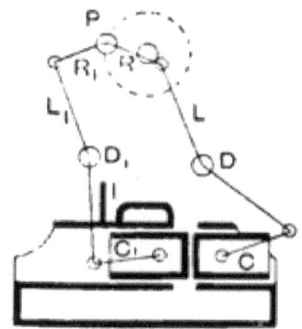 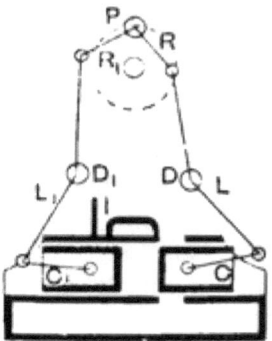

ATKINSON'S DIFFERENTIAL GAS ENGINE.

FIG. 5.—Showing total expulsion of burnt gases.   FIG. 6.—Volume of charge before compression.

TYPES OF GAS ENGINES. 21

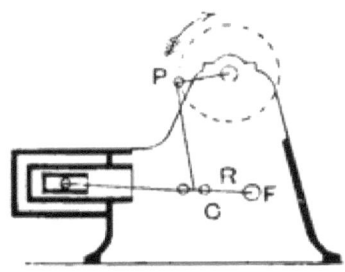 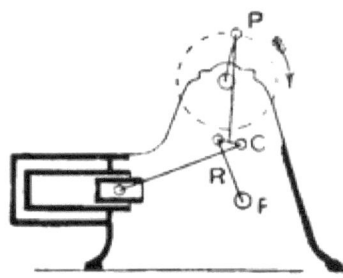

ATKINSON'S CYCLE GAS ENGINE.

FIG. 7.—Showing volume before explosion.   FIG. 8.—Showing volume when expanded.

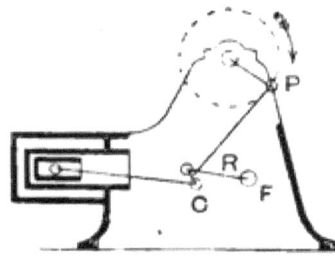 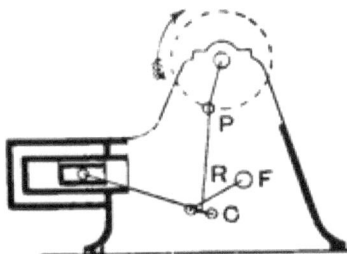

ATKINSON'S CYCLE GAS ENGINE.

FIG. 9.—Showing total expulsion of burnt products.   FIG. 10.—Showing volume of charge before compression.

and the charge between the pistons is expanded, thus giving an impulse to the crank pin in the direction of its motion. The effect of the pressure upon the left-hand piston during the time the crank pin moves between the positions shown in figs. 3 and 4 merely produces a downward thrust upon the crank-shaft journals, and only a small resolved force acts against the rotation of the crank pin. On the other hand, the rod R, attached to the right-hand lever L, exerts an almost tangential effort on the crank pin during this quadrant. The exhaust port is now uncovered by the piston c, and remains so during the next quarter revolution. In the mean time the left-hand piston c_1 moves rapidly to the right, and expels the whole of the burnt gases. The piston c now moves *slowly* to the left, covering the exhaust port, while c_1 moves *rapidly* to the left, drawing in the fresh charge. Fig. 6 shows the position of the pistons when the charge is complete, and it should be observed that the volume enclosed by the pistons is here *less* than in fig. 4, just when the exhaust opens. It therefore follows that the charge is expanded beyond its original volume at atmospheric pressure, thus carrying out the principle of maximum expansion laid down by Beau de Rochas.

The four characteristic features of this engine are—an ignition per revolution, the expulsion of the burnt gases, expansion to greater than the original volume, also perfectly automatic valves and means of timing the ignition. Notwithstanding the mechanical defects, this engine was the most economical of its time, for it consumed only 26 cubic feet of gas per brake horse power in small engines, and this was reduced to 24 cubic feet in large engines. This engine was first exhibited at the Inventions Exhibition held in London in 1885, and was there awarded a gold medal.

Its mechanical defects were so obvious that its manufacture was abandoned in favour of another type, patented by Mr. Atkinson, and known as the Cycle engine. Here the patentee sought to combine the advantages of the Differential engine with more durable mechanism, and he was able, by the arrangement shown in figs. 7 to 10, to reduce the gas consumption to 22 cubic feet per brake horse power per hour. Fig. 7 shows the position of the piston when ignition takes place. The fixed centre F being rather below the horizontal centre line of the cylinder causes the rod R to rise through a greater angle above than below F. By this means the explosion stroke was 11·1 in. Fig. 8 gives the position of the links at the end of the explosion stroke.

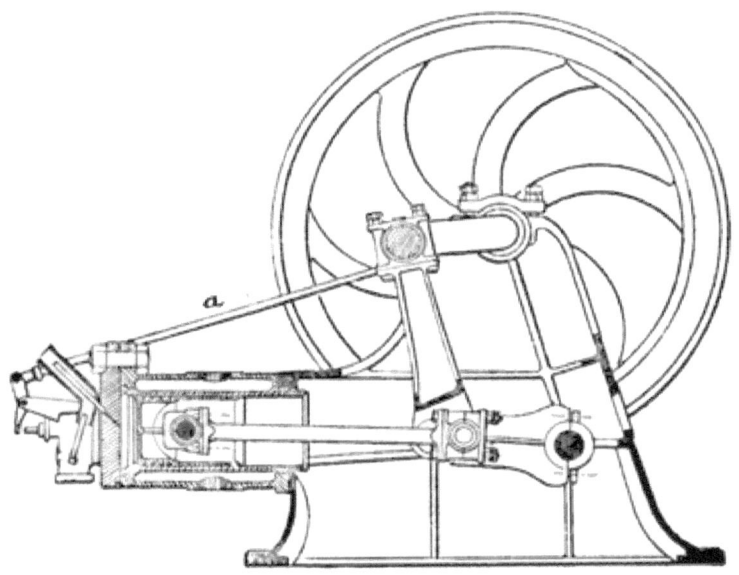

FIG. 11.—ATKINSON'S CYCLE GAS ENGINE.

During the exhaust stroke it will be noticed (fig. 9) that the joints at C are inclined instead of horizontal, as in fig. 7, thus increasing the length of the backward stroke to 12·4 in., and bringing the piston close to the back of the cylinder. The whole of the burnt gases being driven out, the piston makes another forward stroke, but, as before mentioned, owing to the smaller angle made by the link R below the horizontal, this stroke only measures 6·3 in. Fig. 10 shows the position of the crank pin when the charge is completed. Fig. 11 gives a more complete view of the Cycle engine, many of which are at the present time working.

The rod a operates the gas valve by means of a cam on the crank shaft. A similar rod in front of a operates the exhaust valve. The ignition tube in this engine is screwed direct into the back of the cylinder, the time of ignition being determined by the length of the tube. The hot ignition tube communicates with the combustion chamber by means of the small hole, through which passage the fresh charge is compressed into the tube. After the explosion, expansion, and exhaust have occurred, the tube remains full of products of combustion, and it is evident that, before a fresh charge can be ignited, these products must be so far driven to the end of the ignition tube as to allow the fresh mixture to come in contact with the red-hot portion of the tube. Hence the length of an ignition tube plays an important part in determining the amount of compression necessary, and consequently the time of an explosion. In the Cycle engine the firing of the charge is regular, and little trouble is experienced with it. This is probably, in a great measure, due to the pure charge put into the cylinder. There is much diversity of opinion upon the value of a timing valve.

To show the result of the application by Mr. Atkinson of the principles laid down by Beau de Rochas, the following figures may be quoted. A 6 horse power Cycle engine was put down by the Hampton Wick Local Board to drive a single-acting air compressor in connection with the Shone pneumatic sewage system. This was tested against a duplicate set of pumps driven by a Crossley Otto engine under precisely similar conditions. It was found that the Cycle engine consumed 18·4 per cent less gas than the Crossley engine. Notwithstanding the high efficiency of the Cycle engine with regard to gas consumption, it has been found to be costly in up-keep, requiring more lubrication and more frequent repairing, consequently, now that the Otto patents have become public property, the Cycle engine is not manufactured. It is nevertheless worthy of careful study as an example of a very successful attempt to put into practice the true theory of an economical gas engine.

It has been stated previously that the majority of gas engines now being manufactured work on the Otto cycle, but owing to the irregularity of the impulse given to the piston it is certainly desirable to aim at a more equal distribution of the turning effort exerted upon the crank pin. This object may be to some extent attained by building an engine with two Otto cycle cylinders instead of one, and a still greater regularity in the impulses has been attained by the construction of double-acting cylinders, made possible by improvements in details relating to lubrication and glands.

COMPARATIVE CYCLES OF GAS ENGINES.

The following diagram, fig. 12, shows the steadiness of running with the various cycles now used. The shaded squares represent indicator diagrams taken from the back or front of the piston when an explosion takes place. It is seen that in the Otto cycle single-cylinder engine, in six revolutions, only three impulses are given to the piston. The Griffin engine, about which more will be written, has a double-acting cylinder. The series of operations on one side of the piston only is as follows :—

1. Outstroke : Explosion and expansion.
2. Instroke : Products of combustion expelled.
3. Scavenger stroke—outstroke : Draws in pure air only.
4. Scavenger stroke—instroke : Clears out the cylinder.
5. Outstroke : Draws in gas and air.
6. Instroke : Compresses ready for explosion.

It is therefore evident that the back of the piston receives one impulse every three revolutions. Similarly, the front of the piston receives one impulse every three revolutions; consequently during the six revolutions two impulses are received by one side of the piston, and two by the other, making in all four. The object of the third outstroke for drawing into the cylinder a charge of pure air will be fully

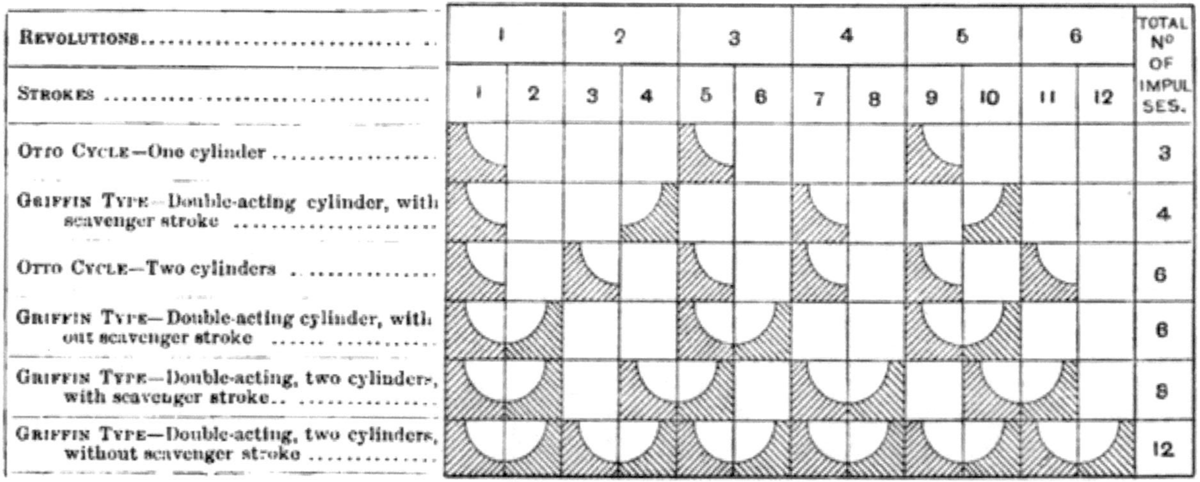

26   TYPES OF GAS ENGINES.

Revolutions	1		2		3		4		5		6		TOTAL Nº OF IMPULSES.
Strokes	1	2	3	4	5	6	7	8	9	10	11	12	
Otto Cycle—One cylinder													3
Griffin Type—Double-acting cylinder, with scavenger stroke													4
Otto Cycle—Two cylinders													6
Griffin Type—Double-acting cylinder, without scavenger stroke													6
Griffin Type—Double-acting, two cylinders, with scavenger stroke													8
Griffin Type—Double-acting, two cylinders, without scavenger stroke													12

Fig. 12.—Diagram Showing Comparative Cycles of Gas Engines Running at Full Load.

treated later; but here it may be stated that if all the products of combustion are entirely swept out of the cylinder by this means, it is generally believed that the efficiency of the next charge of gas is increased. This is no doubt true when Dowson gas is used, but experiments carried out by the author upon mixtures of coal gas and air point to the conclusion that the deleterious effect of burnt products is much overrated, excepting when the gas is more than $7\frac{1}{2}$ per cent of the air by volume.

The Otto cycle, when applied to an engine having two cylinders, gives an impulse every revolution of the flywheels in the order shown upon the diagram. The Griffin type, having but one double-acting cylinder, and working without a scavenger stroke, gives an average of one impulse every revolution, though the sequence of the working stroke is perhaps somewhat less conducive to steady running. This is, however, improved by the use of two cylinders, each with its scavenging strokes, giving eight impulses in six revolutions. And, lastly, the Griffin engine, with two double-acting cylinders and no scavenger stroke, gives twelve impulses during six revolutions. Regarding only the number and sequence of motor strokes per revolution, the above-mentioned cases afford an example of what may be done by the various combinations of cylinders; but it will be understood that there are other engines, which, whilst fulfilling one set of conditions indicated by the diagram, are distinct in design, and possess advantages peculiar to themselves.

THE CROSSLEY ENGINE.

The modern Otto, as built by Messrs. Crossley Brothers Limited, Manchester, is very different from that illustrated in fig. 1. The old method of flame ignition is now entirely superseded by allowing the explosive mixture in the cylinder to enter a red-hot tube attached to the cylinder. The slide valve controlling the admission of the air and gas has been replaced by two simple mushroom valves, somewhat similar to the exhaust valve on the original Otto engine. There are many objections to the employment of a slide valve on a gas engine, and it is probable that a change would have been made much earlier had it not been generally believed that the slide valve effected a better distribution of the gas in the cylinder than was otherwise possible. In describing the original Otto, it was pointed out that the spacing of the port edges, admitting the air and gas, was such that air entered the cylinder first, then air and gas, and lastly pure gas only. It was believed that when the full charge had entered the cylinder it existed in three distinct layers—the purer gas assisted the ignition, the more dilute mixture spread the flame, and, lastly, the pure air deadened to some extent the percussive effect upon the piston. A deceptive experiment in support of this theory may be made by fitting a simple piston in a glass tube. Let a cork be fitted tightly to the end of the tube beneath the piston, and into a hole in the cork pass a cigarette. Push the piston to the bottom of the tube, and then withdraw it *slowly* to about half the length of the tube. Upon lighting the cigarette, and completing the slow movement of the piston to the end of the tube, smoke will follow in a distinct stratum, and will remain unmixed with the air for some time. This slow movement, however, does not exist in a gas engine, and, moreover, the gas more readily follows the piston than in our experiment, and consequently a practically homogeneous mixture is contained in the cylinder before ignition takes place. That there is no stratum of pure air next the piston of a gas engine has been proved by igniting the charge at the forward end of the cylinder, instead of at the back of the clearance space.

As the theory of stratification was proved to be a fallacy, there appeared no reason why the mechanical difficulties of the slide valve should not be overcome by the use of separate gas and air valves. By the use of mushroom valves leakage is entirely prevented, rendering it possible to compress up to about 80 lb. or more per square inch before ignition,

TYPES OF GAS ENGINES.

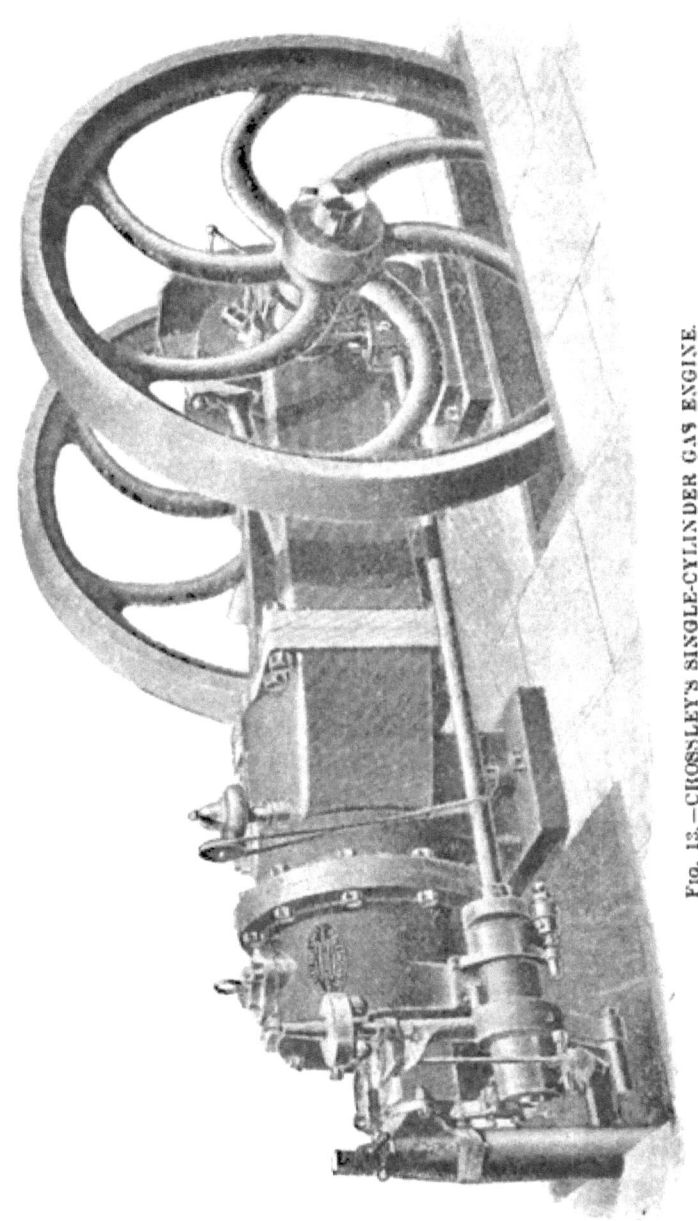

Fig. 13.—CROSSLEY'S SINGLE-CYLINDER GAS ENGINE.

whereas in the old slide engines a pressure of only 40 lb. was obtained. These valves are invariably held upon their seats by a spiral spring, and lifted by levers actuated by cams on the lay shaft.

According to their latest designs, Messrs. Crossley are building engines with one cylinder indicating up to 100 horse power, fitted with one or two flywheels, according to the requirements. Engines indicating 250 horse power are built with two cylinders placed opposite each other, their connecting rods working on the same crank pin. One specially heavy flywheel, supported by an extra bearing, is fitted to these engines for electric lighting purposes. Figs. 13 and 14 show the general external appearance of these engines. Small vertical engines, indicating up to 8 horse power, are built for various purposes. Those fitted with hoisting drums are geared to the latter by friction wheels, and an engine indicating 6 horse power may be calculated to lift 1,110 lb. at the rate of 60 ft. per minute, whereas a 2 horse power engine will lift 280 lb. at 80 ft. per minute. These figures depend to some extent upon the gearing used, and it is probable that under favourable circumstances both the weights and speeds might be increased, for it will be found from the above-quoted figures that the mechanical efficiency is from 33 per cent to 53 per cent, a somewhat low estimated efficiency for a direct-driving motor.

The ignition tube now used on the Crossley engines is a modified form of fig. 15. The central tube T is maintained at a bright red heat by means of a bunsen flame. A cylindrical cover R of non-conducting material serves to concentrate the heat. The action when working is as follows: During the compression stroke the small valve E closes upon the upper orifice by the upward movement of the lever L. The compressed mixture enters the cavity G. The moment ignition is required, the valve E descends by the pressure exerted by the spring S, when the lever L drops. The compressed gas then rushing into the tube T is ignited, and the flame strikes back into the cylinder. The valve E now

TYPES OF GAS ENGINES.

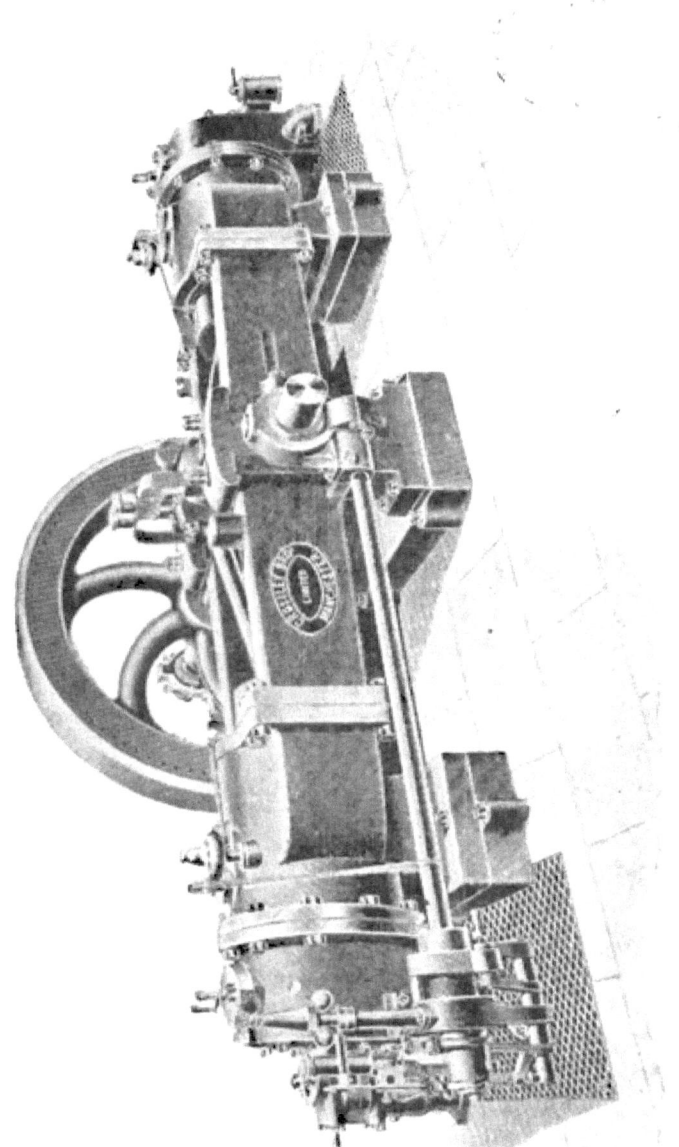

Fig. 14.—CROSSLEY'S DOUBLE-CYLINDER GAS ENGINE.

rises, and the burnt products in the tube T escape through the lower orifice of the valve E. In this design a rather long ignition tube is required, to ensure the fresh mixture reaching the hottest part of the tube T, by forcing to its upper closed end any of the burnt products remaining in the tube.

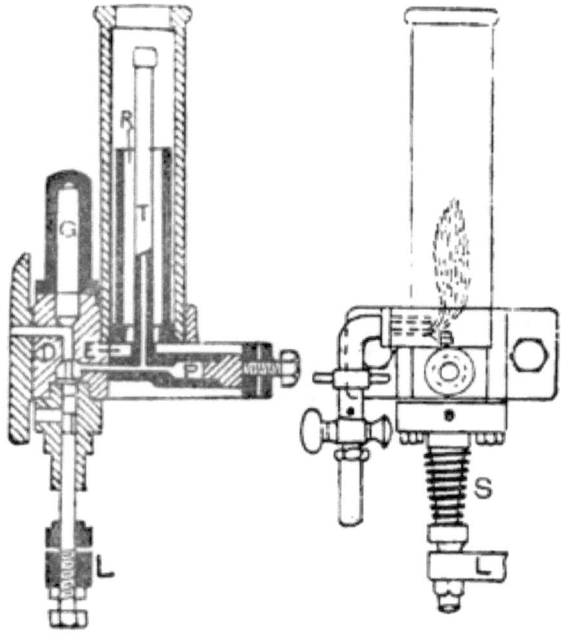

FIG. 15.—Otto Tube Igniter.

In 1893 Messrs. Crossley patented a self-starting arrangement for their gas engines, which consists essentially of a hand pump for forcing a charge into the cylinder when the crank is in a proper position for receiving an impulse. The exhaust cam on the lay shaft is so constructed as to prevent excessive compression when starting. When a charge has been pumped by hand into the cylinder, a timing valve is opened, and the charge fired by contact with the ignition tube. When the engine has acquired a considerable momentum, the exhaust valve is made to close early, and so give the required compression for continuous running.

The latest improvement in the Crossley engines is said to be due to the introduction of a scavenging arrangement, by which the exhaust gases usually remaining in the clearance space are drawn away at the end of the stroke. The innovation is fully described in a paper read by Mr. J. Atkinson, M.I.Mech.E., before the Manchester Association of Engineers, from which the following description and illustrations have been derived.

Referring to fig. 16, which shows a diagrammatic view of the piston, cylinder, and path of the crank, we may take the

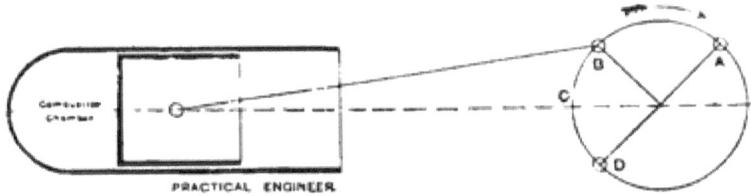

FIG. 16.—Diagram of Atkinson and Crossley's scavenging arrangement.

point A as the position of the crank pin when the exhaust valve opens for the discharge of the products of combustion. In the ordinary Otto engine this valve would close at the point C, and at the same time the air admission valve would open. But in the engines now made with Messrs. Atkinson and Crossley's scavenging arrangement, the exhaust valve remains open until the crank pin is at B, whilst the air admission valve opens at D. Thus, it will be noticed, both the air and exhaust valves are open during one-quarter of a revolution. When the exhaust valve first opens at A there is a pressure in the cylinder of about 35 lb. This is discharged into an abnormally long exhaust pipe, about 65 ft., through which it is driven by the returning piston. When the velocity of the piston approaches zero at the end of the instroke, this long column of exhaust gas, by virtue of its inertia, causes a slight vacuum to be formed in the combustion chamber. At this time the air valve is opened (see position marked D), and a draught of fresh air is drawn through the combustion chamber into the exhaust pipe, sweeping out all the remaining burnt products and replacing them with fresh air. The exhaust valve closes at B, and the gas for the next charge may then enter through the gas valve.

The variation of pressure in the cylinder is clearly shown by the accompanying indicator diagram, fig. 17, taken with a $\frac{1}{8}$ in. spring, in order to show only the effect of the long exhaust pipe. The top line of the diagram has no significance, for the indicator piston is merely pressing upon a stop provided in order to prevent damage to the weak spring during the compression and explosion strokes. The

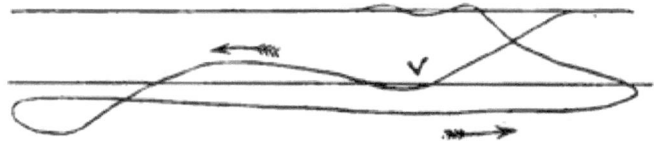

Fig. 17.—Diagram taken with $\frac{1}{8}$th spring.

pencil of the indicator leaves this horizontal line on the exhaust stroke of the engine, and the effect of the first puff of the exhaust is to set in motion a long column of gas, the inertia of which causes the slight vacuum shown at V. After this point the engine piston, travelling at its maximum velocity, causes a slight increase in the pressure, and the consequent acceleration of the gases in the exhaust pipe, which finally produces about $3\frac{1}{2}$ lb. vacuum, when the air valve admits fresh air. The suction stroke is completed at from 1 lb. to 2 lb. below the atmospheric line.

In order to assist the draught of air through the cylinder, the piston is specially shaped as shown in figs. 18 and 19. This drawing, together with fig. 20, also illustrates the usual style of mushroom valves used in nearly all modern gas engines. It will be noticed that no stuffing boxes are used,

TYPES OF GAS ENGINES. 35

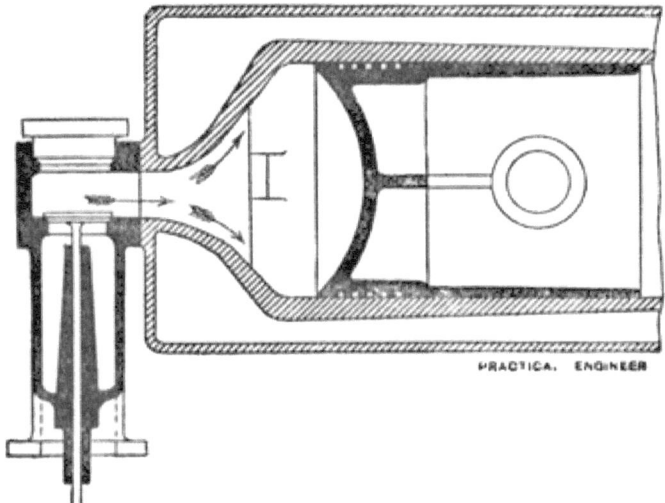

Sectional elevation.

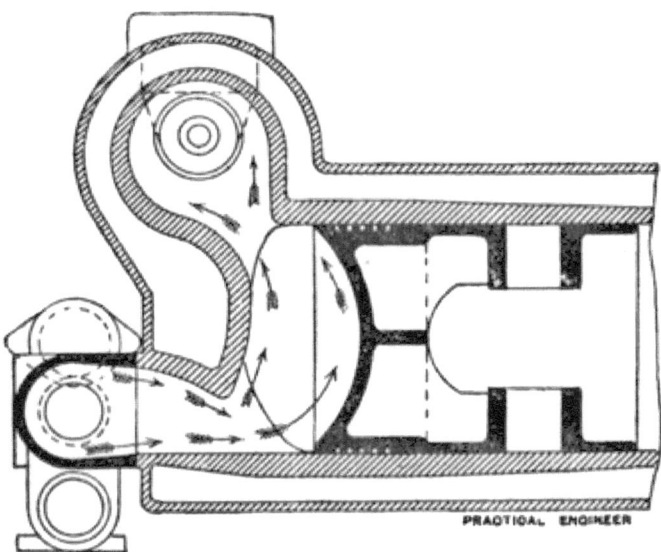

Sectional plan.

FIGS. 18 and 19.—Arrangement of air passages in Atkinson and Crossley's scavenging arrangement.

but that specially long, well-fitted spindles, working in long sleeves, are sufficient to prevent escapes. The valve spindles are always on the face subjected to the least pressure. Mr. Atkinson states that silencers and quietening chambers do not prevent the action of the exhaust, provided they are

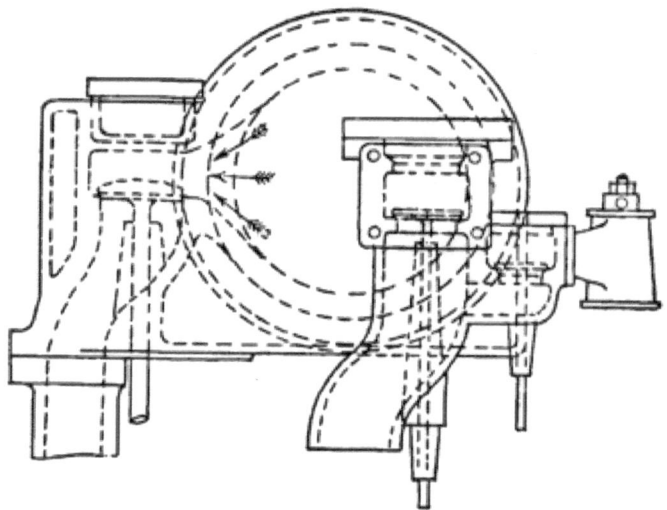

FIG. 20.—Mushroom valves used in gas engines.

placed at the end of a 65 ft. length of exhaust pipe of uniform diameter. No sudden enlargements are permissible within about 65 ft. of the engine, although drain pockets may be inserted for the collection of condensed moisture.

THE "STOCKPORT" GAS ENGINES.

The Stockport gas engine is manufactured by Messrs. J. E. H. Andrew and Co. Limited, Reddish, and works upon the Otto cycle. This firm commenced the manufacture of the "Bisschop" engine—a small motor not much used at the present—in 1878, and from that time have built over 7,000 motors of the Bisschop and Stockport design. The latest Stockport is a horizontal engine, the general features of which may be seen from the engraving (fig. 21).

The following table, supplied by the makers, is of use in the arrangement of details external to the engine itself:—

Effective horse power.	Revs. per minute.	Size of flywheels.		Standard size of pulley.		Overall dimensions, engine only.				Approximate weight.	
		Diam. One:	Width One:	Diam.	Width	Length.		Breadth.			
		Ft. In.	In.	In.	In.	Ft.	In.	Ft.	In.	Cwt.	Qr.
Vertical:											
1½	220	3 1½	4	10	6	3	4	3	0	13	2
5	200	4 0	5	18	7	3	6	3	3	22	2
Horizontal:		two:	Two:								
1	240	2 6	3½	9	5	4	9	2	6	9	2
2	220	2 11	2¾	10	6	5	3	3	0	13	2
3	220	3 2	3	14	6	5	9	3	9	18	0
5	220	3 6	4	16	7	6	9	4	0	27	3
7	220	3 11	4	18	7	7	0	4	3	32	2
9	200	4 3	5	21	8	8	0	4	6	40	0
11	200	4 3	5	21	8	8	3	5	0	45	0
13	190	4 8	5½	23	9	8	6	5	3	54	2
15	190	4 9	5½	23	10	8	9	5	6	58	2
17	185	5 2	6¼	27	12	8	10	5	9	66	0
19	185	5 3	6¼	27	12	9	0	6	0	70	0
22	185	5 3	6½	32	12	9	3	6	3	75	3
26	180	5 3	6	36	12	9	9	6	6	90	0
30	180	5 4	6	42	14	10	0	6	9	100	0
35	170	5 5	6	48	15	10	6	7	0	112	2
42	160	6 2	9	54	19	11	10	7	3	145	0
55	160	6 3	9	54	23	12	0	8	3	190	0
67	155	6 10	10	Special pulleys to suit.		13	0	8	6	210	0
80	150	7 0	10			13	3	8	9	245	0
100	150	7 2	10			17	0	10	0	361	0

The construction of the Stockport gas engine now built, may be followed by an examination of the accompanying

Fig. 21.—"Stockport" Gas Engine.

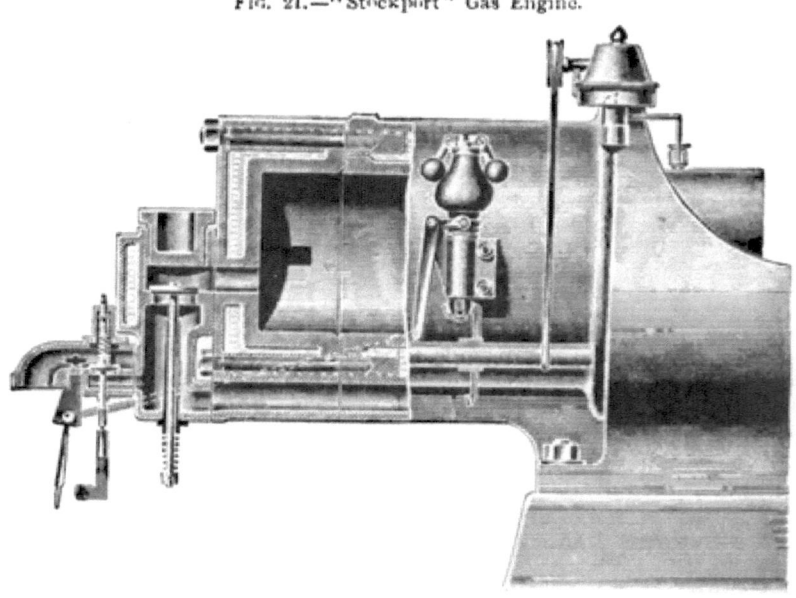

Fig. 22.—"Stockport" Gas Engine—Sectional Elevation.

drawings. Fig. 22 shows a section through the back of the cylinder, with the gas and air valves. It will be noticed that the back of the cylinder is cast separately from the remainder of the cylinder and engine framing; and further (see fig. 25) that the metal forming the back of the water jacket is specially thin. By this arrangement the casting and boring of the cylinder is much facilitated, and in the event of frost getting to the jacket, when full of water,

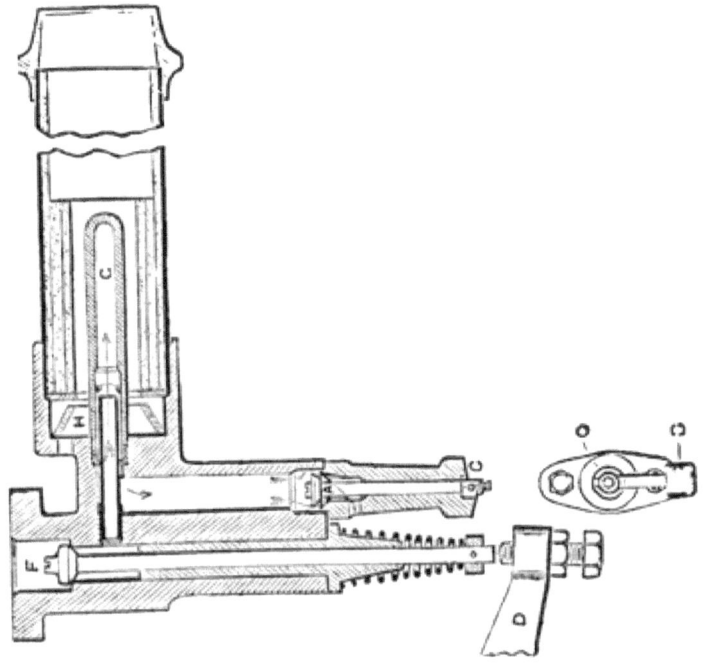

FIG. 23.—"Stockport" Gas Engine—Section of Timing Valve Bracket and Self-starter combined.

fracture due to the formation of ice will occur only at the thin wall of the jacket. This is easily and cheaply replaced, whereas if fracture occurred in the forward end of the cylinder, a large and expensive casting would be ruined.

In fig. 22 the supply of gas is coupled to the mouth of the pipe shown downwards. In this pipe is a wing throttle valve actuated by a lever from the governor. The gas passes through the mushroom valve, when the latter is lifted by a cam, and passes into a chamber beneath the air valve. Here it mixes with the air, as both are drawn into the cylinder through the upper mushroom valve. This valve is lifted by a cam shown in fig. 24, and closes by its own weight, assisted by the spiral spring upon the spindle. When the mixture is compressed by the return stroke of the piston, it is forced up to the face of the timing valve shown in the end sectional view, also in detail in fig. 23. At the end of the stroke the timing valve F is pushed from

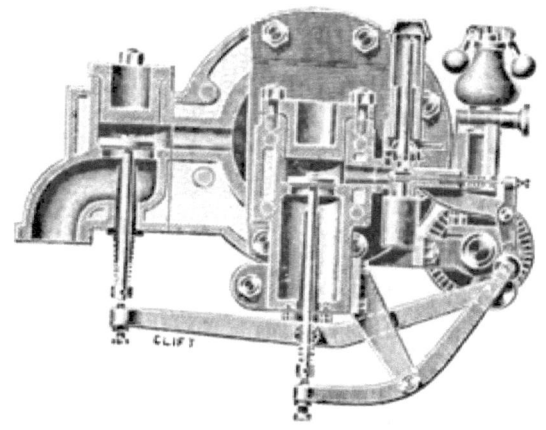

FIG. 24. – "Stockport" Gas Engine—Sectional End Elevation.

its seat by the lever D, and the gas entering the red-hot tube G is exploded. The timing valve may be adjusted by the set screw on the end of the lever D. If the explosion occurs too early, the set screw should be slightly withdrawn, if too late it should be slightly screwed forward and locked by the nut for that purpose.

The ignition tube G has an internal tube of smaller diameter entering its lower end. This affords an annular space communicating with the valve A. This valve, when down upon its seat, permits the escape of the gas in the tube after explosion, through a groove cut in the seating. This renders the tube more certain in its action, for it is obvious that if the burnt products were pent up in the tube at a high pressure, the fresh mixture to be exploded would not enter, and would therefore not ignite. Messrs. Andrews make their ignition tubes of a special alloy of silver, which they maintain will resist the corrosive action of the explosive gases at high temperatures. The valve A, fig. 23, is of special use to assist the self starting of the engine. This is done in the following way. The engine is barred round until the connecting rod is on the top throw and about at right angles to the crank. The best position for starting is governed to a great extent, by the nature and quality of gas used, but

FIG. 25.—"Stockport" Gas Engine—Section of Cylinder End.

a few trials will enable the attendant to secure the best position for a given case. The exhaust valve lever is geared to the starting cam to prevent excessive compression at starting. After taking the precaution to admit gas gradually to the gas bags and to have the ignition tube at a bright red heat, the valve C, fig. 23, may be opened by raising the weighted lever B into a vertical position. The timing valve F will be open with the crank in the position for starting; consequently if gas is admitted to the cylinder by means of a special starter pipe, it will find its way, together with displaced air, through the valve F, up into the ignition tube, downwards as indicated by the arrows, and out at A.

This stream of air and gas continues until the mixture becomes rich enough in gas to explode. The engine will then start, and receive its next charge of gas through the main gas valve supplying the engine. The exhaust lever bowl is put to run upon the ordinary working cam; the valve A is closed by the action of the weighted lever B pressing the inclined plane at C. It will be noticed that if,

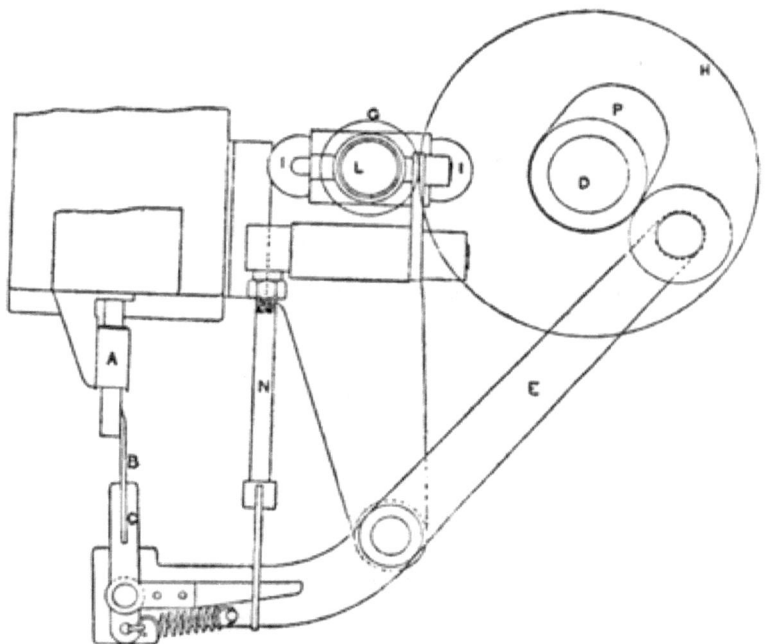

FIG. 26.—"Stockport" Gas Engine—Governing Arrangement.

in attempting to start, the gas enters the cylinder very rapidly, it may displace all the air first and not be sufficiently diffused to effect combustion when it passes into the hot tube. For this reason the gas is not turned fully on to the gas bags, so that it may have time to diffuse somewhat with the air in the cylinder before passing into the ignition tube. Immediately after the first impulse the gas should be fully turned on.

The engine is governed by first throttling the gas in the inlet pipe when the governor rises. Should the speed increase after throttling has taken place, the governor, still rising, brings the throttle-valve lever, fig. 22, in contact with the bell-crank lever actuating the gas-valve spindle, and so cuts off entirely the gas supply. The most recently

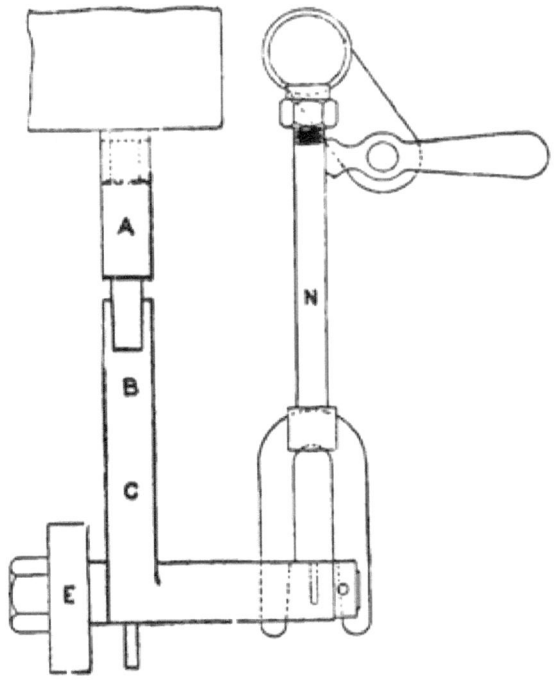

Fig. 27.—"Stockport" Gas Engine—Governing Arrangement.

designed governor used upon the Stockport engine is of the horizontal type, shown in figs. 26-27. A cam on the lay shaft drives the gas-valve lever E. At the end of E is a bell-crank lever, held in the position shown by the spiral spring. The rod N, actuated by the governor, terminates in a fork, which when moved sideways (see fig. 27) engages the end of the bell-crank lever, overcomes the tension of the spiral spring, so that when the tripper blade rises it misses the notch under A on the gas-valve spindle, thus cutting out entirely the gas supply. The range of action of the throttle valve depends to some extent upon the width of the fork on the lever N, and when its limit is reached the gas is entirely cut off. The speed of the engine is raised

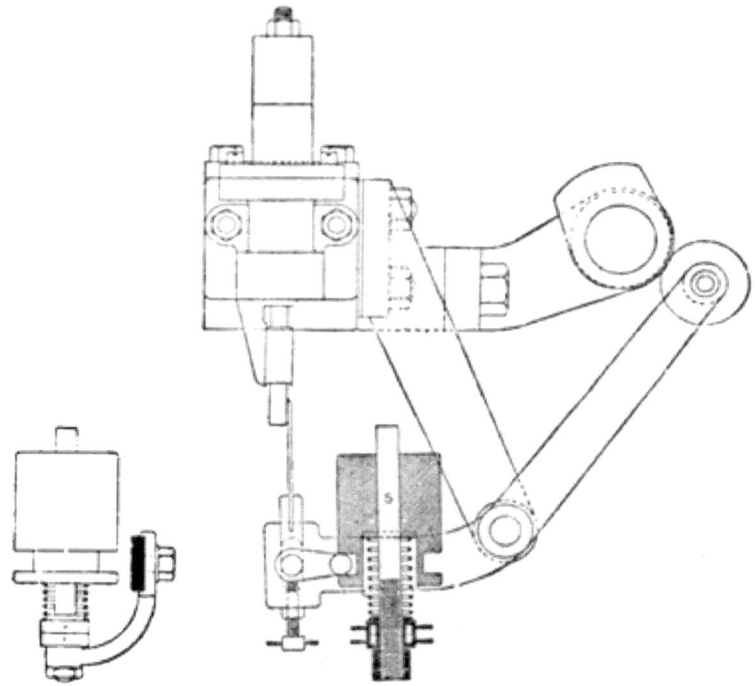

Fig. 28.—"Stockport" Gas Engine—Arrangement of Governor for Small Engines.

by compressing the spring on the governor spindle by means of two adjusting lock nuts.

The peculiar and sudden action of cam-driven levers renders it possible to entirely cut out the gas supply, when the speed increases, by a simpler mechanism than that just described. Fig. 28 shows a form of simple vibrating governor, which is fitted to the smaller engines of Stockport design. The valve lever carries a vertical spindle S. Upon this spindle a cast-iron weight slides freely, but is supported by a spiral spring, the height of which may be adjusted by the two lock nuts shown. If the speed of the engine increases beyond the limit, the inertia of the weight upon

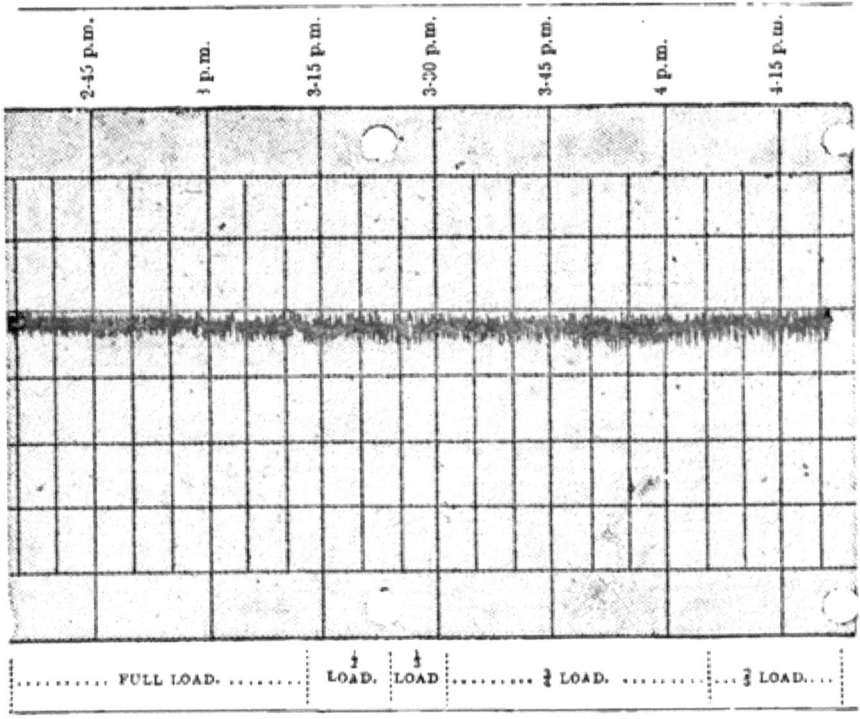

Fig. 29.—Moscrop Recorder Diagram.

the spindle S overcomes and compresses the spring supporting it. This in effect rotates the bell-crank lever slightly in a clock-wise direction, causing the tripper blade to miss the notch on the gas-valve spindle.

CHAPTER IV.
THE "GRIFFIN" ENGINE.

This engine has already been mentioned, and the cycle has been explained in the text relating to fig. 12. The Griffin engine is manufactured by Messrs. Dick, Kerr, and Co., of Kilmarnock, and since its introduction has been much simplified, and has had a considerable sale in England. Amongst other special features of the engine, the steadiness of running under varying loads is noteworthy. Fig. 29 is a Moscrop recorder diagram taken from a double-acting engine with single cylinder, developing 70 horse power on

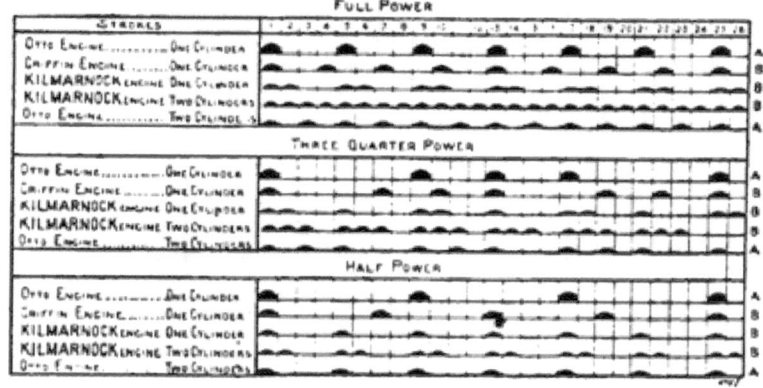

FIG. 30.

A. Single-acting engines.   B. Double-acting engines.

the brake, and fitted with a special electric lighting governor. The distance between the horizontal lines represents a variation in speed of 5 per cent, and the distance between the vertical lines is traversed by the paper in five minutes. The trial lasted 1¾ hours, and the loads were varied between full load and one-third load, with a variation in speed of about 2¼ per cent. The following diagram, fig. 30, supplied to the author by the makers, shows the impulses given to the pistons of various types of engines running at full, three-quarter, and half power. It will be noticed here that the Kilmarnock engine, running at half load, has twice as many impulses as the ordinary Otto engine running at full load, and $3\frac{1}{2}$ times as many at half load. All the engines constructed by Messrs. Dick, Kerr, and Co. larger than 12 brake horse power are double acting. The double-acting six-cycle engines, having two

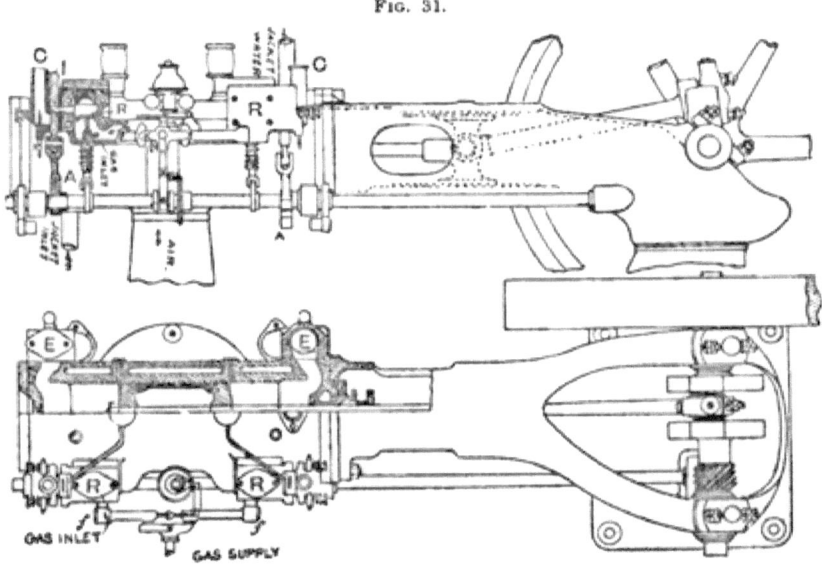

Fig. 31.

Fig. 32.

Sectional Elevation and Plan of Griffin Double-acting Gas Engine.

idle strokes, for scavenging purposes, are termed the "Griffin" motor, and the double-acting engines, dispensing with the idle strokes, are called the "Kilmarnock." In the latter type the turning effort exerted upon the crank pin is more regular, though, according to accepted theory, some loss in efficiency may be occasioned by the presence of burnt gases in the cylinder of this latter type.

The details of a double-acting engine will be understood on reference to fig. 31. This is an illustration of a recent design of Griffin engine. The engine is of the horizontal pattern, with balance weights on the crank webs. The side shaft is driven by a 3 to 1 worm gearing on the crank shaft, shown in fig. 32. The cylinder is closed at both ends, and is consequently kept free from the grinding action of dust, which in some factories may have a very serious effect upon an open-ended cylinder. The cylinder is water jacketed, together with the piston-rod gland. From the one side shaft all the valves and governor are driven. The two exhaust ports are shown at E E, and are operated by cams, acting on levers passing under the cylinder, lifting plain mushroom valves. On the opposite side of the cylinder are placed the governor gear, distribution valves, and igniting slides. At f in fig. 32 the exterior of the gas-valve boxes are shown. After passing through the valves at f, the gas meets air drawn up through the bed, as indicated by the arrows in fig. 31. Mixing with the air, it now passes through the inlet valve R into the cylinder, the valve R closes, and the charge is compressed in the combustion chamber and the space above the valve R.

The ignition slide I is now opened by the eccentric A, and makes communication between the flame in C and the compressed mixture. The governor controls the gas supply by throttling its passage through the valves in f and f until the gas is entirely cut off. Referring only to the back end of the cylinder, the sequence of operations is as follows: The gas valve f is opened by its cam, and gas, mixing with air, passes through R into the cylinder, R closes, and the charge is compressed on the return stroke of the piston. Ignition takes place, driving the piston forward. The exhaust opens, and the products of combustion are expelled. The exhaust valve E closes and R is opened, but as the gas valve f remains closed, air only is drawn into the cylinder. This in turn is expelled through the exhaust port E, and the cycle being completed, a fresh charge is again drawn

TYPES OF GAS ENGINES. 49

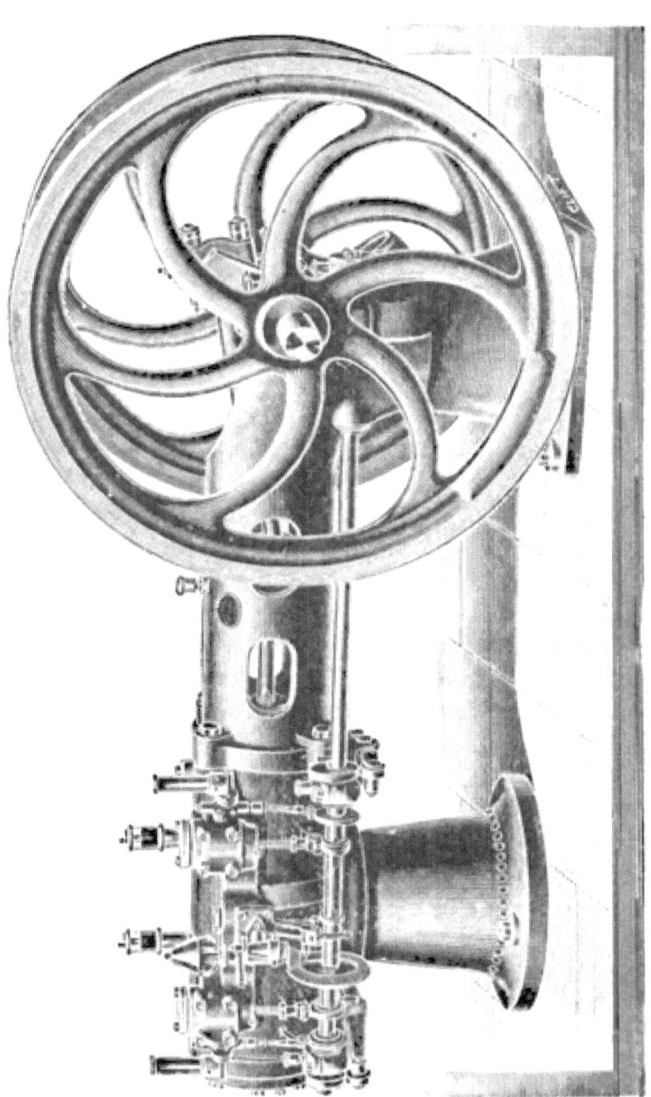

FIG. 33.—KILMARNOCK DOUBLE-ACTING GAS ENGINE.

into the cylinder. Precisely the same action takes place in the front end of the cylinder, thus giving two impulses to the piston every six strokes.

Fig. 33 shows an outside view of the Kilmarnock engine, the details of the valves and igniting arrangements being somewhat revised. A timing valve, of the mushroom pattern, is substituted for the slide, and a hot tube is substituted for the flame shown in the previous illustrations.

Fig. 34 is an illustration of a recent design of engines as supplied to the Corporation of Belfast for the generation of electricity for lighting purposes. Four of these engines, each indicating 120 horse power, are driving four 60 kilowatt dynamos, and two smaller engines, having single instead of tandem cylinders, are driving two 26 kilowatt dynamos. The efficiency of the engines and dynamos combined proved to be 76 per cent, and the gas consumption per electrical horse power was less than 24 cubic feet. This value might be somewhat reduced if rich coal gas were used, instead of, as in the present instance, the gas being composed of coal gas and enriched water gas. The tandem design has been adopted by Messrs. Dick, Kerr, and Co. because of its narrow width, and consequent economy of space. The increase in length, consequent upon the position of the tandem cylinder, is utilised by placing the cylinders between the dynamo and the engine crank shaft— an arrangement advocated upon a previous page. Each dynamo is driven by eight $\frac{7}{8}$ in. ropes, and for this reason it is essential to run the engine contra-clockwise, in order that the tight side of ropes shall be at the bottom. This precaution, as has been already pointed out, is not essential with a belt drive, but when ropes are used there is a danger of them leaving the grooves if not kept tight at the bottom. Each engine is fitted with a flywheel on the opposite end of the shaft occupied by the rope-driving pulley.

In this design of engine there is an explosion every stroke, but no scavenging strokes are made. In the front

TYPES OF GAS ENGINES. 51

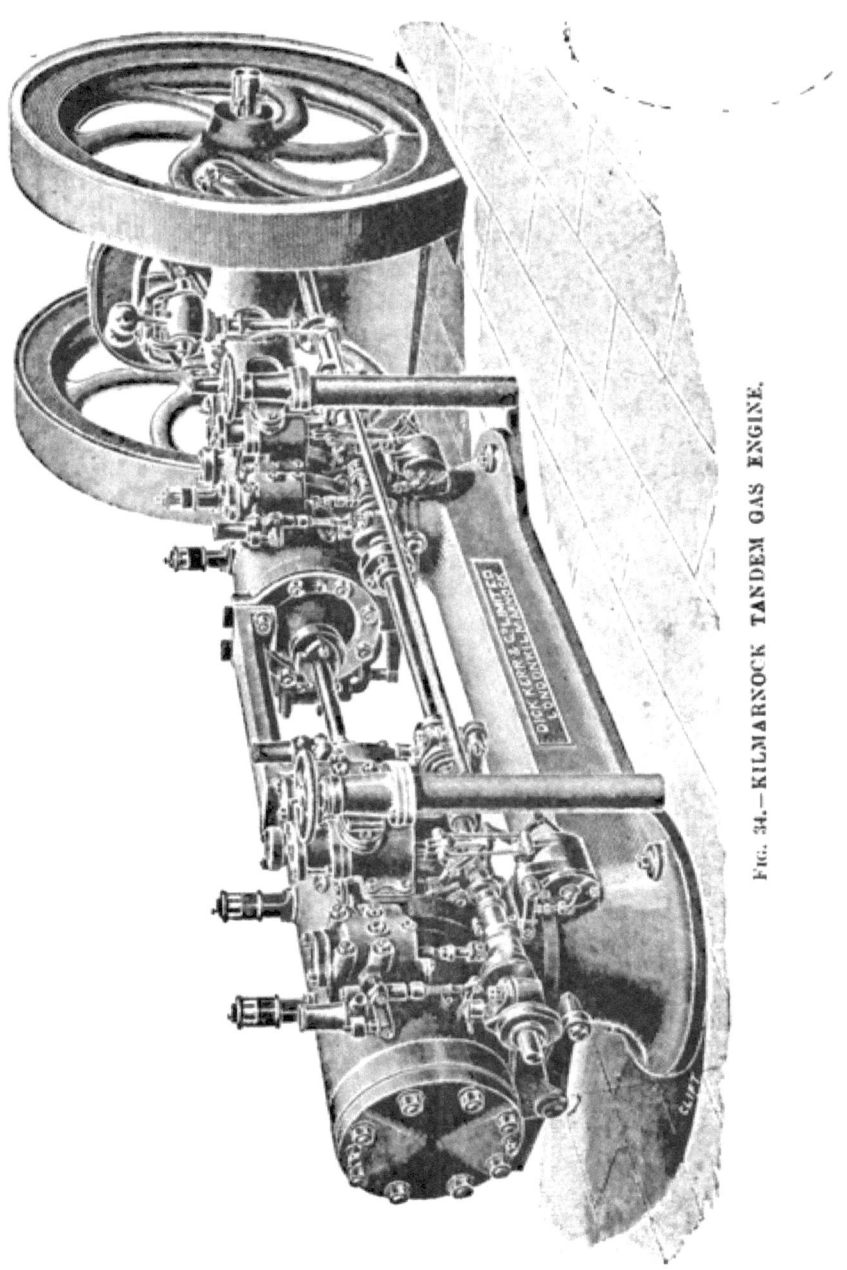

Fig. 34.—KILMARNOCK TANDEM GAS ENGINE.

and back of each cylinder a complete Otto cycle is carried out once in two revolutions in the following order: First, the charge in the back end of the back cylinder is fired; second, that in the front end of the forward cylinder; third, that in the back end of the forward cylinder; and lastly, the charge is fired in the front end of the back cylinder. The governing is carried out by a special electric light governor, reducing the quantity of gas supplied to each of the cylinders. This method is found preferable to one in which the gas supply is entirely cut out. At Belfast the starting of the engine is effected by utilising electric energy stored in the batteries, by sending a current through the dynamos, converting them for the time being into motors, and so driving the gas engines, until a charge is drawn into the cylinder and ignited.

The exhaust pipe of each engine communicates with a main exhaust pipe, to which a silencer is fitted, but it is found that there is less probability of noise when two or more engines are working than when only one is exhausting, for the flow of exhaust gas is then more regular, and does not cause that coughing noise often so objectionable.

Besides a large circulating tank for supplying the water jackets, provision is made for admitting water from the town mains direct to the jacket; and as a still further precaution, each engine is provided with a circulating pump for driving water through the jacket.

At Coatbridge,* near Glasgow, Messrs. Dick, Kerr, and Co. have supplied engines for driving the electric light, worked by producer gas. In this installation each engine has two cylinders placed side by side instead of tandem. The starting of the engines is effected by utilising the pressure in the steam boiler used in connection with the gas-producing plant, about which more will be written. A special valve is fitted to the back of one cylinder of the engine, and is operated entirely by a hand lever. A steam pipe is connected to each of these valves, and steam enters

---

* Since the publication of the first edition of this book, these engines have been removed and steam substituted.

the cylinder when the operator opens the starting valve. The operator, performing the work of the eccentric on a steam engine, opens and closes the starting valve until the engine has acquired a momentum sufficiently great to draw into the cylinder, and compress, a charge. Ignition then takes place. The largest gas engine made by this firm indicates over 700 horse power, and is specially interesting, inasmuch as it is constructed upon a compound principle. The engine somewhat resembles a large triple-expansion horizontal steam engine, and has two 10 ft. diameter by 14 in. face flywheels. Two 21 in. diameter by 30 in. stroke cylinders are placed one on each side a 32 in. diameter cylinder having a 36 in. stroke. One of the high-pressure cylinders only exhausts into the central cylinder, the other being kept separate for starting the engine by the application of steam pressure, as above described.

CHAPTER V.

THE TANGYE ENGINE

MESSRS. TANGYE'S gas engines work upon the Otto cycle, but improvements have been made in the igniting and governing gear, and in a self-starting arrangement. Fig. 35 shows an outside view of an engine which will give a maximum indicated horse power of 115. Messrs. Tangye construct single-cylinder engines, indicating $\frac{1}{2}$ H.P. to 150 H.P., all of which work with either town or other gases made by their own producer plant. The combustion chamber is specially formed to prevent shock to the working parts during explosion, and also assists in making the charge more homogeneous. Messrs. Tangye claim that these improvements render their engines specially useful for electric lighting, a large number having already been made for that purpose. It is stated that, working with gas costing 2s. 6d. per 1,000 cubic feet, a 30 H.P. engine will produce 1 kilowatt for each penny expended, which works out to about 2 cubic feet of gas per 10 candle power lamp. The weight of anthracite coal used in the producers for running an engine of about 70 brake horse power is said to be less than 1 lb. per B.H.P. per hour.

The large engines are now started with a new and very powerful starter, which is capable of starting the engine against half its working load. A charge of gas and air is pumped by hand into a detached receiver, there being an excess of gas present, thus rendering the charge inexplosive in the receiver. The engine is barred round into the position for the commencement of a forward stroke. The charge in the receiver is pumped up to a pressure of about 40 lb. per square inch. At this pressure communication is made with the working cylinder, and the charge enters the combustion chamber, and by mixing with the air present in the combustion chamber forms a strong explosive mixture. This, however, is at first prevented from igniting by the closed ignition valve being tightly held upon its seat by a lever operated by a cam upon the side shaft. Under the initial pressure of the gas entering the combustion chamber the piston moves forward; the cam then releases the ignition valve, and explosion takes place.

By setting the engine in motion before igniting the charge, excessive stress upon the working parts is greatly avoided. Fig. 36 is a drawing of the self-starter patented by Mr. C. W. Pinkney, to whom many other improvements in Messrs. Tangye's gas engines are due. In the drawing, the ignition tube I and starting pump are shown together; this arrangement is, of course, subjected to modifications necessary in special cases. The valves a and b are the suction and delivery valves respectively of the starting pump P. The valve a, shown separately, is contained in the same valve box as b, and is in communication with the passage c. A gas pipe is coupled to g, and by the small port shown the gas mixes with the air drawn in

TYPES OF GAS ENGINES.

FIG. 35.—THE TANGYE GAS ENGINE.

through the valve a. The gas port terminates in an annular space, to facilitate the mixing with the air. The proportion of these valves is such as to admit a mixture of about four volumes of air to one of gas. This may be delivered to the receiver, as previously mentioned, or may be pumped directly into the combustion chamber. In the latter case

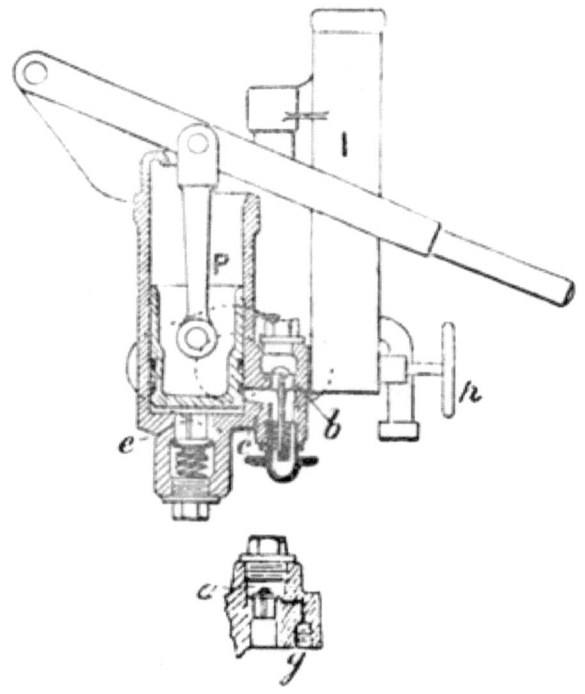

Fig. 36.—Pinkney's Self-starter for Gas Engines.

the handwheel h controls admission to the ignition tube, and the engine is arranged to fire only when the hand wheel is turned. The valve e is held up to its seating by a spiral spring beneath it, and the spring is adjusted so that the valve e may open when the desired pressure in the pump and combustion chamber, or receiver, has been acquired, thus giving an indication that the mixture is ready for firing. In connection with this starter, Mr. Pinkney has patented an arrangement for preventing the movement of the engine piston when the pressure of the hand pump is first felt in the combustion chamber; for it is obvious that, when the hand pump delivers directly into the combustion chamber of a small engine, the crank will slowly move towards the forward dead centre, and be in that position when the charge is ready for firing. To obviate this, a stud upon the crank web engages with a spring catch of sufficient strength to hold the crank in its starting position until the greater pressure of the explosion causes its release. The bar, with its catch, then falls clear of the crank as it revolves. This gear is only suitable for

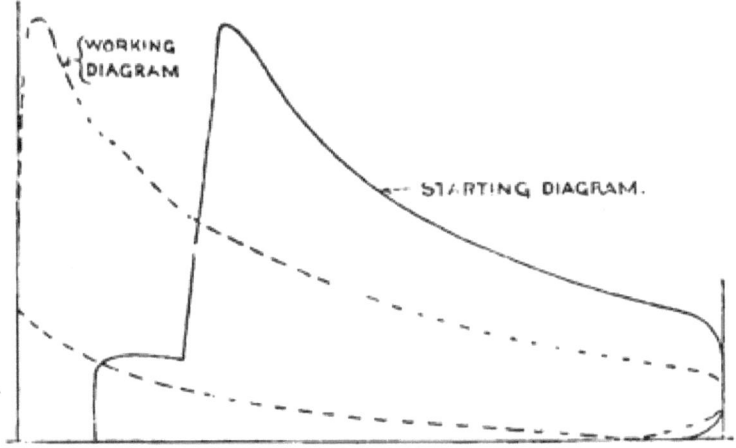

Fig. 37.—Starting and Working Diagram taken from Tangyes' Gas Engine.

small engines fitted with self-starters, larger engines being fitted with a special receiver to contain the charge until it is admitted to the combustion chamber by means of a valve operated by hand.

An indicator diagram taken from an engine of this latter type is shown in fig. 37. It is seen from this diagram that the engine piston is standing in a position equal to one-ninth of its forward stroke before communication is made between the combustion chamber and the receiver. The pressure immediately rises when the communicating valve is opened to about 40 lb. per square inch. The diagram also shows that two-ninths of the forward stroke are completed before ignition takes place. The remainder of the full-line diagram shows the explosion and expansion during the first revolution. The dotted diagram has been taken after the engine has acquired its proper working speed. The latter shows a maximum pressure of 200 lb. per square inch, and a compression pressure of 72 lb. per square inch.

Messrs. Tangye's engines have a specially hard metal liner fitted to the cylinder, which can quickly be replaced. Lubrication is effected by motion derived from the side shaft. A ratchet wheel, shown on the lubricator in the external view of these engines, slowly revolves, and thereby raises a plunger against the resistance of a strong spiral spring. Oil follows into the plunger chamber, and is injected into the cylinder by the release of the plunger from the top of its stroke. The worm wheels driving the side shaft are cut from solid metal, and run in an oil bath, the casing of which can easily be removed for examination of the wheels. The governor is of the centrifugal high-speed type, and acts directly upon the gas supply without throttling.

THE FIELDING GAS ENGINE.

This engine is made by Messrs. Fielding and Platt, of the Atlas Works, Gloucester, and is constructed upon the Otto cycle. Fig. 38 shows an outside view of the engine. The valves, which are of the plain mitre type, are driven in the usual way from the crank shaft, by means of cams on a side shaft. The governor is of the ordinary high-speed type, and is driven from the side shaft by bevel wheels. Another type of governor used on Messrs. Fielding and Platt's earlier

TYPES OF GAS ENGINES.

FIG. 28.—THE FIELDING GAS ENGINE.

engines was actuated by a cam on the side shaft. In this case the governor consisted of a simple dashpot and piston, the rod of which was connected to a lever working the gas

FIG. 39.—Indicator Diagram from Fielding and Platt's Engine, running with no load.

valve. If the speed of the engine increased beyond that to which the dashpot was adjusted, then the cam left the piston at the top of its stroke, coming round into its lifting

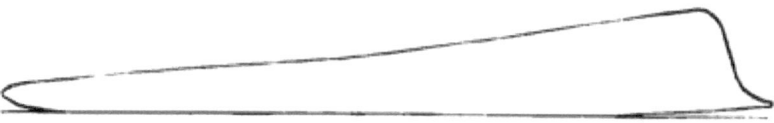

FIG. 40.—Indicator Diagram from Fielding and Platt's Engine, running at about one-third load.

position before the piston had time to descend; consequently the gas valve was not opened.

A feature in the governing of this firm's electric lighting

FIG. 41.—Indicator Diagram from Fielding and Platt's Engine, running at nearly full load.

engine is illustrated by the accompanying indicator diagrams, figs. 39, 40, and 41. The governor is of the ball type, and regulates the gas and air supply, so that even when running light an explosion is never missed. This arrangement, though possibly slightly increasing the consumption of gas, undoubtedly conduces to steady running under a fluctuating load. It is stated by Messrs. Fielding and Platt that the variation in speed between light and full load is about $3\frac{1}{2}$ per cent. The gas consumption in an engine of this type, of 100 B.H.P., is claimed to be under 20 cubic feet per hour per B.H.P.

Messrs. Fielding have recently patented an efficient system of starting their larger gas engines by the use of compressed air. When the engine is about to be stopped after its first run the gas is turned off, and the piston and engine cylinder, by a slight alteration in valves, is converted into an air compressor, which discharges into a reservoir until a pressure of about 60 lb. is obtained. In this way the energy stored in the flywheels is utilised until the engine comes to rest. The charge of air thus obtained is sufficient to start from six to twelve times. The starting is effected in the following way: The crank is barred just over the back dead centre, and gas is admitted by a hand gas tap to the combustion chamber. The displaced air is allowed to escape through an open cock until gas which will burn with a clear blue flame begins to issue from the open cock. These cocks are now closed, and compressed air from the reservoir is admitted to the combustion chamber, forming a rich mixture. The igniting valve is now opened, and a powerful impulse is given to the piston. It is said that the engine will start by this means even against half the full load.

THE "PREMIER" GAS ENGINE.

The "Premier" gas engine, patented by Mr. J. H. Hamilton, B.Sc., is manufactured by Messrs. Wells Brothers, Sandiacre, near Nottingham. An external view is shown in fig. 42, with modified valve gear. Its characteristic feature is the scavenging arrangement. Fig. 43 is a sectional view of the engine, and from it the working of the scavenging stroke

62   TYPES OF GAS ENGINES.

Fig. 42.—WELLS' PREMIER GAS ENGINE.

may easily be followed. There are two pistons, C and D, cast together with a cylindrical connection. The piston C receives the impulse due to the explosion of the charge, whilst the piston D acts merely as an air pump. The exhaust valve E is actuated by a lever driven by a cam on the side shaft (see fig. 44). The gas and air valves are driven by one lever, and are arranged, as shown, upon the same spindle. The gas valve is made an easy fit upon the air-valve spindle, but is held up to its seat by a spiral spring. Upon the outstroke of the pistons, air is drawn through rubber or leather valves in the bed plate, shown at A. The chamber marked A has a free communication with the chamber marked B. When the air valve is depressed beyond the position shown in the drawing, the gas valve is opened by contact with the collar shown upon the spindle. The exhaust valve E being closed during the outstroke of the pistons, air, mixing with the gas, enters the combustion chamber, as indicated by the arrows. When sufficient gas to form a charge has entered, the air-valve spindle slightly lifts, closes the gas supply, but still admits air to complete the charge. Upon the instroke of the pistons, the charge is compressed in the combustion chamber to about 60 lb. per square inch ; at the same time the air entrapped between the two pistons becomes compressed to about 9 lb. per square inch. Thus the air valve has upon its lower face a pressure of 60 lb. per square inch, and upon its upper face 9 lb. per square inch ; the difference, 51 lb. per square inch, tends to keep the valve tight upon its seat. In order to control the action of the air valve, and to make its movement independent of the difference of pressure upon its upper and lower faces, a strong spiral spring is attached to the lever L, fig. 44, tending always to force the air valve on its seat. The cam driving L gives the air valve a long and a short stroke alternately, the former for the admission of the charge, the latter for the admission of air only.

When the charge is compressed it is fired by a timing valve, and both pistons travel outwards. During this out-

64   TYPES OF GAS ENGINES.

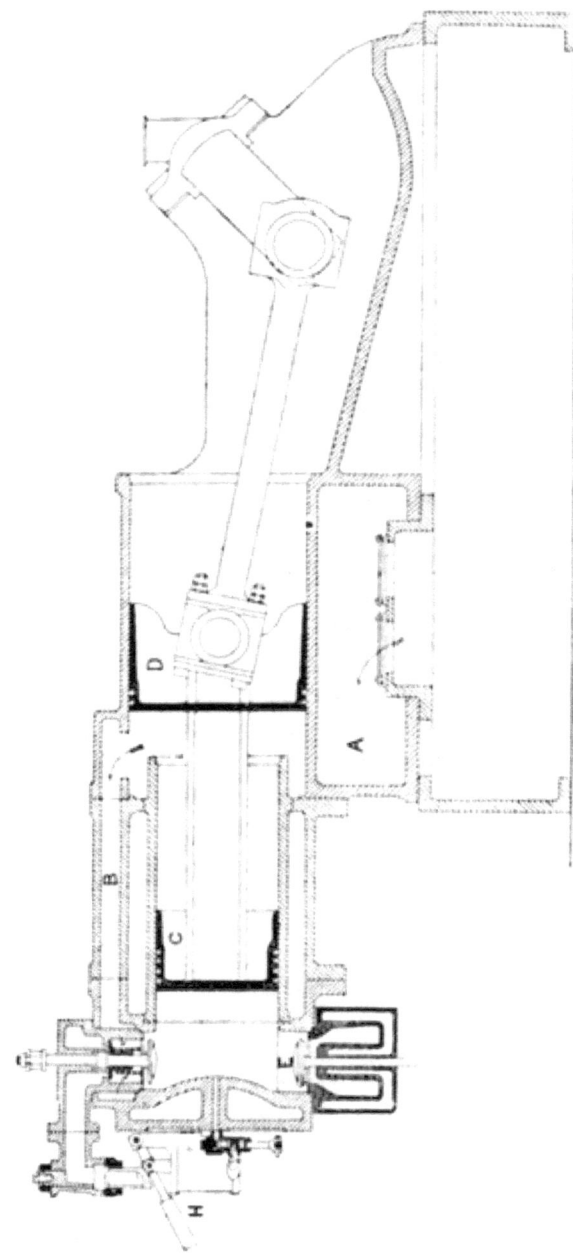

FIG. 43.—LONGITUDINAL SECTION OF PREMIER GAS ENGINE.

stroke the air already compressed by the larger piston D expands, and gives back to the engine the energy stored in it by compression. At the end of the outstroke the exhaust valve opens, and releases the pressure in the combustion chamber. It is evident that so long as the pressure in the combustion chamber during the exhaust stroke is nearly atmospheric, the piston D will displace a volume of

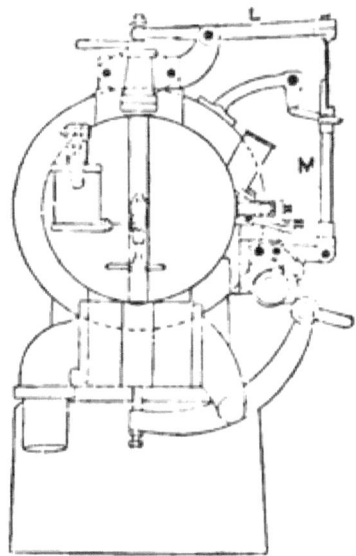

FIG. 44.— End View of Premier Gas Engine.

air and drive it through the combustion chamber into the exhaust pipe. This effectually clears the combustion chamber of its burnt products, and this done, the exhaust closes, and the cycle is repeated. The indicator diagram shown in fig. 45 has been taken from the working cylinder, whilst the diagram shown in fig. 46 has been taken from the pumping cylinder. Following the direction of the arrows on fig. 46, it will be seen that little or no work is lost in compressing the entrapped air in the chamber B, for the air-expansion curve nearly coincides with the compression curve. At the commencement of the exhaust stroke the pumping piston raises the air pressure, the air valve opens, and air is forced into the combustion chamber *against the*

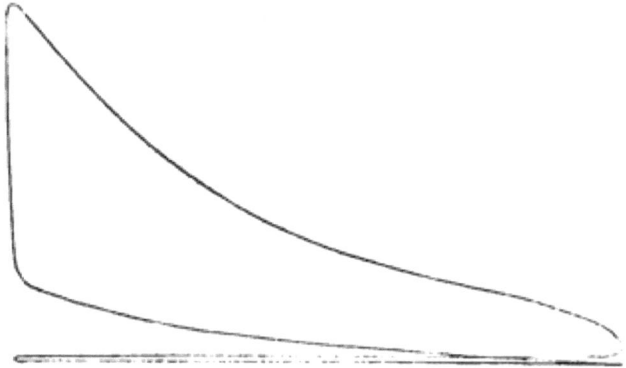

Fig. 45.—Working Diagram from Premier Gas Engine.

pressure of the exhaust. This point is shown on the diagram at P; the area P A S E of this diagram gives the work done by the pump in retarding the motion of the engine; and the net indicated horse power is found by subtracting from the

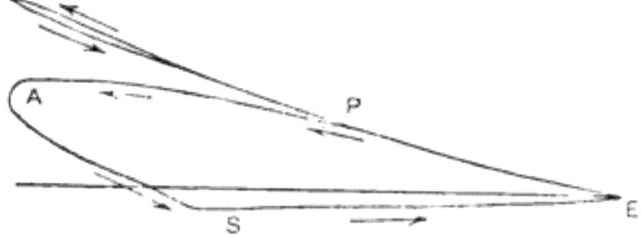

Fig. 46.—Pumping Diagram from Premier Gas Engine.

I.H.P. of the working cylinder the I.H.P. of the pumping cylinder. It must be remembered that the area P A S E of the pumping diagram occurs only at every alternate revolution; consequently, in obtaining the H.P. the revolutions per minute must be divided by 2. It must also be noted that the effective area of the piston D, fig. 43, is not its whole area, but only that which remains after subtracting from it the area of the piston C.

In engines of this type it is extremely important, from the makers' point of view, to have a free exhaust pipe, for cases are not unknown in which the undue throttling of the exhaust pipes has so raised the back pressure as to cause the burnt products to enter the chamber B as soon as the air valve opens, thus entirely preventing the scavenging action. It is, for another reason, highly important to keep the exhaust pressure low, for the area of the pumping diagram depends upon it, and represents lost work.

This engine is started by means of a hand pump in the following way: The bowl on the exhaust lever is made to engage with a projection on its cam, so that the compression of the charge may be relieved. The engine is then barred round until the crank has turned through about 45 deg. of its forward *working* stroke. It is very important that the engine should start from such a position that all the valves are ready for the impulse, for it is obvious that by careless handling the engine might be started from the position corresponding to the suction stroke. In the latter case the exhaust valve would not open at the end of the stroke, and the burnt products would enter the chamber B, and probably damage the valves at X. When the engine is in the correct position, the timing valve is closed by a short lever inserted by hand. Gas is then turned to the hand-pump suction valve, and two or three strokes taken with the lever H. The gas supply to the pump is then turned off, and the main gas cock to the engine opened. The hand-pump lever is again worked, and the pump delivers air to the combustion chamber. As soon as the engine piston commences to move forward under the pressure of the charge, the timing valve is released by hand, the charge enters the ignition tube, and a strong forward impulse is given. When the engine has acquired some momentum, the exhaust bowl is put into its working position, and gives the correct compression to the charges. The relative number of strokes of the hand pump when drawing gas and air respectively must be determined for each case by trial, as the quality of gas varies considerably.

The governing of the engine is effected by the movement of the rod M, fig. 44, actuated by an ordinary high-speed centrifugal governor. When M is moved to the right its knife edge acts upon the gas lever L at a greater distance from its fulcrum; consequently the gas valve is not fully

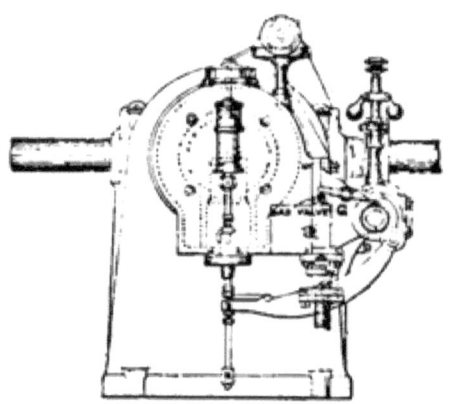

FIG. 47.—End of View of "Forward" Otto Gas Engine.

opened. It is merely a matter of arrangement whether the gas supply be entirely cut off or gradually decreased. In fig. 44, the lever M would first throttle the gas supply, and after a further increase in speed cut it off entirely.

The ignition tubes supplied by this firm are made in nickel, and will stand continuous use for several months.

The "Forward" gas engine is manufactured by Messrs. T. B. Barker and Co., of Birmingham. Figs. 47 show a sectional elevation and end view of this engine. The cylinder is 10 in. diameter by 20 in. stroke, and running at a speed of 180 revolutions per minute the engine will develop about 25 I.H.P., and about 20 on the brake.

TYPES OF GAS ENGINES.

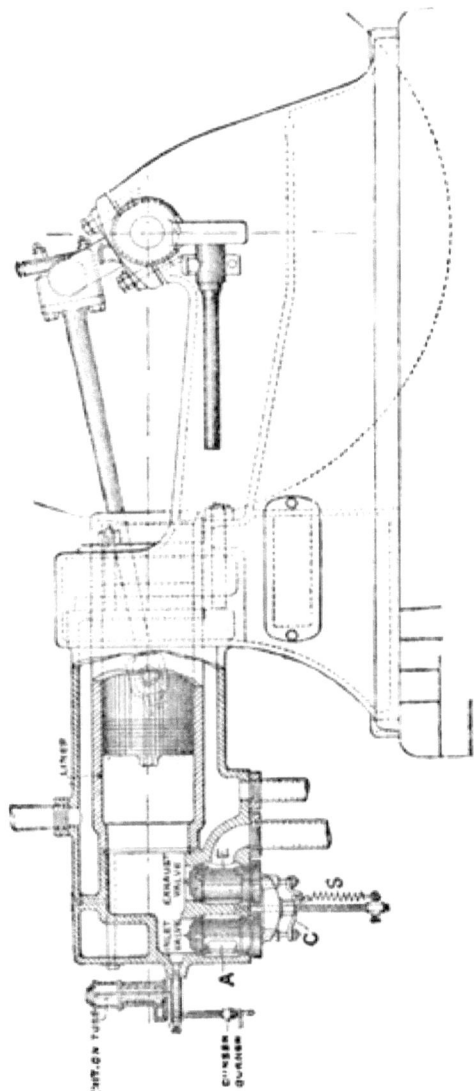

FIG. 47A.—LONGITUDINAL SECTION OF "FORWARD" OTTO GAS ENGINE.

An important feature in this design is the reduction of port surface to a minimum. It will be noticed that the air and exhaust valves A and E, fig. 47A, are placed as near the combustion chamber as possible. They are fitted to separate seatings, as shown at A and E. The gas is admitted by the valve G, fig. 47, and mingles with the air on its way to the valve A. The spring S is connected to a bar, one end of which rests upon the crossbar C, and the other upon the levers driving the valves. By this arrangement one spring suffices. Messrs. Barker and Co. do not use an ignition valve, but rely entirely upon the compression of the charge into the ignition tube for the correct timing of the explosion. The cylinder is formed by a liner of special cylinder metal, having an asbestos joint where it is attached to the combustion chamber. This to some extent prevents the conduction of heat from the combustion chamber to the fore end of the cylinder. The joint at the front end of the cylinder is made with indiarubber, and the liner is free to expand in the direction of its length as it becomes heated. As the function of this joint is merely to retain the jacket water, there is no necessity for an exceedingly tight fit. The crank shaft is of forged Siemens-Martin steel, and is fitted with phosphor-bronze bearings, the mean pressure upon the bearings being 100 lb. per square inch during the working stroke. The crank-pin pressure allowed is about 370 lb. per square inch, whilst the piston pin carries a mean pressure of 530 lb. per square inch.

These figures are worked out on the mean effective pressure given by the indicator diagram during a working stroke. The piston is packed with three cast-iron rings $\frac{3}{8}$ in. wide, having a baffle groove $\frac{1}{8}$ in. wide cut in each ring, dividing the bearing surfaces into two bands, each $\frac{1}{4}$ in. wide. The pressure exerted upon the walls of the cylinder amounts to about 5 lb. per square inch of surface. The piston speed of this engine running at 180 revolutions is nearly 600 ft. per minute, and the velocity of the inlet and outlet through the valves is about 100 ft. per second.

The following figures are quoted from a trial of a "Forward" engine of 30 B.H.P., conducted by Messrs. Morrison and Lanchester for the City of Birmingham Gas Dept. in 1894. When running with no load, the ratio of air to gas by volume was 14·5 to 1; when running with full load, the ratio was 9·9 air to 1 volume of gas. In the latter case the products of combustion were not swept out as the engine fired every cycle; consequently the volume of air plus products to that of the gas was 11 to 1. The gas consumption in cubic feet per hour per I.H.P. was 17·75, and per B.H.P. 21·05 cubic feet. To this should be added a total of 5·25 cubic feet per hour used by the burner for heating the ignition tube. The mechanical efficiency worked out to 84 per cent, and the thermal efficiency calculated on the I.H.P. was 22·2 per cent, and 18·6 when calculated on the B.H.P. The engine was governed when running light by cutting out the gas supply.

CHAPTER VI.

Self-starters.

The Forward engine is fitted with Lanchester's patent self-starting gear, the application of which is shown in the following drawing. Fig. 48 shows a general view of the arrangement fitted to the engine. Gas enters the combustion chamber from a ½ in. branch through the valve A. The stream of gas and air passes out of the cylinder through the cock C, and ignites, when rich enough in gas, at the naked flame shown at F. The mixture burns at the orifice, at first with a pale blue flame, which becomes deeper in colour as it becomes richer. When the flame burns with a roaring noise the valve A should be closed. The flame at the orifice will now strike back into the cylinder and ignite the entire volume of the mixture in the combustion chamber. The action of this starter depends entirely upon the size of the outlet through the cock, for if this outlet were large in diameter the velocity of the gas would be less than the velocity of flame propagation; consequently, immediately the gas ignited at the orifice, the flame would strike back and ignite the mixture in the cylinder before it was rich enough to give a starting impulse to the piston. This

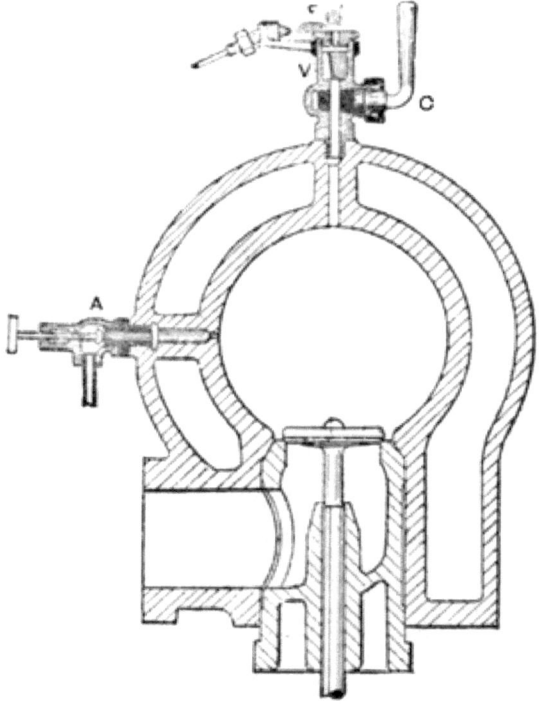

FIG. 48.—Lanchester's Self-starter for Gas Engines.

is prevented by the contracted area of the outlet nozzle, causing the gaseous mixture to flow rapidly from the orifice. This is, of course, the principle upon which all atmospheric burners depend, and the slight report which is always heard when turning out an atmospheric gas stove, is due to the return of the flame along the pipes towards the stop cock at the moment the latter is turned off.

To prevent the escape of the pressure through the cock from the engine cylinder, when the first ignition takes place, an automatic valve is placed inside the chamber in the cock C. This valve is shown at V, and rests upon its lower face, excepting when its weight is overcome by the

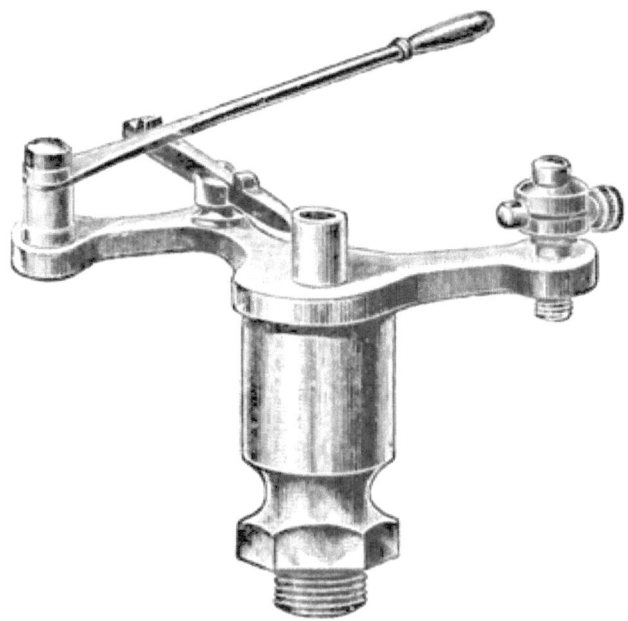

FIG. 49 —Green's Self-starter for Gas Engines.

rush of an explosion. Grooves cut in this valve allow the passage of gas through the open cock so long as the valve remains in its lowest position. Immediately the starting impulse is given this valve is projected upwards, and as the grooves are not deep, the centre of the valve entirely closes the orifice, thus preventing the escape of the pressure. The cock C may now be turned off. In using this starter the engine must always be barred round to the commencement of its *working* stroke, otherwise serious damage may be done to the gas bags and other fittings.

A self-starter similar in principle to that already described is shown in figs. 49 and 50. This is known as Green's self-starter. It differs from that already described in the construction of the automatic valve. Referring to fig. 50, the passage marked 17 communicates directly with the combustion chamber. The valve B is cylindrical, and hollowed out to the point C, but solid at the lower end. The holes 4_1, 4, when the valve is in position for starting, form a passage for the gas and air, which rise to the orifice 6, and ignite by the naked flame issuing from the gas burner E. When the mixture issuing from the orifice 6

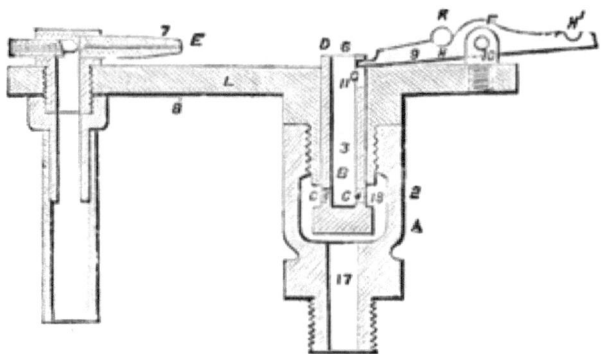

FIG. 50.—Green's Self-starter for Gas Engines.

burns with a dark blue flame, the gas supply to the combustion chamber is shut off, the flame strikes back through the passages 4, 18, 17, and ignites the charge in the combustion chamber. The pressure thus generated forces up the valve B, thereby closing the passages 4_1, 4. The hand lever shown in fig. 49 is made of spring steel, and when in the position shown presses downwards upon the lever engaging with the automatic valve, thus effectually keeping it in its highest position, and preventing the escape of pressure from the combustion chamber when the engine is working. When the starter is in use, the hand lever is drawn forward, and holds the automatic valve in the position shown in fig. 50. The advantages of this form of construction are that the automatic valve serves to throw the starter out of use, and being at the same time accessible from the outside, there is no inconvenience occasioned by the valve sticking.

The self-starters we have described ignite the mixture at atmospheric pressure; hence the impulse of the starting stroke is limited, and the maximum pressure in the cylinder will not usually exceed 80 lb. per square inch. In order to increase this pressure, Mr. Dugald Clerk was the first to apply the apparatus shown diagrammatically in fig. 51, which is known as the Clerk pressure starter. A chamber C is connected to the engine cylinder by the pipe P and a check valve V. The passage H leads into C from a hand

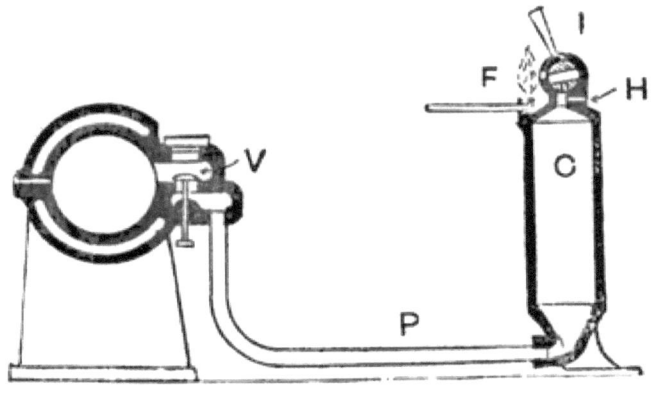

FIG. 51.—The Clerk Pressure Starter.

pump, which is used to charge C and the engine cylinder with an explosive mixture *slightly* above atmospheric pressure. I is an igniting valve, through which the mixture passes when open, and comes in contact with the flame F, which causes the ignition. The action of the starter is as follows: The cylinder and chamber C being filled at atmospheric pressure with an explosive mixture, the igniting valve is opened, the mixture fires at the orifice, and the flame strikes back into the chamber C. As the gas burns downwards it expands, driving a large portion of the mixture yet unburnt through the pipe P into the cylinder. In this way the pressure of the mixture in the cylinder is considerably raised before the flame reaches it. When, therefore, the mixture in the cylinder ignites, it explodes

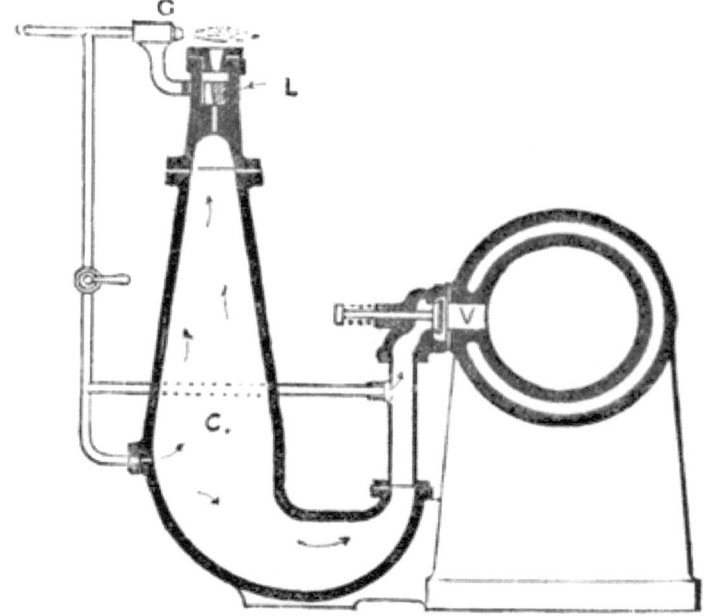

FIG. 52.—Clerk-Lanchester High-pressure Self-starter.

violently, developing a maximum pressure of 190 lb. per square inch, instead of 80 lb., as with the low-pressure starters of Lanchester and Green.

The self-starter shown in fig. 52 is known as the Clerk-Lanchester. It is, as will be seen, a combination of the Clerk pressure starter and the Lanchester automatic valve. It is otherwise more convenient than the Clerk starter, as no pump is required to fill the cylinder and chamber C with an explosive mixture. The action of this starter is as follows: The engine cylinder and chamber C are filled with air at atmospheric pressure. To ensure pure air occupying these spaces, it is usual to open the valve V before the engine is stopped, thus drawing pure air through C into the cylinder. When ready for starting, the engine is barred round to the commencement of its working stroke, the valve V opened, and gas turned on; the gas jet G is lighted, and serves to ignite the mixture as it issues from the orifice. Immediately the flame strikes back into the chamber C the valve L lifts and closes the orifice. The action is now precisely the same as already described in the Clerk pressure starter.

All makers supply with their larger engines some self-starter, which, though differing in detail from those already described, may nevertheless be recognised as dependent upon one or other of the principles explained.*

CHAPTER VII.

Two-cycle and other Engines.

The large number of gas-engine makers who are now competing has given rise to a variety of distinguishing names, which the author ventures to think are far in excess of the corresponding differences which those names are supposed to characterise. Having now fully described a variety of engines which may be considered typical, but little will be gained by dwelling at length upon minute details. It will be advisable, before leaving the descriptive side of the subject, to touch briefly upon points of interest in connection with engines not already described.

The Day gas engine, made by Messrs. Day and Co., Bath, is illustrated in fig. 53. This engine is noticeable for its simplicity and fewness of parts. Though not suitable for

---

* Other methods of starting gas engines are described on pages 41, 52, 54, 56, 61, and 67

large powers, it is a moderately efficient engine where only light work is done. It will be noticed that the crank and connecting rod run in a closed space, into which is fitted one mushroom valve. Through this valve both gas and air are

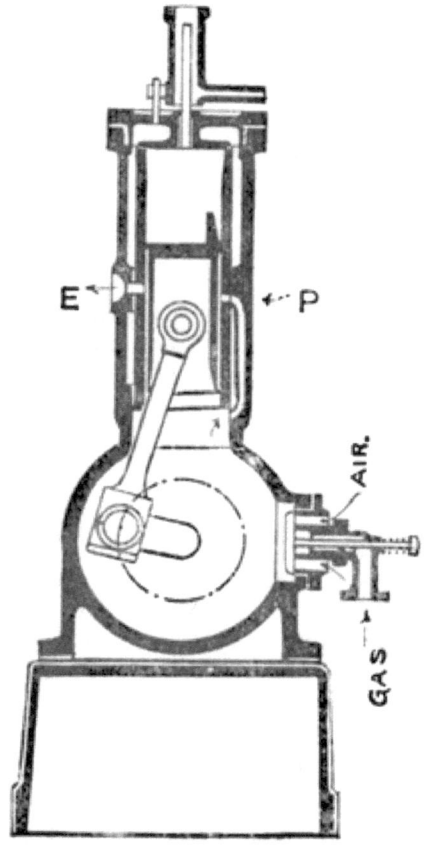

FIG. 56.—The Day Gas Engine.

sucked during the up stroke of the piston. On the down stroke this mixture is slightly compressed. When the piston descends, the port P is uncovered, and the mixture flows from the lower chamber into the working cylinder.

On the return stroke the port entrance to the cylinder is covered by the piston, and the charge being compressed into the ignition tube I, is fired without the use of a timing valve. The piston is moved downwards by the expanding gases, which escape through the port E when uncovered by the piston. It will be observed that the exhaust port is uncovered before the inlet, and therefore the pressure of the expanding gases is released before the end of the stroke. The inlet and exhaust are open together for a short period of time, and the first rush of fresh mixture is deflected upwards into the cylinder; in this way the greater portion of the burnt products are displaced. As the working of the valve is entirely automatic, the engine may be run in either direction without any alteration whatever. This engine gives an impulse every revolution.

The Palatine gas engine is constructed somewhat upon this principle, the crank shaft running in a closed chamber. The object of this design is to supply a scavenger stroke, and the impulse only occurs every two revolutions. The objection to these designs is the inaccessibility of the connecting rod.

Messrs. Alfred Dougill and Co., Leeds, make an Otto cycle engine, which is noticeable for its patent governor gear. This gear is shown in figs. 54 and 55. The object of the arrangement is to keep the ratio of air to gas uniform throughout all variations of load. Instead of merely intercepting the gas supply, the governor acts on both the air and gas valves, and when the speed rises the total volume of the charge admitted to the cylinder is decreased, but the ratio of air to gas remains unchanged. The essential parts of the gear are the stepped cam O and the sleeve L. The lever P lifts both the gas and air valve spindles N and M, and is driven by the stepped cam O operating upon the movable sleeve L. In fig. 55, L is shown in line with the highest step; consequently the admission of the charge is a maximum. When the governor balls F rise the sleeve is drawn towards the lower steps, and

DOUGILL'S GOVERNOR.

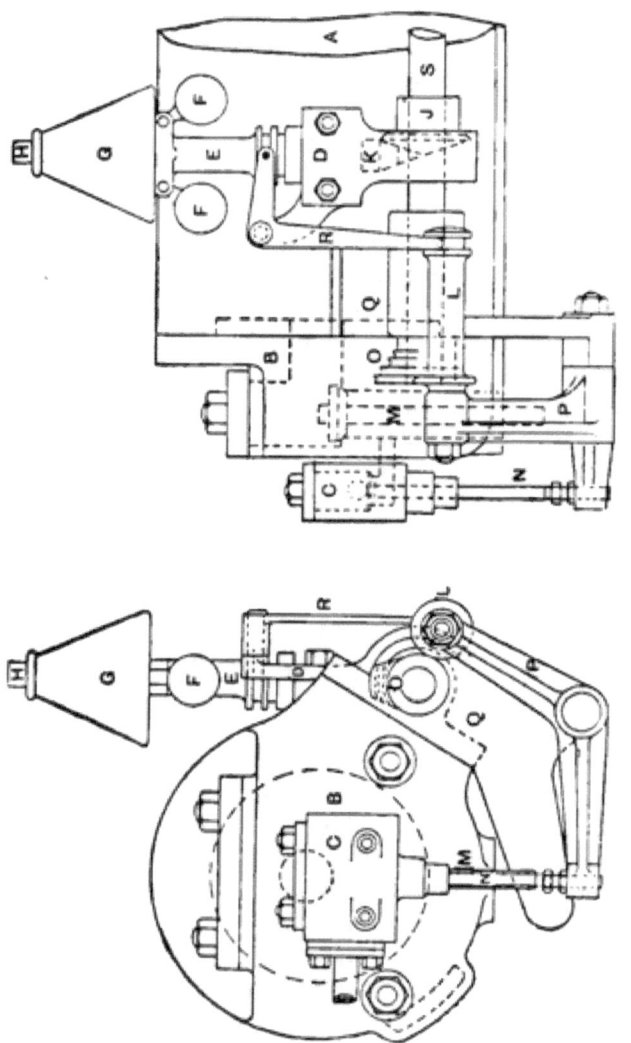

FIGS. 54 AND 55.—DOUGILL'S GOVERNOR.

the lift of the valves is diminished. It will be observed that since an increase in speed must take place on the explosion stroke, the roller of the sleeve L is at the time of the increase running upon the cylindrical portion of the cam O. For this reason it is perfectly free to move sideways when the speed varies. Diagrams obtained from this engine are shown in fig. 56. From these it will be seen that the compression is reduced when running light, and the explosion is nearly as rapid as at full load. This governor is said to prevent a variation in speed of more than 2 per cent on account of the continuity of the impulses even at

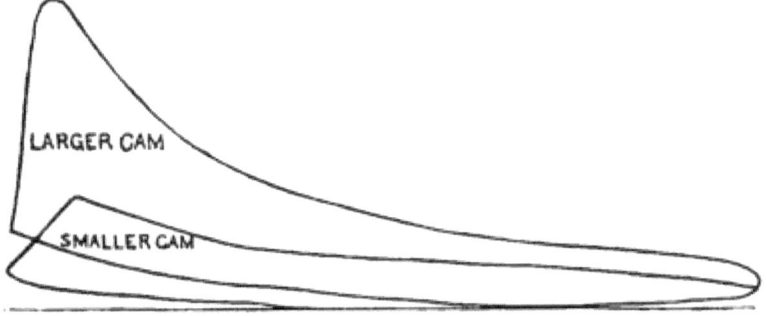

FIG. 56.—Diagram taken from Dougill's Otto Gas Engine.

light loads, and it is therefore highly suitable for electric lighting purposes.

The Acme engine, made by Messrs. Alexander Burt, Glasgow, was designed with the object of obtaining maximum expansion. This engine comprised two cylinders, working with two crank shafts. The shafts were geared together with two to one gearing, so that one piston made twice the number of strokes of the other. The gases expanded from the higher speed cylinder to the lower one, and the exhaust was said to be much cooler than usual. The results obtained showed the engine to be economical; but the noise of the gearing, and the extra wear of these parts, probably operate against the more general adoption of the engine.

During the last few years there has been a growing tendency for all makers to adopt the Otto cycle in preference to their own particular makes. We have already mentioned that this cycle leaves much to be desired in regard to steadiness of running. It is not surprising, therefore, that a reaction is taking place, and not a few are trying to solve the problem of constructing a satisfactory engine having an impulse every revolution. The Griffin engine, as already described, gives an average of one impulse every revolution, but utilises both ends of the cylinder for the combustion of the charges. For more reasons than one it is desirable to utilise only the space at the back of the piston as an explosion chamber, the forward end merely acting as a pump.

The first engine built, in 1878, to give an impulse every revolution was designed by Mr. Dugald Clerk, Assoc.M.Inst.C.E. It will be well to describe briefly the working of this and other two-cycle engines, not because they are regarded as modern gas engines, but because the author believes that the gas engine of the future will probably be a combination of past and present attempts to construct an engine having an impulse every revolution.

Mr. Dugald Clerk's first engine consisted of two cylinders, one of which was used as a motor cylinder, the other as a pump to deliver the mixture into a reservoir at a pressure of about 70 lb. per square inch. The motor piston travelled nearly to the end of the cylinder. The usual combustion chamber was dispensed with. When the motor piston had moved forward about 2 in. on its working stroke, a slide valve admitted the mixture from the reservoir. The supply being cut off, ignition took place. In this engine the inventor sought to combine the advantages of compression before ignition with the complete expulsion of the exhaust gases by minimising the clearance at the back of the cylinder. The difficulties met with in this engine were chiefly due to back ignition in the compression reservoir, and to excessive shock in the motor cylinder. The former of these difficulties was never overcome, though the latter was minimised by modifying the shape of the combustion chamber.

In 1880 Mr. Clerk designed another engine, in which the pump delivered its charge directly into the motor cylinder slightly above atmospheric pressure. The exhaust ports were uncovered by the working piston, and just before being closed by the return of the piston the displacer pump delivered its charge into the working cylinder. This was compressed on the return stroke and ignited at the commencement of the forward stroke. Many engines of this pattern were made, and in the larger sizes worked quite as economically as the best engines of their time, though there were difficulties in the governing. It is also obvious that there was great risk of delivering the unburnt mixture into the

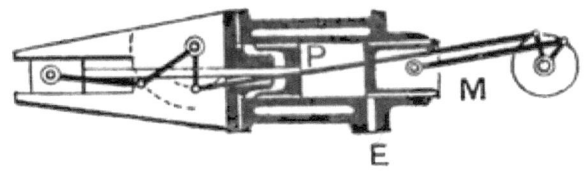

FIG. 57.—The Clerk Two-cycle Engine.

exhaust ports, and Mr. Clerk states that in the smaller engines this could hardly be avoided.

In 1890 Mr. Clerk built another engine, which is shown diagrammatically in fig. 57. Here M is the motor piston, P the charging and expelling piston. The link work is so arranged as to give a maximum speed of motion to one piston whilst the other remains almost stationary. Thus, when M uncovers the exhaust E, P travels rapidly towards it and expels the burnt gases; at the same time P is drawing a fresh charge into the back of the cylinder. The two pistons then travel back together, and the charge passes from the back of piston P to the space between the pistons. Upon ignition, M moves forward, whilst P remains practically stationary. The inventor believes that this engine is well adapted for both moderate and large powers, and that it will give exceptionally economical results when given a thorough trial. It seems hardly probable that its mechanical efficiency will be high after a short period of use, though the engine is no doubt very effective in design from a thermal, if not from a mechanical point of view.

Messrs. Robey and Co., of Lincoln, have for some years manufactured an engine upon the Otto cycle, with improvements introduced by Messrs. Richardson and Norris. An important feature of the engine is the ease with which it can be reversed. The cams are made to run in either direction, so that the alteration can be effected in a few moments. The speed is regulated by Richardson's high-speed governor, similar to that used on other Robey engines, fully described and illustrated in the *Engineer* of October 14th, 1892. The governor is loaded partly by dead weight and partly by springs, which latter can be regulated whilst running to give the required speed. The governor acts upon the gas valve, cutting off the supply of gas when the speed increases. Many of the Robey engines are specially designed for electric lighting, and for this purpose Mr. Richardson has introduced an electrical governor. This, in principle, consists of a solenoid wound as a shunt from the current generated by the engine and dynamo. A soft iron core is sucked into the solenoid as the voltage rises. Its movement is connected by a bell-crank lever to the pecker operating the gas valve, causing it to hit or miss the knife edge on the gas-valve spindle. By this means the gas supply may be entirely cut out.

Mr. Norris is now perfecting a two-cycle engine, with the object of increasing the steadiness of running and increasing the power derived from a given weight of engine. The arrangement is briefly as follows : The front end of the cylinder is closed, and acts as a pump for drawing in the charge and expelling it to the combustion chamber at the back of the cylinder. The piston rod carries a slight enlargement upon it, which traverses a cylinder attached to the front cover. This small cylinder is used to pump in the gas.

The cycle of this engine is carried out in the following order: The return stroke of the piston draws air into the front end of the cylinder through an automatic valve, whilst gas is drawn into the small cylinder attached to the inside of the front cover. The next outstroke compresses the air into an intermediate chamber at about 5 lb. per square inch above atmospheric pressure, until the piston has completed nine-tenths of its outward stroke. At this point a port in the engine piston connects the combustion chamber with the receiver. The exhaust valve is opened a little before nine-tenths of the outward stroke, and a column of exhaust gases is therefore already in motion by the time air enters the combustion chamber from the receiver. Air continues to flow from the receiver through the combustion chamber until one-tenth of the inward stroke is complete, when the exhaust valve closes. At this time pure air only occupies nine-tenths of the cylinder volume. After the air and exhaust valves are closed, gas from the small pump is admitted to form an explosive mixture, which is compressed during the remainder of the instroke. The compression, in the opinion of Mr. Norris, should not exceed 95 lb. per square inch.

In larger sizes of this engine a differential piston is used, in order to increase the volume of air pumped into the receiver.

CHAPTER VIII.
FRENCH ENGINES.
SIMPLEX GAS ENGINE.

THE Simplex gas engine was patented by Messrs. Edward Delamare and Malandin, in 1884. Whilst resembling in many respects the Otto engine, this motor has several distinctive features. It works upon the usual Otto cycle, but the charge is fired just after the commencement of the outstroke of the piston, instead of, as usual, on the dead centre. It is stated that this modification greatly reduces shock upon the working parts. The ignition of the charge is effected by means of an electric spark produced by a battery and induction coil. The difficulty usually met with in electric igniters is found to be due to the inefficiency of the *make and brake* mechanism. This is obviated in the Simplex engine by the generation of a continuous spark within a specially-formed chamber. The entrance to this chamber is controlled by a slide valve, and the charge in the cylinder can only come in contact with the continuous spark when the port through the slide opens communication between the cylinder and sparking chamber. Many of the continental engines fire by electricity, but this method has been little used in this country. There are points in favour of electric ignition; but the maintenance of the battery, the possibility of the sparking points becoming coated with deposit, and the difficulty of maintaining the insulation are serious objections, and it is probable that as the hot tube is made more durable it will entirely supersede electric ignition.

The governing of this engine is effected by the use of an air cylinder and piston. The piston is stationary, and the air cylinder moves backwards and forwards with the igniting slide spindle. Air enters the cylinder through an orifice regulated by a micrometer screw. If the speed of the engine increases, the air in the cylinder is unduly compressed, and so forces outwards a second piston, which is in communication with the air cylinder. This latter piston carries the knife edge for actuating the gas valve. The micrometer screw can be so regulated as to cause the outward motion of the second piston at any desired maximum speed. In this way the knife edge is moved out of line with that on the gas-valve spindle, and the entire supply of gas is cut off. On larger engines of the Simplex pattern a form of pendulum governor has been adopted.

The self-starter fitted to the Simplex engine consists of a three-way cock, suitably proportioned to admit a charge of gas and air to the cylinder. The cock is opened when the piston is at the commencement of its forward expansion stroke, and when charged the current is turned on. The high temperature of the electric spark renders the ignition of a weak mixture certain.

LENOIR ENGINE.

This is another engine in which electric ignition is used to fire the charge. The chief object of the designer was to obtain a very high compression and temperature of the charge before firing. This was effected by jacketing the working part of the cylinder only. The compression chamber was bolted to the cylinder casting, with an asbestos joint to prevent the transmission of heat from the compression chamber to the jacketed cylinder. The compression chamber was cast with a series of deep ribs outside, to distribute the heat by convection of air instead of by the use of a water jacket. By this means the combustion chamber was kept at a much higher temperature than the working cylinder, and a weak mixture was easily ignited by the electric spark.

CHARON ENGINE.

An attempt is made in this design of engine to expand the charge beyond its volume at atmospheric pressure when drawn into the cylinder. To effect this, the air admission valve remains open during part of the compression stroke, and through it a portion of the charge is driven into a long spiral tube open to the atmosphere, and of sufficient length to retain the mixture forced into it. The valve then closes, and the charge is compressed. After expansion and exhaust the gases in the spiral pipe are drawn into the cylinder with the new charge, and the cycle is repeated. The engine is governed by reducing the gas supply and by allowing more of the charge to enter the spiral pipe, thus reducing the quality and volume of the gas ignited.

NIEL ENGINE.

In this engine the charge is admitted through a conical revolving plug, which is kept tight during the compression and explosion strokes by the pressure generated in the cylinder, acting upon the back of the plug so as to force it into its seating.

LALBIN ENGINE.

This engine is designed with the object of equalising the turning effort upon the crank shaft. It consists of three cylinders, one placed vertically with the crank shaft beneath it, and one at each side inclined at an angle of 60 deg. with the horizontal. Each cylinder works upon the Otto cycle; hence in two revolutions the crank shaft receives three impulses, instead of only one. The mechanism is so arranged as to permit of the engine being reversed.

GERMAN ENGINES.
BENZ ENGINE.

Of the German engines perhaps the Benz is one of the most interesting from a constructional point of view, inasmuch as the cylinder is arranged to give an impulse every revolution, without the aid of a separate large pump, such as used upon the early gas engines of the Clerk type. The engine is horizontal, and has electric ignition. The cylinder is closed at both ends; the back of the piston receives the impulse from the ignition of the mixture, and the front of the piston drives, at each forward stroke, a volume of fresh air through a suitable valve into an air reservoir formed in the bed plate of the engine. A small plunger, worked from the crosshead, acts as a gas pump, and the plunger cylinder becomes filled with gas during every forward stroke of the engine. It is possible with this arrangement to produce an explosion at the commencement of each outstroke of the piston. Imagine the gases to have ignited and driven the piston forward. By this stroke the air reservoir is replenished and the gas pump charged. On the return stroke the exhaust valve opens, and just before the end of the stroke the air from the reservoir is admitted to the combustion chamber. This effectually clears out the burnt gases and replaces them with fresh air, which at the same time tends to cool the cylinder. The air and exhaust valves then close, and the gas pump forces its charge into the combustion chamber. The air and gas mingle sufficiently to permit of ignition by means of the electric spark. The consumption of gas in these engines is said to be about 23 cubic feet per indicated horse power.

KOERTING-LIECKFELDT ENGINE.

The first of these engines was designed with vertical cylinders, and is specially interesting for the method of ignition of the charge. By a special apparatus, shown in fig. 58, the external flame F ignites the charge. The chamber C is in direct communication with the motor cylinder during the compression stroke and at the time of ignition. The cylindrical piece B is free to move upwards under the pressure of the mixture. The rod R is worked up and down by a lever, thus opening and closing the port P opposite the naked flame. When compression commences the rod R is raised, so that the port P is open to the flame. The mixture enters the chamber C, and raises the plug B. It is then forced through the small entrance of the cone, and, expanding, arrives at P at nearly atmospheric pressure, where it is ignited by the flame F. The flame then travels a little way down towards the small end of the cone, but cannot get very far, because the velocity of the outcoming gas is greater at the lower end of the cone than the rate of flame propagation. The rod R descends at the end of the instroke of the piston, and, covering the port P, effectually stops the flow of gas; the pressure within the cone becomes equalised, the

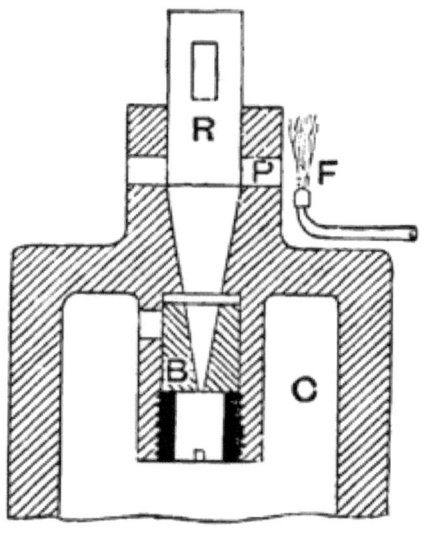

FIG. 58.—Koerting-Lieckfeldt Igniter.

piece B drops, and the flame travels downwards towards the chamber C, and so ignites the entire charge.

The governing is effected by a somewhat novel arrangement of the centrifugal type, which cuts out the gas and air supply, and at the same time keeps the exhaust open, so that the products of combustion are drawn back into the cylinder. This method is advantageous in oil motors, inasmuch as it helps to maintain the temperature of the combustion chamber; but it is a doubtful practice in connection with gas engines.

THE DAIMLER GAS ENGINE.

This engine was first exhibited in 1889, and is specially noticeable for its high speed and simplicity of parts. The later designs have two cylinders, placed nearly vertically over one crank shaft. The connecting rods work upon one crank pin, set between heavy balanced crank webs. The connecting rods and crank are entirely encased in an airtight covering, in a similar way to the engine shown in fig. 53. An automatic air valve admits air only to this casing as the pistons rise. The gas and exhaust valves are placed at the upper end of each cylinder, the gas valve being automatic, whilst the exhaust is lifted by the equivalent of a cam on the disc crank web. Instead of the air port P, shown in fig. 53, a valve is placed in the centre of each piston, for passing the air from the crank chamber to the combustion chamber. The action of the engine is as follows: Upon the down stroke one cylinder expands its burning charge, whilst the other draws in gas, and at the same time passes air from the crank casing into the working cylinder through the valve in the piston. On the return stroke the one cylinder exhausts, whilst the other compresses. In this way an impulse is received every revolution, although each individual cylinder works upon the Otto cycle. The governing is effected by holding open the exhaust valve every revolution when the speed rises, thus preventing the automatic gas valve from being opened by the formation of a slight vacuum in the cylinder. This engine is worked entirely without jacket water. This is no doubt possible on account of the high speed at which it is run (from 500 to 700 revolutions per minute), coupled with the fact that only very small powers are attempted. It is claimed that the engine will consume about 33 cubic feet of gas per hour per I.H.P., and when it is remembered that the engines only range from 1 to 2 horse power, this figure is not very excessive.

THE CAPITAINE GAS ENGINE.

The Capitaine gas engine is designed to give a high speed of revolution with a nominal piston speed. This is done by increasing the diameter of the cylinder, whilst decreasing the length of stroke. The combustible mixture is drawn into the cylinder through an enlarging entrance, so that its velocity is decreased, the object being to prevent the mingling of the new charge with the exhaust gases. How far this arrangement is effectual it is difficult to estimate, though it is certain that the time of combustion is lengthened by the presence of burnt products in a rich mixture of, say, eight volumes of air to one of gas. The ignition tube in the Capitaine engine is of porcelain, and is claimed to be very durable and efficient.

CHAPTER IX.

TESTING GAS ENGINES.

THE testing of gas engines specially fitted up for experimental work is a comparatively easy task, and involves but little forethought from the experimenter; when, however, complete tests are to be made by the use of improptu apparatus, there is ample scope for the ready exercise of one's wits in arranging simple and reliable means of measuring the quantities to be dealt with. In what follows we shall confine our attention to testing a gas engine alone—that is, not in conjunction with the machinery it may be driving. There may be cases in which the work done by the driven machine is easily ascertained. The horse power obtained from the terminals of a dynamo driven by a gas engine affords a measure of the useful work done, and, making allowance for the efficiency of the dynamo, gives the work transmitted from the engine flywheel to the dynamo pulley. The work done in pumping a certain weight of water against a known head, in a given time, is easily converted into useful horse power. But in all such cases the efficiency of the machines has to be allowed for, and as this may be a rather uncertain quantity, the only reliable method of testing is to run the engine separately, and to measure the power derived from the flywheels by suitable means.

The simplest and most reliable form of absorption dynamometer is illustrated in fig. 59. It consists of two or more

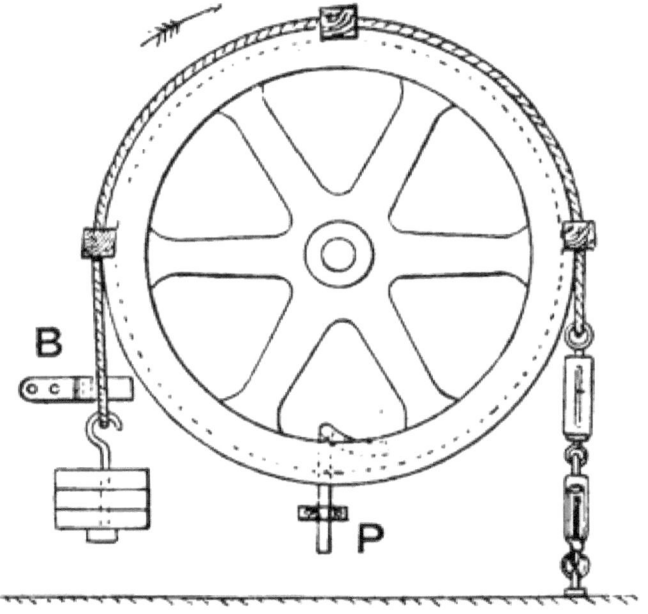

FIG. 59 —Friction Brake.

lengths of good hemp rope placed over the upper semicircumference of the flywheel, and guided by wood blocks. The ends of the ropes are spliced together so that a spring balance may be attached at one side of the wheel, whilst a hook for carrying weights may be attached to the other side. The spring balance is anchored to the ground by means of a hook and adjustable screw. The latter is of great convenience, for without means of adjustment the ropes often stretch and allow the weights to touch the ground. The weights for loading the brake should be cast with slots in, so that they may be placed upon the hook. When putting on the weights it is important that the slots should *not* coincide, for if they do the vibration will invariably cause the weights to fall over.

As a precaution against accident, the bar shown at B, fig 59, should be fixed to a suitable place and pass between the brake ropes. This prevents the undue lifting of the weights should the friction increase, and has often been the means of preventing a serious accident.

When absorbing large powers the rim of the wheel will become much heated, and its undue expansion may lead to fracture. It is therefore better to cast the rim in the form of a trough (⌐⌐), and arrange for the delivery of cold water to the rim. When the wheel is revolving the water will follow it in the direction of rotation and completely line the trough; centrifugal force, acting upon the water, will prevent its displacement from the trough. In order to change the water in the rim the pipe shown at P, fig. 59, is fixed so as to skim the surface and drain away the water so caught. In this way a constant circulation may be maintained.

It is important that the brake weights be removed when the engine is being stopped, for if not the spring balance will be broken by their sudden fall. Another arrangement of the brake ropes is shown in fig. 60. This is more suitable for large powers, but whether one form or other is adopted is largely decided by convenience of arrangement, though for very small powers this latter form of brake is unsuitable.

When an economy trial is to be made the brake should be loaded, with the gas cock fully open, until the engine runs at its nominal speed, and fires every cycle with a full charge of gas. To adjust the brake and other measuring gear, a preliminary trial is invariably necessary.

In calculating the load upon the brake, the weight of the hook supporting the load should, of course, be included, and allowance should be made for any unbalanced part of the brake rope. The spring balance should always be tested before use, as the spring often gets a slight permanent set, and the index does not usually read *zero* when the balance is unloaded. It is of the highest importance that the weights hang freely, otherwise serious errors may arise. Although these remarks deal with details apparently trivial, we cannot too strongly urge the necessity of their strict

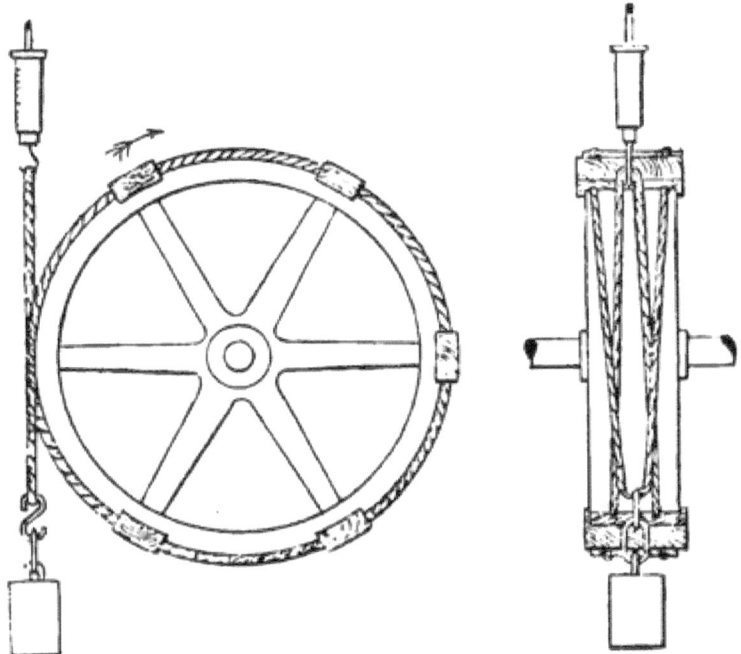

FIG. 60.—Friction Brake.

observance. A successful trial depends entirely upon the immediate observation of any disturbance of the measuring apparatus, and this can only be detected by constant watching.

During the trial the reading of the spring balance should be taken every five or ten minutes, according to the duration of the test, and from these an average may be calculated.

Let S = the mean spring balance reading in pounds;
W = the *total* weight hanging upon the brake in pounds;
R = effective radius of brake wheel in feet,
    = radius of brake wheel + radius of brake rope;
N = revolutions of wheel per minute;

then the brake horse power

$$= (W - S)\frac{2 \pi R N}{33000}.$$

For the same brake gear the factors

$$\frac{2 \pi R}{33000}$$

remain constant; hence they may be worked out once for all, and the result be booked as the *brake constant* = C. The formula for the B.H.P. may then be written

$$B.H.P. = (W - S) N C.$$

INDICATING.

Indicator diagrams obtained from gas engines cannot be entirely relied upon, though they may, with careful manipulation and a suitable instrument, be considered accurate enough for practical purposes. Before any important trial is to be made the indicator springs should themselves be tested under the conditions of temperature likely to occur. The average difference in the deflections of indicator springs when hot and cold amounts to as much as 5 per cent, and more in some cases; a cold test is therefore no guarantee. In the case of a gas engine, a simple method of testing the springs is as follows: Construct a stirrup of brass, as shown in fig. 61, having a hole in it sufficiently large to allow the indicator piston rod to pass through it. This stirrup is placed in position by disconnecting the links attached to the pencil lever Next obtain a 100 lb. spring balance, and carefully test it, with the stirrup attached, against standard weights, noting the plus or minus errors, if any. Then pass the cord attached to the

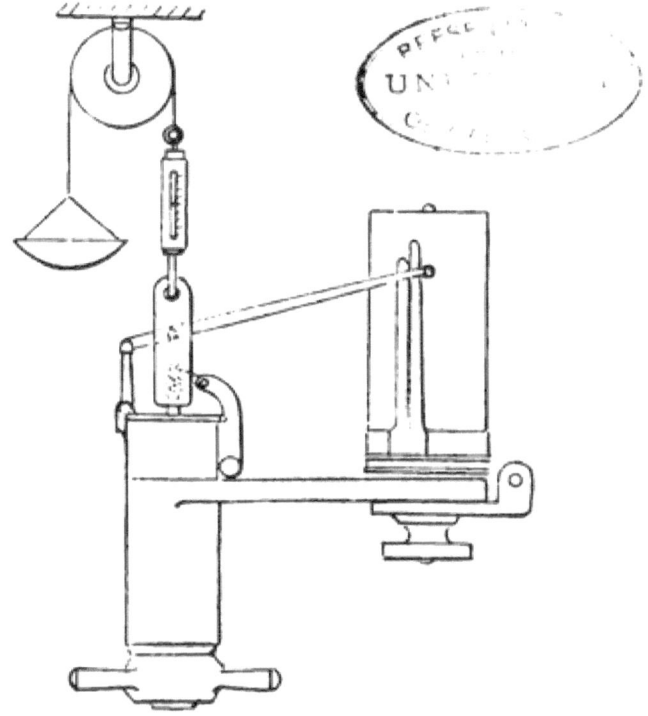

FIG. 61.—Arrangement of Indicator for Testing Gas Engines.

upper end of the balance over a suitable pulley, as shown. Weights may then be placed upon a scale pan at the end of the cord, and adjusted until the balance reads various definite loads. The use of an accurate balance can hardly be dispensed with, as otherwise the friction of the pulley will give an error of probably 5 per cent. By the arrangement shown this is eliminated. Suppose a spring is being tested which is supposed to register 100 lb. per square inch for every one inch vertical movement of the pencil on the drum. Put the indicator on the engine, and arrange the tackle above it as shown in fig. 61. Start the engine, and whilst running *slightly* turn on the indicator cock so as to heat up the spring. When the indicator is at its working temperature, close the indicator cock and mark off the atmospheric line on the drum, revolving the latter by hand. Now load the balance until it reads 10 lb., and mark off the corresponding height of the indicator pencil. Proceed in this way by increments of 10 lb. at a time until the limit of the instrument is reached. Carefully measure the diameter of the indicator piston and obtain the area. In our example, suppose the area of the piston to be 0·5 square inch, and suppose when the balance reads 50 lb. the movement of the pencil above the atmospheric line measures 1·03 in. The pressure per square inch at 1·03 in. rise

$$= 100 \times 1\cdot03 = 103 \text{ lb. per square inch.}$$

But the actual pressure upon an area of 0·5 square inch is 50 lb., which is equivalent to

$$\frac{50}{0\cdot5} = 100 \text{ lb. per square inch.}$$

We see, therefore, that the indicator is recording a pressure 3 per cent in excess of the real pressure acting upon the piston.

When testing springs by this method, care must be taken not to overload the instrument, for it must be remembered that the whole stress is transmitted through the small piston rod of the indicator.

CHAPTER X.

INDICATORS FOR GAS ENGINES.

CROSBY INDICATOR.

THIS instrument, shown in figs. 62 and 63, has a well-earned reputation of being both durable and accurate at high speeds. The heavy stresses brought to bear upon the working parts of the instrument when used for gas-engine indicating has led to modifications in design, rendering it in every way more adaptable to gas-engine work. The most obvious alteration is the adoption of the straight link in the parallel motion, in place of a longer and curved link attached to the extreme end of the pencil bar. The indicator shown in fig. 63 is specially designed for the gas engine, but

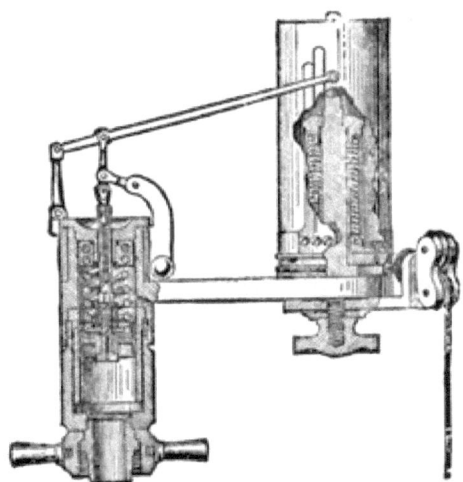

FIG. 62.—Crosby Indicator.

it can be used with equal efficiency upon a steam-engine cylinder. It will be observed that the barrel of the indicator is bored out to two diameters, the larger part having an area equal to twice that of the smaller. Two pistons are supplied, to either of which the same spring may be fitted. In this way a spring marked 100 will register 100 lb. per square inch for each inch of vertical movement of the pencil when the spring is fitted on the *larger* piston. If, however, this spring is fitted to the *smaller* piston, as recommended for gas-engine work, then

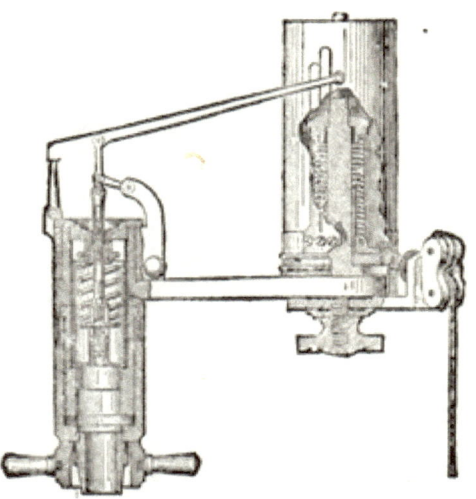

Fig. 63.—Crosby Indicator.

1 in. vertical movement of the pencil corresponds to 200 lb. pressure per square inch. With this instrument a variety of pressures may be dealt with by a small assortment of springs, a feature which readily recommends itself to the economist. In both designs the working cylinder is jacketed, to enable it to expand readily with the piston, and so obviate undue friction. All the piston springs are double spiral, to prevent the slight rotation and tilting of the piston which is inevitable with a single spiral. A very light pencil bar is used upon these indicators for steam-engine work, but for gas-engine work a bar of L section is necessary to withstand the sudden jar due to the explosion.

INDICATORS FOR GAS ENGINES

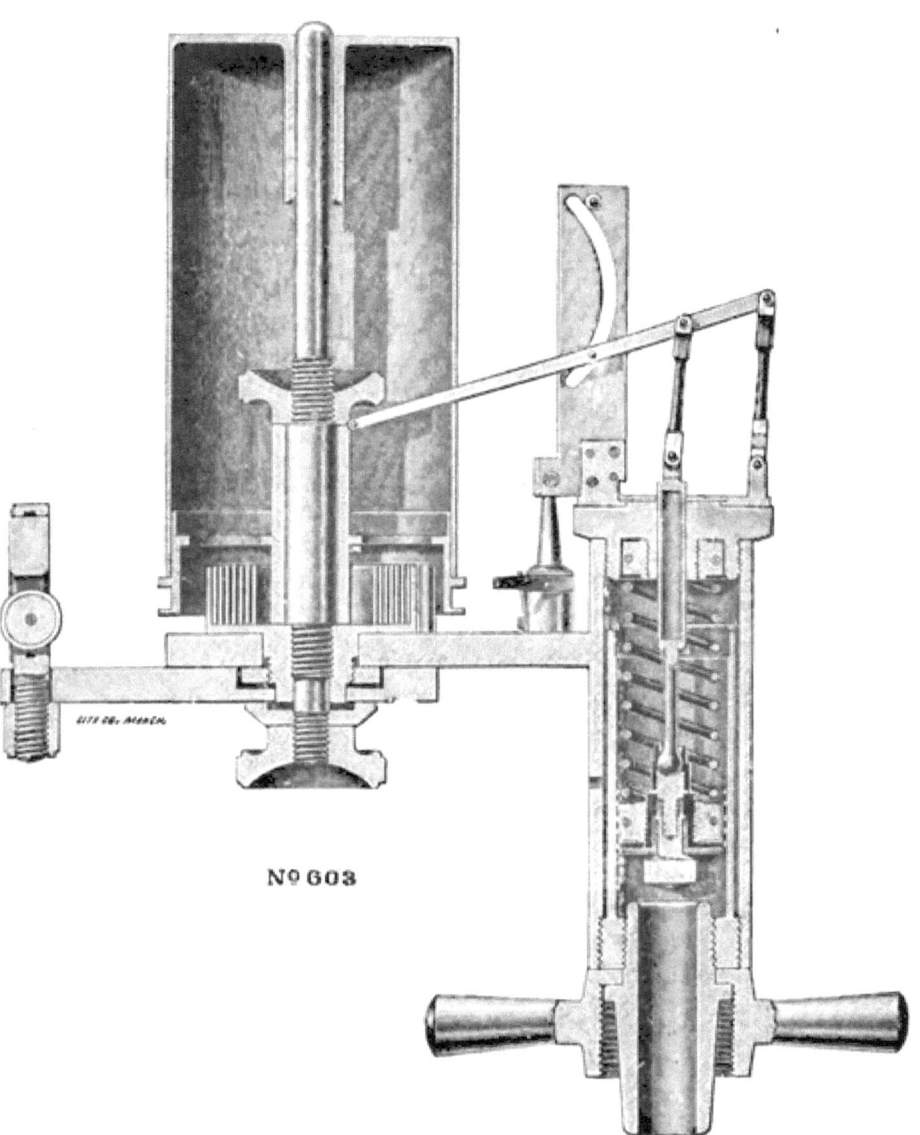

Fig. 64.—Section of Tabor Indicator.

The general construction of the indicators will be gathered from the illustrations.

THE TABOR INDICATOR.

The Tabor indicator is shown in fig. 64. Its three most characteristic features are the straight-line motion, the working cylinder, and the involute spring used to actuate the drum. The vertical movement of the marking point is secured by the curved slot, in which runs a small roller attached to the pencil bar. The cylinder in which the indicator piston works consists of a thin tube att·ohed to the body of the indicator at its lower end only. The air jacket around the tube admits of free expansion of the tube when in use, and the thin walls of the latter assist in equalising the temperature. These indicators are somewhat larger than the Crosby, and will give diagrams 5 in. long at slow speeds, though when working at 200 revolutions per minute the makers recommend a 4 in. diagram, reducing it to 2 in. at 500 revolutions in order to minimise the effects of inertia of the drum.

The indicator illustrated in fig. 65 requires no reducing motion as usually fitted. It will be seen that the worm R engages with a worm wheel upon the drum B. The cord from the pulley O is attached to the crosshead of the engine, and travels through its entire stroke. Various lengths of diagrams are obtained by altering the size of the pulley O. The cage d contains the spring which gives the return motion to the pulley. The backlash of the worm gear is taken up by a spring within the drum B. By a simple movement of the milled head, shown at n, the pulley O disengages with the worm, and revolves freely upon its spindle. The drum B then remains stationary. This gear is very convenient for indicating at high speeds; but it is obvious that the speed of the engine must be considerably reduced to enable the hook from the indicator pulley to be attached to the crosshead.

The only automatic gear for attaching and detaching

the reducing motion from the engine is that now being introduced by Messrs. Crosby and Co. This gear, which we shall describe, enables the operator to attach a complete

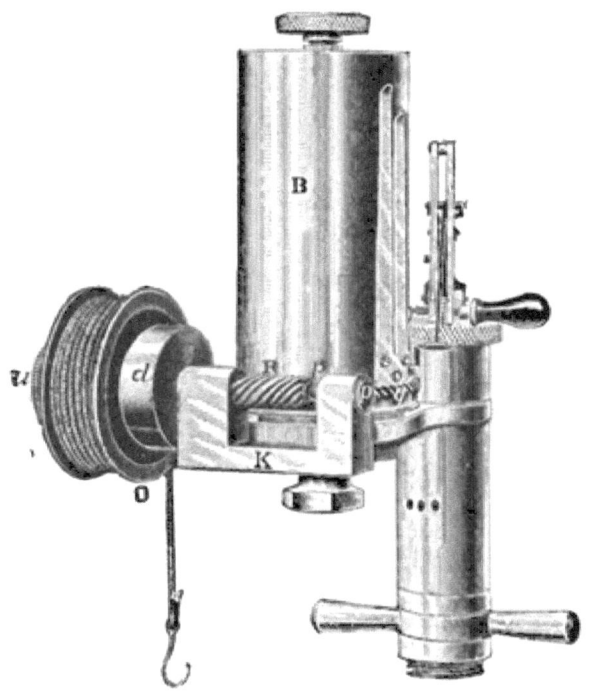

FIG. 65.—Tabor Indicator with Reducing Gear.

indicator gear to any high-speed engine whilst running at full speed Another important feature is that the reducing motion is thrown out of action immediately after the diagram has been taken.

THE WAYNE INDICATOR.

The design of this instrument, which is made by Messrs. Elliott Brothers, is a complete departure from the usual lines. Two views are shown in figs. 66 and 67, from which the general appearance may be gathered. It will be seen that the paper upon which the diagram is traced is fixed by two spring clips to an aluminium guide, and forms a

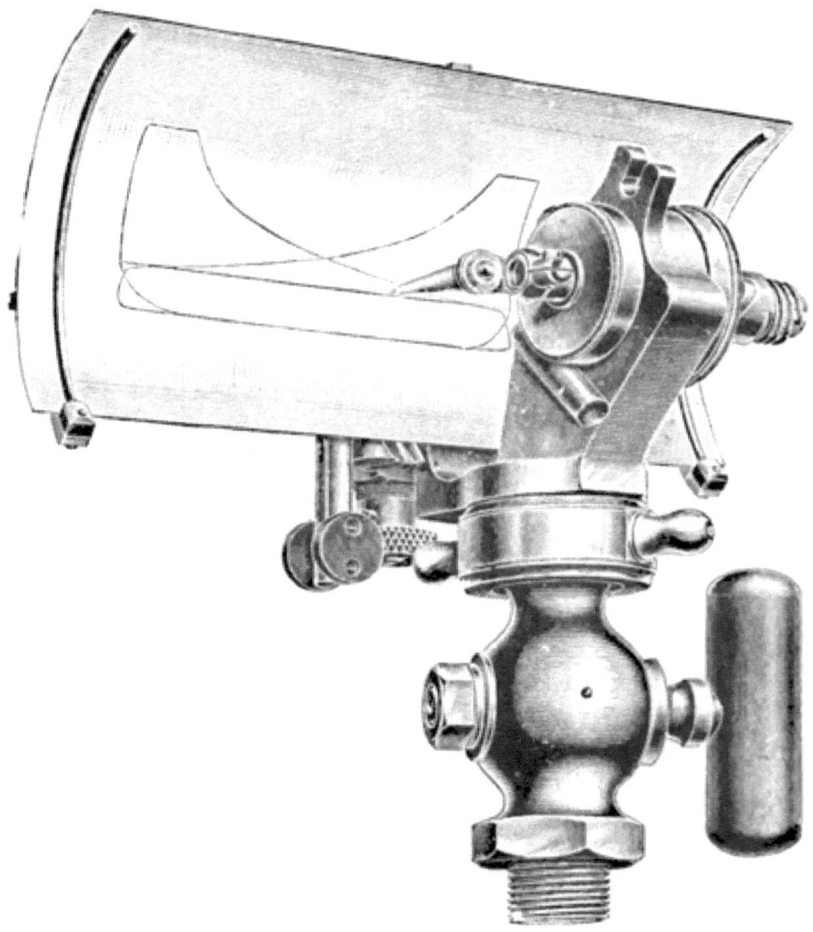

Fig 66.—Wayne Indicator.

concave surface. The latter moves horizontally by means of a cord passing over a spring pulley and attached to any convenient reducing gear. The marking point traverses the arc of a circle, its movement being resisted by the torsion of a spiral spring shown on the right of the illustrations. This spring may be changed to suit the

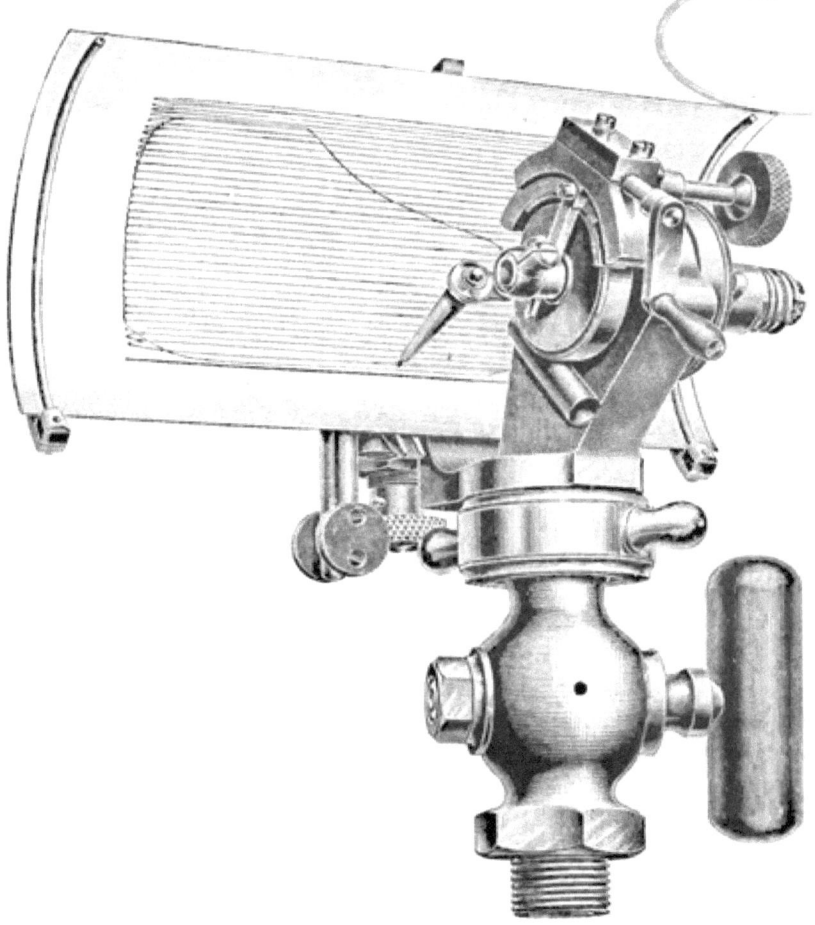

FIG. 67.—Wayne Indicator.

pressures dealt with, and determines the scale of the pressure ordinates. The circular movement of the pencil is produced by the pressure of the steam upon two steel tongues a, fig. 68, projecting from a horizontal rod passing through the cylinder. This rod carries the pencil at one end and the spiral spring at the other. The diagrammatic sketch, fig. 68, will show how the pressure acts upon the steel tongues, and how the steam which passes the tongues escapes through the holes e, e. The chief features in this indicator are: The absence of joints or parallel motion, small movement of working parts, and accessibility

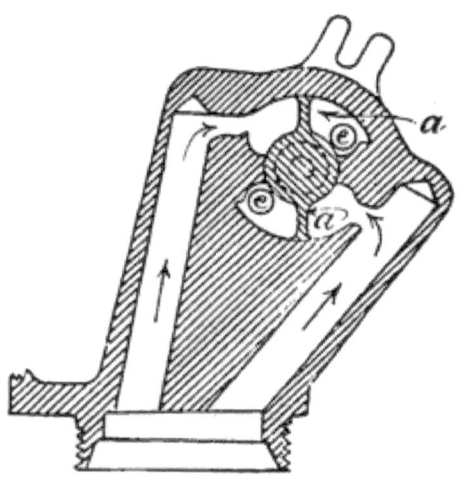

FIG. 68.—Sectional Elevation of the Wayne Indicator.

of the pressure spring. For indicating engines at very high speeds, such as 600 revolutions per minute, an ingenious fitting is added to the instrument, termed by the makers "the lining attachment." By this gear, shown in fig. 67, the indicator diagram is built up line by line, the movement of the pencil for each part added being about one-twentieth of an inch. By turning the handle shown in the front of fig. 67 a worm is rotated. This gears with a segment of a worm wheel, which in turn rotates in a concentric circle with the cylinder. A radial arm, visible in the illustration, fits into a hole in the piston rod, and is attached to the worm-wheel segment by means of a screw passing through a slotted hole. This slotted hole enables the pencil to move a distance of ⅛ in. when the worm wheel is stationary. The method of taking a "line" diagram is as follows : First turn the handle operating the worm and worm segment until the slot in the radial arm stands quite free of the set-screw passing through it. This enables the atmospheric line to be accurately taken. Then turn on the indicator cock, and commence to rotate the handle before mentioned. The distance between the horizontal lines of the diagram will depend entirely upon the loss of time occasioned by the slot in the radial arm, and consequently upon the speed of rotation of the handle operating the worm-wheel segment. For any given case a few trials will enable the operator to accommodate the movement of the handle to produce a distance of about one-twentieth of an inch between the horizontal lines, as recommended by the makers. A line diagram is shown in fig. 69. It is

FIG. 69.—Diagram taken with Wayne Indicator.

noticeable that a weaker spring may be used with the line attachment ; at the same time a much more accurate diagram is produced. The author has found the lining attachment extremely efficient and simple to work. It may be attached or removed from the instrument in a few seconds, and certainly produces a most perfect diagram at all speeds. The accessibility of the pressure spring is a great convenience, and its uniform temperature should

FIG. 70.—Simplex Indicator.

increase the degree of accuracy obtained. For convenience in adjusting the instrument it is attached to the cock with a swivel joint.

THE SIMPLEX INDICATOR.

A photograph of this instrument is shown in fig. 70. The instrument is made by Messrs. Elliott Brothers, and is exceedingly strong. The chief departure from the usual construction is in the arrangement and form of spring used to record the pressures. This spring is visible at S. The upper limb is held in the upright standard, which is rigidly attached to the body of the instrument. The lower limb is held in the top of the piston rod of the indicator. When pressure is exerted upon the piston, its movement is resisted by the spring. The spring is quite easily removed by a slight pressure upon its side. Various strengths of springs are supplied.

The pencil levers, which are somewhat heavy, pass through a wide slot cut in the upper part of the instrument, and are attached to the piston rod by a collar, which is free to rotate upon the piston rod. The straight line motion is obtained by four parallel bars, three of which are visible in the photograph.

CHAPTER XI.

REDUCING GEAR FOR GAS ENGINES.

IT is invariably necessary to attach to an engine some mechanism to cause the drum of the indicator to reproduce the motion of the piston to a small scale. Such mechanisms are numerous, and for a complete description of the various types the reader is referred to text-books on indicating. The essential requirements of a reducing gear are simplicity, durability, and accuracy. The great fault of nearly all reducing gears arises from the necessity of stopping the engine to attach the gear. This also necessitates the gear running until the engine may be stopped. The wear of the parts thus becomes abnormal, causing considerable shake and inconvenience, especially in high-speed engines.

Motion for the gear is usually derived from the crosshead of a steam engine or trunk piston of a gas engine. A convenient attachment for the latter is illustrated in fig. 71, at X; the pipe shown is welded to the adjusting screw of the piston pin, and carries the upright bar Y. The lock nuts shown serve to adjust the position of the bar. The motion of Y may be reduced to suit the stroke of the indicator drum in a variety of ways, and a practical

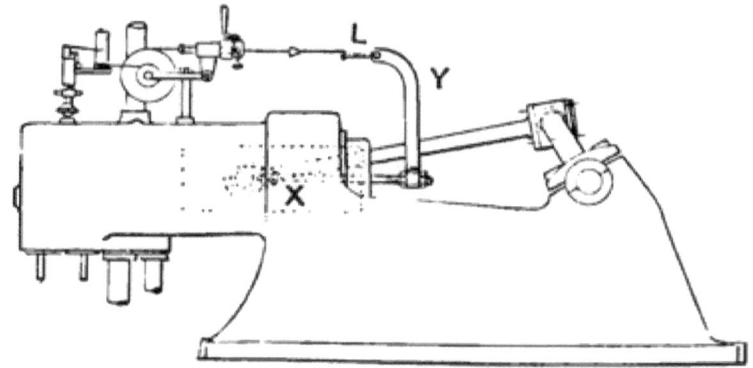

FIG. 71.—General view of Grover's Indicator Gear.

engineer will often be able to devise means suited to individual cases. It is, however, almost essential, to ensure economical working, to have a gas engine tested periodically in order to detect defective valves, and in view of this it is convenient to be able to fit up an entire indicator gear without stopping the engine. In order to secure this condition the author has recently designed and provisionally protected the arrangement illustrated in figs. 71, 72, 73. A number of these gears are being made by Messrs. Crosby and Co., for use in connection with their roll reducing gear and improved indicator.

Referring to fig. 72, it will be seen that the cord from the reducing wheel W passes through a tube, to which a handle

GROVER'S INDICATOR GEAR. 111

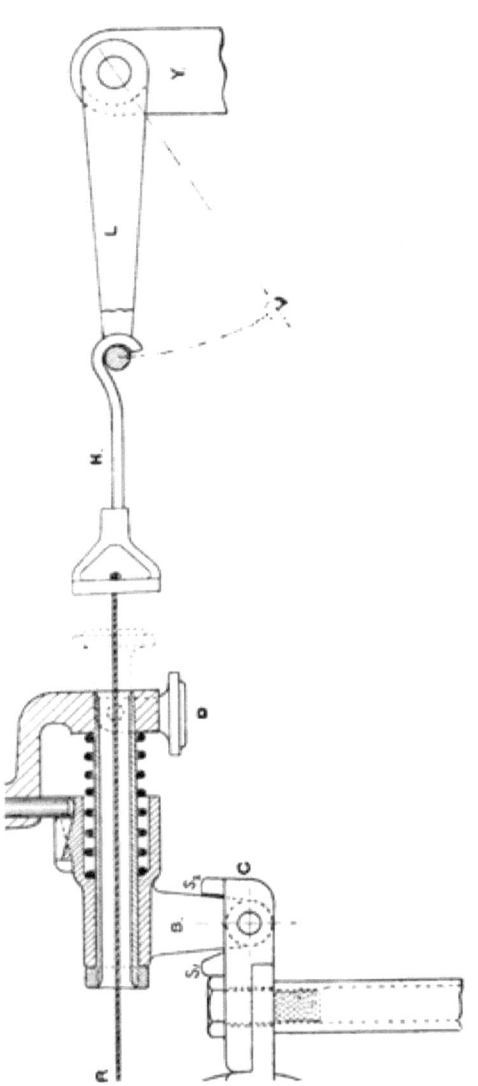

Fig. 72.—Elevation of Grover's Indicator Gear.

is attached. The tube slides in a boss upon the rocking lever B, and is pressed outwards by the spiral spring shown. When the spring is compressed, the bolt fitted in the handle rides up the incline, and, dropping over the edge, prevents the release of the spring. By pushing the handle over, as indicated by the arrow in fig. 73, the spring is released and the bolt in the handle runs up an opposite incline, dropping over its edge, as before. The handle must be pulled back again before the spring can be compressed. Upon the front of the tube a distance piece D is pivoted. This part drops downward by its own weight, but may occupy the horizontal position shown dotted.

A coiled spring inside the reducing wheel W causes the cord R to be in tension; hence the hook H, resting against the front of the handle, tilts the lever B against the stop S_1. When the hook is drawn forward, B rests against the stop S_2.

An important part of the arrangement is the swinging link L attached to the bar Y, figs. 71 and 72. This link, by reason of its inertia, swings from an angle of about 45 deg. into a horizontal position at the end of each instroke. By this means it is made to engage with the hook H when the latter is in position for coupling up.

The only permanent attachment to the engine is the bar Y, with its link L, and in the hands of a skilful operator the whole of the preliminary adjustments of the gear may be made even when running at full speed, though it is advisable to keep a record of the length of hook required for each engine, and to make such observations as will assist in quickly replacing the gear when once adjusted.

We will suppose that our cord from the indicator drum is attached to the reducing wheel, and that all is ready for taking a diagram. The first thing to be done is to compress the spiral spring. If this is omitted the gear may couple up, but it will immediately uncouple itself on the return stroke. Next, draw forwards and *upwards* the hook H, at the same time lifting the distance piece D until it is in the dotted position, fig. 72. Now allow the hook H to return until it presses against the distance piece D. It will now be found that the distance piece and the hook remain in line, but the hook is tilted upwards because the tension of the cord pulls B against the stop S_1. The gear is now ready for coupling, and this is effected by bringing B gently against the stop S_2. Immediately the hook leaves the distance piece, the latter

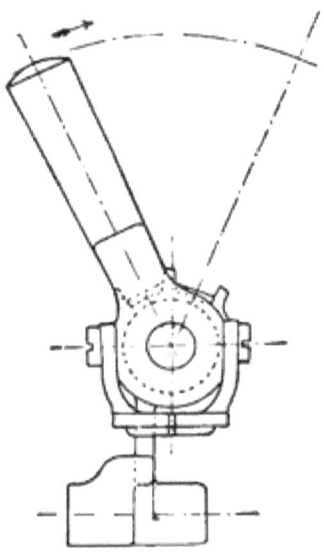

FIG. 73.—End view of parts A, B, and C of Grover's Indicator Gear.

drops down by its own weight, and when next the hook H returns there is a quarter of an inch clearance between it and the face of the tube. The hook therefore remains coupled to the link until the diagram is taken.

To uncouple the gear it is merely necessary to rotate the handle in the direction of the arrow on fig. 73. The spiral spring is then released, the handle flies out, and occupies the position shown in fig. 72. It is obvious that the hook H will now collide with the handle, and its further inward movement will be arrested. Hence the tension of the cord

R will again tend to bring B against the stop S_1. In consequence, the hook H tends to lift from the link L, and when L completes its inward stroke the clearance is so arranged that H is free to tilt upwards, and thus automatically uncouple itself.

CHAPTER XII.
Gas-Engine Trials.

WHEN taking indicator diagrams from a gas engine, it is advisable to keep the pencil upon the diagram paper for about half a minute, in order that a series of diagrams may be taken. If the engine is running at full power, the pencil will traverse the same path during each cycle and trace one distinct diagram. If, however, the engine is running lightly loaded, it is possible that it may not receive a full charge of gas, owing to the action of the governor; hence the pencil will trace out a fresh diagram for each cycle. Methods of working out the cards will be given later; at present we shall treat only of the practical details of a test; suffice it to say here that the object of the experimenter should be to obtain a set of diagrams at each operation of the indicator, ranging from a maximum to a minimum area.

The springs used for indicating gas engines are necessarily heavy (from $\frac{1}{120}$ to $\frac{1}{250}$); hence only the compression, explosion, and expansion curves are clearly shown upon the diagram. It is nevertheless important that the small variations in pressure during the exhaust and suction strokes should be ascertained as a check against bad valve setting and undue throttling in the pipes. This is usually done by using a light spring in the indicator (say a $\frac{1}{8}$th). In order to prevent the excessive compression of the spring during the explosion it is usual to pass a $\frac{1}{2}$ in. length of $\frac{3}{16}$ in. or $\frac{1}{4}$ in. brass pipe over the indicator piston rod before putting the instrument together for use. This acts as a distance piece between the piston and top cover of the indicator cylinder, and thus prevents the spring from being crushed. The length of the brass pipe will depend upon circumstances. In the Crosby indicator a $\frac{1}{16}$ in. length suffices. A diagram taken in this way has been given in fig. 17, and is explained in the text relating thereto. The excessive throttling of a silencing chamber, exhaust pipe, or valves is at once detected by a light spring diagram, and no engine should escape this test after it is completely fitted up.

Measurements of the Jacket Water—In a gas-engine trial there are three observations to be made with respect to the jacket water :—

1. The quantity (measured in pounds).
2. The temperature of the inlet (measured in deg. Fah.).
3. The temperature of the outlet (measured in deg. Fah).

The Quantity.—The most convenient method of measuring the weight of jacket water depends so much upon local conditions that no specific advice may be given. The author has found the following method convenient, and of wide application : Most engines not specially fitted for testing will be arranged as in fig. 2. This being so, empty the tank B by syphon or otherwise, and plug the orifice of the upper circulating pipe leading into tank A. No circulation through the jacket is now possible without opening the feed cock to A. The feed water delivered to A will pass through the jacket and find its way into tank B. This tank may be calibrated to read pounds of water, either by means of a float or by the insertion of a glass tube passing up the outside of the tank. In some instances it has been less trouble to uncouple a union on the pipe *e* and conduct the water to a tank resting upon a weighing machine. In either case the quantity should be regulated by the feed pipe to A, until the temperature of the outlet water is about 150 deg. Fah. Observations of the weight of water may be taken every ten minutes, though with a steady flow this is not necessary. When short handed only the total weight at the end of the trial need be observed.

Jacket Temperatures, Inlet.—The inlet temperatures should be taken on the inlet pipe near the tank A. If convenient, insert a ⊥ piece in the inlet pipe, and through a cork in the ⊥ place a Fahrenheit thermometer vertically, so that the mercury bulb is directly in the stream of water. Many errors arise through inattention to this. If the vertical part of the ⊥ is long, a small volume of stagnant water remains in it and gathers heat from the engine. The thermometer readings may be affected by this, and become altogether unreliable. In most cases the inlet temperatures may be observed from the water in the tank A, thus obviating any alteration to the pipes.

The Outlet Temperature.—This should be taken as near the exit from the jacket as possible. A convenient place is in the bend at the top of the pipe *e*. The thermometer should be placed vertically, especially if permanently fitted, as, if not, the column of mercury tends to stick at the maximum temperature recorded. It has been stated above that the usual outlet temperature is about 150 deg. Fah. The thermal efficiency of an engine may be increased by raising the temperature of the jacket. There is therefore a tendency to raise the temperature of the jacket beyond its safe working limit when running short economy trials. An increase in efficiency acquired in this way is sometimes ignorantly ascribed to other causes, and fair comparisons cannot be made without regard to the temperature of the jacket outlet water. No doubt a time will come when the jacket, as now usually fitted, will be dispensed with; for, although the gas engine is—theoretically and practically—the most efficient heat engine, it is nevertheless a humiliating admission that provision must be made for wasting between 30 and 40 per cent of the heat generated. Where hot water is required in factories there is no reason why this heat should not be utilised by a convenient arrangement of service pipes. The author has arranged a plant to work upon this system, which will effect a considerable saving in fuel, and be otherwise extremely convenient.

Measurement of the Gas.—The number of cubic feet of gas used, also the temperature and pressure of the gas in the meter, require to be known. The index of an ordinary gas meter is usually provided with a set of three or four pointers indicating respectively thousands, tens of thousands, hundreds of thousands, &c., of cubic feet of gas. Besides these, there is a smaller pointer placed above, which revolves once for, say, 10, 20, or 30 cubic feet according to the size of the meter. Besides these, another figure, which is frequently misleading, will be found printed upon the dial. This figure refers to the capacity of the measuring chamber inside the meter, and this is frequently noted upon the dial in the following way: "1·32 cub. ft. per rev." Mistakes occur in supposing this figure, 1·32 cubic feet, to refer to a revolution of the small pointer, instead of, as above mentioned, to the capacity of the measuring chamber. It should, therefore, always be remembered that this figure has absolutely no reference to the pointers on the dial.

When the meter is situated in a room of practically uniform temperature, the meter may be assumed to be of the same temperature as the air in the room. It is, however, more satisfactory to have a thermometer fitted to the exit pipe from the meter, so that the temperature of the gas may be more accurately ascertained. The pressure of the gas is best ascertained by the application of a manometer, or U tube filled with water, to some connection close to the meter. The head of water sustained by the pressure of gas should be noted a few times during the trial, to see that no variation of pressure takes place. In connection with the observation it is also necessary to take the height of the barometer, so that all readings may afterwards be reduced to one standard of atmospheric pressure.

Junker's Calorimeter.—In very complete trials it is necessary to know the average composition of the gas during the trial, though in most tests the calorific value of the gas (which, for general purposes, is the only figure required) may be ascertained by means of an instrument known as Junker's calorimeter. This instrument, which may be obtained from the sole agent, Hermon Kühne, New Broad Street, E.C., is illustrated in figs. 74 and 75. The principle of the instrument is that the heat generated by a gas flame is absorbed by a water jacket. The quantity of water, its inlet and outlet temperatures, and the quantity of gas passing through the instrument, afford data from which the calorific value of the gas may be determined to within 0·5 per cent of any other determination. Radiation is prevented by surrounding the apparatus by an air jacket formed by a nickel-plated cylinder. The flame shown at 28, fig. 74, is surrounded by a water jacket, through which pass a number of vertical copper tubes. The flame burns in the central chamber, and the products of combustion pass down the inside of the tubes to the outlet at 33. By this arrangement the gases at the highest temperature meet the hottest water, whilst as the gases cool they meet the colder inlet water. This, of course, favours the transmission of heat, and the products of combustion escape at the throttle at atmospheric temperature, having parted with the heat of combustion to the jacket water. In order to obtain accurate results, it is necessary that the flow of water through the instrument should be perfectly uniform. This is secured by leading the water into a tank shown at 3, fig. 74. This tank is kept slightly overflowing, thus producing a constant head. Two thermometers are fitted for measuring the temperatures of the inlet and outlet, and a graduated measuring glass is supplied for water measurements. It is highly important that the gas pressure remain constant, and for this reason a suitable regulator is required to be used with the calorimeter. An external view of the apparatus showing the gas meter and regulator is given in fig. 75. Water formed by the combustion in the central chamber is collected in a small measuring glass at d, fig. 75.

GAS ENGINE TRIALS. 119

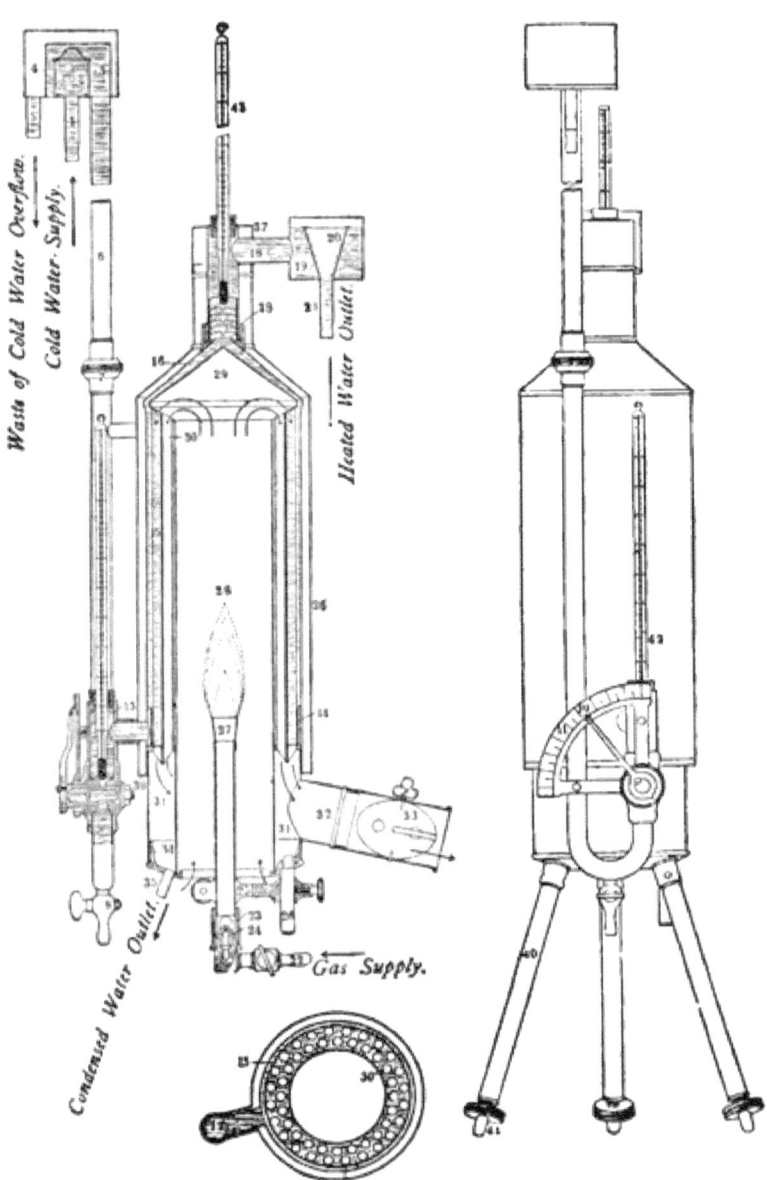

Fig. 74.—Section and Elevation of Junker's Calorimeter.

The calibrations of the instrument have been made in the metric system, and the unit of heat has been taken as the quantity required to raise the temperature of 1 kilogramme of water 1 deg. Cen. This unit is termed a calorie, and is converted into British thermal units* by multiplication by 3·96.

In fixing the apparatus, the chief points to be observed are as follow :—

No draughts must be allowed to strike the outlet of the exhaust gases. The quantity of gas passed through the calorimeter should be at the rate of

    4 to 8 cubic feet per hour of illuminating gas,
    8 to 16 ,, ,, hydrogen,
    16 to 32 ,, ,, Dowson gas.

Always light the burner outside the combustion chamber, to avoid explosion due to accumulated gas.

Regulate the water passing through the jackets until its rise of temperature is from 10 to 20 deg. Cen.

Having set up the apparatus and regulated the quantity of gas and water, a test may be made in the following way: Observe the reading of the gas meter at a convenient figure, and at the same time remove the tube C, fig. 75, to discharge into the graduated glass. Then take the readings of the inlet and outlet thermometers. Take a few intermediate readings of the outlet thermometer, and immediately the water reaches, say, the 2 litre mark, turn off the gas and read the quantity of gas shown by the meter. The readings may be booked as follow :—

Gas meter.	Cold water thermometer.	Hot water thermometer.	Water jacket.
4 cubic feet	7·98	27·54	0
	,,	27·52	...
	,,	27·53	...
4·268 cubic feet	,,	27·55	2 litres
Gas burnt 0·268 cubic feet	7·98	27·53 (mean)	2 litres

* The heat required to raise 1 lb. of water of maximum density 1 deg. Fah. is equal to one British thermal unit.

Mean rise in temperature
$$= 27\cdot53 - 7\cdot98 = 19\cdot55.$$

Calorific value of gas in calories per cubic foot
$$= \frac{\text{mean rise in temperature} \times \text{litres of water}}{\text{cubic feet gas burnt}}$$
$$= \frac{19\cdot55 \times 2}{0\cdot268} = 145\cdot8 \text{ calories}$$
$$= 145\cdot5 \times 3\cdot96 = 577 \text{ B.T.U.}$$

So far we have obtained a calorific value of the gas without regard to any condensed water which may have collected

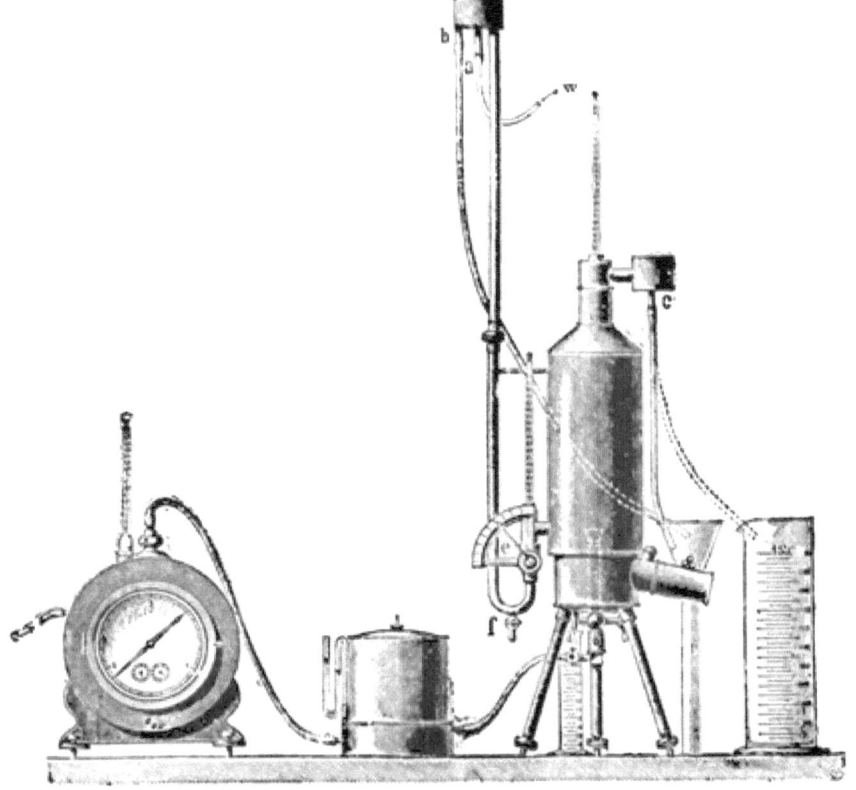

Fig. 75.—External View of Junker's Calorimeter.

in the small measuring glass marked D, in fig. 75. Now, this moisture is the result of the combustion of hydrogen with the oxygen of the air, and at the moment of combustion steam is formed. In the calorimeter this steam is condensed, and gives up its latent heat to the calorimeter; hence the calorific value above obtained is the total heat evolved per pound of gas when all the products of combustion are cooled to atmospheric temperature.

In nearly all industrial processes the steam formed by the combustion of hydrogen with oxygen passes away as steam; consequently some of the heat is not available unless the steam is all condensed to water. The number of British thermal units carried away per pound of hydrogen is, in round numbers, 10,000. This is obtained in the following way: 1 lb. of hydrogen requires eight times its weight of oxygen to completely burn it; hence 9 lb. of steam would be produced. Suppose this to be cooled to water at 60 deg. Fah., and at atmospheric pressure, the heat evolved by the process would be equal to $9 \times \{966 + (212 - 60)\}$ units per pound of hydrogen, which amounts to 10,062 British thermal units. It is evident, therefore, that two calorific values may be obtained—the one the *total*, the other the *available*. In gas engines the heat of the exhaust does not permit of condensation of the steam produced; hence the latent heat should be subtracted to give the available heat for use in the gas engine.

For this determination it is advisable to continue the operation of the calorimeter for a longer time, because of the small quantity of condensed water produced. Suppose the measuring glass D contains 60 cubic centimeters after burning 3 cubic feet of gas; then the correction in calories

$$= \frac{\text{cubic centimeters of water} \times 0\cdot 6}{\text{cubic feet gas burnt}}$$

$$= \frac{60 \times 0\cdot 6}{3}$$

$$= 12 \text{ calories.}$$

Then the net available heat

$$= 145{\cdot}8 - 12 = 133{\cdot}8 \text{ calories}$$
$$= 529 \text{ B.T.U.}$$

It is sometimes argued that in estimating the efficiency of a gas engine the total heat, and not the net available heat, should be taken as the basis. Nearly all efficiency trials have hitherto been worked upon the available calorific value of the gas used, and for the sake of uniformity we shall adopt this standard. After all, the question is merely one of definition, and needs no further discussion here.

Method of Taking Sample of Gas.—Should it be desired to take a continuous sample of gas for future analysis, the following arrangement will be found convenient : Fit an indiarubber cork into a suitable glass jar, and through two holes insert glass tubes. The one tube should be short, and the other should reach to the bottom of the jar. Attach the shorter tube to the gas supply by means of an indiarubber pipe, and form a syphon of the other longer tube by another piece of rubber pipe. Having completely filled the apparatus with water, a pinch cock may be adjusted on the syphon so that the latter draws the water slowly from the bottle or jar. Gas then enters the jar, and by suitably regulating the syphon small quantities of gas may continuously enter the jar during the whole period of the trial. In this way a fair representative sample of gas is obtained for analysis. Mercury is, of course, preferable to water, inasmuch as the constituents of coal gas are more or less soluble in water. No serious errors arise provided the gas is not left for a long period in contact with a large surface of water. Precise instructions for analysing gases will be given in another chapter.

Counting the Revolutions and Explosions.—The revolutions of the crank shaft are usually observed by means of some form of speed counter. The following methods of actuating the counter have been made use of by the author, and are given here as suggestions. It often happens that incidental conditions adapt themselves to the requirements of the experiments, and for this reason it is always well to be on the alert rather than to attempt to laboriously carry out a special method of fixing the measuring apparatus.

Suppose the counter to have a reciprocating lever which requires to be moved through two short strokes at each revolution of the crank shaft. When the reducing gear for indicating is constantly working throughout the trial, motion may be transmitted from some of its bars by a cord attached to the lever of the counter. The cord may be held in tension by attaching a strong indiarubber band to the counter lever. Indiarubber bands are so extremely useful in fixing up testing apparatus that they should be regarded as part of the equipment for an engine trial. Should the reducing gear be unsuitable for driving the counter, motion may be derived from the valve levers. In this case it must be borne in mind that the side shaft of an Otto cycle engine is geared down to run at one-half the revolutions of the crank shaft; hence the counter readings must be doubled. For the *permanent* attachment of a counter it is, of course, better to employ a link or rod for operating the counter lever, though the cord and indiarubber band is much more easily fitted up, and is just as reliable for a three or four hours' test. Small counters are procurable which may be held against the centre of the crank shaft by hand. Some are arranged to give the revolutions per minute on the dial, others give the revolutions during the time the counter is held in position.

The explosions are best counted from the exhaust pipe outlet. If the engine is running at full power, and is working on the Otto cycle, the explosions will, of course, be equal to half the revolutions. The explosions should in any case be counted occasionally, in order to verify the assumption, as derangement of the governor gear and ignition tube may falsify the results if not checked.

Temperature of the Exhaust.—This measurement is difficult to obtain with any approach to accuracy. It is indeed often left to be calculated from the indicator card. This, however, is not satisfactory, because of the alteration of the specific heat of the gases forming the products of combustion. It has been shown by Le Chatelier that the specific heat of carbon-dioxide increases in the ratio of 1 to 1·6 between temperatures of 0 and 1,000 Cen. Until more is known of the specific heats of gases at high temperatures, calculations from the cards can only be regarded as approximating to the results required.

Mr. Burstall has carried out experiments in this direction, using a fine platinum wire suspended in the combustion chamber. The electrical resistance was measured, and from this the temperature deduced. This was found to range from 1,045 deg. Cen. to 1,140 deg. Cen. At the present time there is no simple and reliable instrument which can readily be fitted up for measuring directly the exhaust temperatures; hence most experimenters have to adopt a method of calculation from the indicator diagram.

We may now summarise the observations during a gas-engine trial as follows :—

Time of observations.
Brake readings {Spring balance. Load on brake.
Revolutions of the engine by counter.
Explosions per minute.
Gas meter {Quantity, cubic feet. Temperature. Pressure.
Jacket water {Quantity, pounds. Inlet temperature. Outlet temperature.
Height of barometer.
Indicator diagrams.
Temperature of exhaust (when possible).

CHAPTER XIII.

The Practical Analysis of Coal Gas.

Analysing the Gas.—Hempel's apparatus is most generally used by engineers for the analysis of furnace and coal gases. If carefully handled, the results may be relied upon as being accurate to the half of 1 per cent. The principle upon which the analysis depends is briefly as follows: From a known volume of gas certain constituents are absorbed. The remaining volume is measured after each absorption is complete; hence the volumetric proportion of the constituents may be determined. If there is a residue which cannot be absorbed, as is the case with coal gas, the remaining quantities may be determined by combustion in a manner to be described.

We will suppose that a sample of coal gas has been collected during the trial, as previously described. This sample, we know, consists of carbon-dioxide (CO_2), olefines (C_6H_4), oxygen (O), carbon-monoxide (CO), hydrogen (H), and marsh gas (CH_4). Our analysis will enable us to determine the volumetric proportions of these constituents, but it will be noticed that the method depends entirely upon our knowledge of their presence. The constituents must be absorbed in the following order:—

1. Carbon-dioxide, absorbed by potassium hydrate.
2. Olefines, aborbed by strong sulphuric acid.
3. Oxygen, absorbed by phosphorus or pyrogallic acid.
4. Carbon-monoxide, absorbed by cuprous chloride dissolved in hydrochloric acid.

The apparatus for carrying out these processes is illustrated in figs. 76 and 77. A is a plain tube, called the levelling tube; B is a graduated tube, called the burette. The burette is graduated up to 100 cubic centimetres. The two tubes are connected together by means of a flexible rubber pipe, which may be of comparatively thin section when water is used in the apparatus, but should be much stouter tubing when mercury is used.

There is a cock at the top of the burettes and a pinch cock upon the rubber connection. The level tube is first

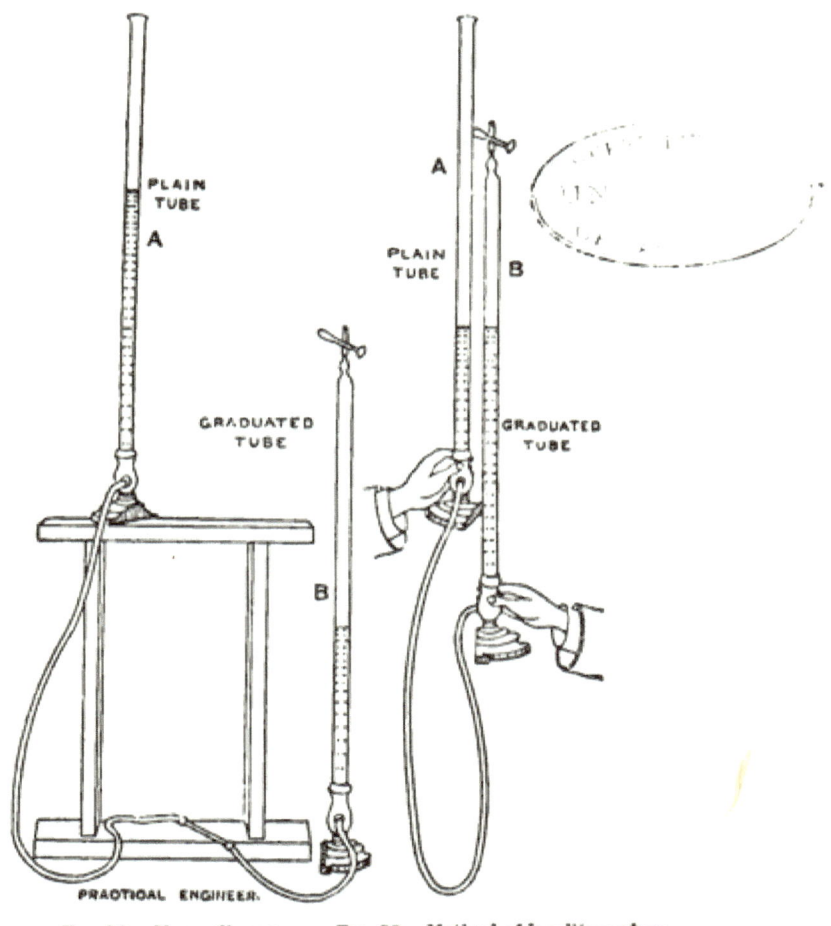

Fig. 76.—Hempel's gas burettes.

Fig. 77.—Method of levelling when measuring volume of gas.

filled with water (or mercury if procurable). The burette is then lowered until the water gravitates into it and completely fills it up to the stop cock. Now connect the syphon tube of the sample bottle to a water tap, and gently turn on the water so as slightly to raise the pressure of the sample gas. Allow a little gas to escape through the other tube from the sample bottle, in order to get rid of any air beyond the pinch cock. The sample may now be connected to the burette, and the water run from the burette back into the level tube. The sample gas will then be drawn into the burette. It is better to draw in rather more than

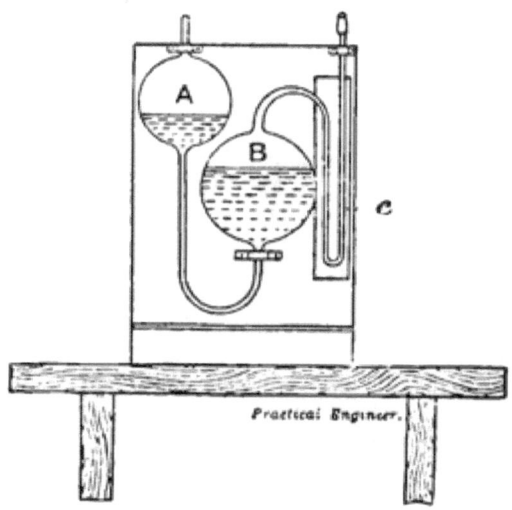

Fig. 72.—Hempel's simple absorption pipette.

100 c.c. before disconnecting the sample bottle. This done, close the stop cock of the burette, and raise the level tube until the surface of the water stands at zero. Close the pinch cock on the flexible tube. The pressure in the burette will now be slightly above that of the atmosphere; hence the stop cock of the burette should be opened momentarily just to allow the excess of pressure to escape. This method of filling contributes towards accuracy, for it is of the highest importance that no measurements of volumes be taken excepting when the gas is at atmospheric pressure. It is

also of the highest importance that the temperature of the burette remain constant, and for this reason the tubes should never be touched; all lifting should be done by holding the wooden stands into which the tubes are fitted. By drawing the hand once or twice down the burette, an alteration of quite 5 per cent will be noticed in the reading, thus showing the importance of uniformity of temperature throughout the analysis.

Having measured off our 100 c.c. at atmospheric pressure, we next proceed to absorb the carbon-dioxide. Each absorption is carried out in a pipette, the forms of which are shown in figs. 78, 79, and 80. Fig. 80 represents two glass bulbs connected together by glass tubes as shown.

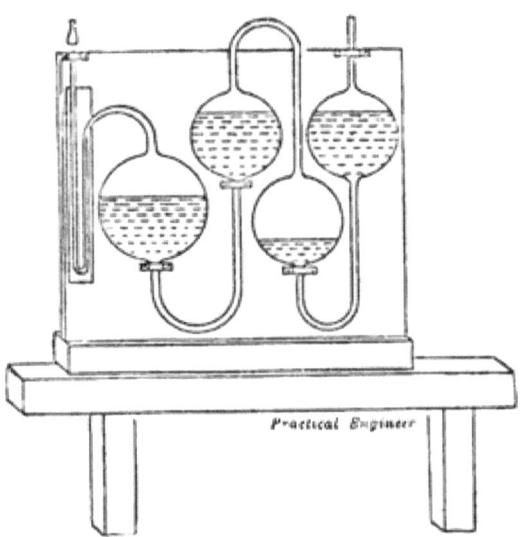

Fig 79.—Hempel's double absorption pipette.

The larger bulb is filled with a strong solution of potassium hydrate until the capillary U tube fills. It is advantageous to place a number of $\frac{1}{8}$ in. solid glass rods inside the long bulb. The solution adheres to the surface of the rods, and thus presents a very large surface for absorbing th CO_2.

10G

After making sure that the solution is well up the capillary tube, couple the burette to the pipette, as in fig. 81, by a very short piece of capillary tube. The admission of air in coupling and uncoupling with the various pipettes used is a frequent source of error, and the utmost care is required. A con-

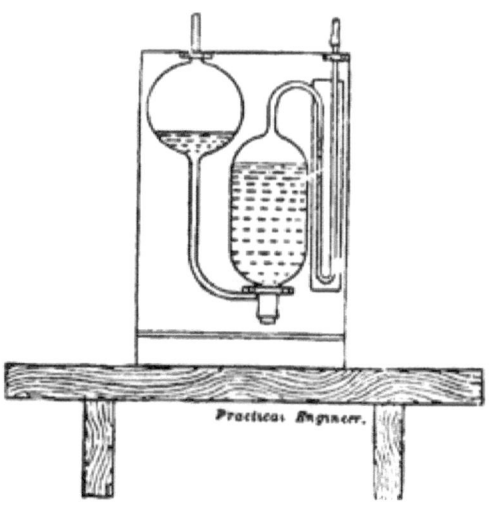

Fig. 80.—Hempel's pipette for solid substances.

venient way of making these joints is to slip a $\frac{3}{4}$ in. length of rubber tube over and beyond the end of one tube. Then butt the two ends together, and by wetting the glass the rubber can be slipped over the joint without enclosing a large volume of air. When the joint is made, open the stop cock, raise the level tube, and drive all the gas over into the pipette. The absorption will be complete in about half an hour. The process will be assisted by shaking the solution or by drawing the gas back into the burette, so that the glass rods may be again moistened.

When the process of absorption is completed, lower the level tube and allow the water to flow from the burette until the caustic potash in the pipette rises up the capillary tube to the position it at first occupied. Now close the stop cock at the top of the burette, and hold the level tube against the burette at such a height that the water in both tubes is exactly at the same level. In this way the gases in the burette are always brought to atmospheric pressure before their volume is measured. In taking the readings great

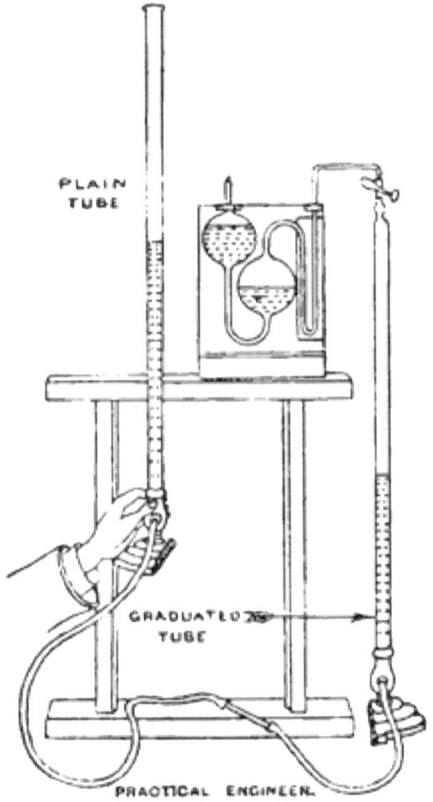

Fig. 81.—Method of using Hempel's apparatus.

care should be exercised. When water is used its surface in the tube will be concave; with mercury the surface is convex. In either case the line of sight when taking a reading should be horizontal and tangential at the *centre* of the concave or convex surfaces. Before taking a reading when water is used in the tubes, the burette should be allowed to stand a few moments to allow drops to run down the sides. It is only by careful attention to such details that any approach to accuracy can be secured. An exactly similar process is carried out in order to absorb the olefines. The pipette used is shown in fig. 78, and contains strong sulphuric acid.

To absorb the oxygen, a pipette similar to fig. 80 is used. This should be filled with water, and contain a number of sticks of phosphorus of about $\frac{1}{8}$ in. diameter. As phosphorus is not readily procured in such thin sticks, it will be well to describe how they may easily be produced from lumps of phosphorus without danger to the operator. Procure a glass tube, the bore of which is equal to the diameter of the sticks required. At the end of this place a short length of rubber pipe. Take a tumbler of water, at about 120 deg. Fah., and quickly drop the lumps of phosphorus into the hot water. The phosphorus will now melt at the bottom of the tumbler. Squeeze the rubber pipe attached to the glass tube, and then immerse the end of the glass tube in the melted phosphorus. Owing to the head of water in the glass, it will be found that the phosphorus will run up the glass tube when the rubber at the other end is released. By suitably arranging the head of water, sticks of phosphorus of the required length may be cast. To get the stick of phosphorus from the glass tube it is advisable to remove the rod into a vessel of cold water, but before doing so take care to pinch tightly the rubber connection, so that the phosphorus does not drop when taken from the water. In a few seconds the phosphorus will set, and will stick in the tube if not prevented. Whilst setting the phosphorus should be kept moving in the glass tube by pressing the rubber tube in one or two places in addition to keeping its end tightly closed. A little practice will enable the operator to cast phosphorus safely and quickly. It is extremely important in dealing with such an inflammable material as phosphorus that it should be handled always under cold water, and never be left exposed to the air for many seconds.

The absorption of oxygen is carried out exactly as previously described.

The carbon-monoxide (CO) is absorbed in a double pipette, as shown in fig. 79. The two bulbs on the right contain water, whilst the two bulbs on the left attached to the capillary tube contain the cuprous chloride and hydrochloric acid. In manipulating this pipette great care should be taken not to pass the cuprous chloride over into the water bulb. If this be done, a white precipitate of cuprous chloride will be formed in the water chamber, and if left may block up the passage between the water bulbs. With this additional caution, the work may be continued as previously described.

We have now absorbed four of the constituents of the gas, and we have a residue of hydrogen and marsh gas. To evaluate these quantities an entirely different method is employed.

To effect the explosion of the hydrogen and marsh gases, a pipette of the form shown in fig. 78 is used, having two platinum wires fused into the bulb B, terminating in sparking points on the inside of the bulb. See that the bulb B and the capillary tube C are filled with water. Then drive from the burette 10 c.c. of the residue into the pipette. Then, either by emptying the burette, or, preferably, by using a second burette, drive seven times the volume of air—that is, 70 c.c. of pure air—into the pipette, as a supply of oxygen for the explosion. It will be found that this charge occupies about half the volume of B. This should not be exceeded. By means of a bichromate battery and induction coil send a spark through the explosive gas, and violent combustion will follow. On account of the sudden pressure, it is well to bind the rubber connection to the pipette with wire. Sometimes a glass stop cock is provided between the chambers A and B. If so, this cock must be *open* when the explosion takes place, or the bulb B will be broken by the pressure. After the explosion measure the volume of the remaining gas by drawing it back into the burette, observing the cautions already given. It will be found that there is a considerable diminution in volume, due to the free hydrogen and the hydrogen in the marsh gas combining with oxygen of the air to form steam, which ultimately is condensed on the sides of the pipette to a negligible volume of water. The gases remaining after the explosion consist of carbon-dioxide—the result of the combustion—nitrogen, which was drawn in with the air, and an excess of oxygen above that required for the complete combustion of the hydrogen and marsh gas. It will be observed that the diminution in volume after the explosion is due to the disappearance of gaseous hydrogen from two constituents, namely, the free hydrogen and that contained in the marsh gas. It is known that one volume of marsh gas when completely burnt with oxygen forms an equal volume of carbon-dioxide. If, therefore, we absorb the carbon-dioxide by means of the caustic potash pipette, we shall obtain the volume of the CO_2 formed by the explosion. This volume gives the required volume of marsh gas. The remainder of the diminution of volume after the explosion must therefore be due to combination of free hydrogen with oxygen. And we know that one volume of oxygen combines with two volumes of hydrogen; hence of the three volumes disappearing due to hydrogen two-thirds of this contraction gives the volume of hydrogen. The nitrogen in the coal gas may be estimated "by difference." But it is preferable to absorb all the oxygen from the residue, and so obtain a residue of nitrogen only. The nitrogen contained in the air used for the explosion may be calculated, and subtracting this from the total remainder of nitrogen gives the volume due to the coal gas.

As an example of the process, the following analysis of Leeds coal gas, obtained by the author in 1895, is fully worked out:—

THE PRACTICAL ANALYSIS OF COAL GAS. 135

90 c.c. of coal gas were taken into the burette.

1. Volume of water in burette before any constituents were absorbed was .... = 10 c.c.
   Volume of water in burette after absorption of carbon-dioxide (CO_2)............ = 10.1 c.c.
   Therefore volume of CO_2 in 90 c.c. of coal gas .... = 0.1 c.c.
   Equivalent volume of CO_2 in 100 c.c. of gas .... = 0.11 c.c.

2. Volume of water in burette before absorption of olefines (C_6H_4) .... = 10.1 c.c.
   Volume of water in burette after absorption of olefines (C_6H_4) .... = 12.6 c.c.
   Therefore volume of C_6H_4 in 90 c.c. of gas............ = 2.5 c.c.
   Equivalent volume of C_6H_4 in 100 c.c. of gas .... = 2.77 c.c.

3. No oxygen was detected.

4. Volume of water in burette before absorption of carbon-monoxide (CO) .... = 12.6 c.c.
   Volume of water in burette after absorption of carbon-monoxide (CO) .... = 20.0 c.c.
   Therefore volume of CO in 90 c.c. of coal gas............ = 7.4 c.c.
   Equivalent volume of CO in 100 c.c. of gas .... = 8.22 c.c.

10 c.c. of residue were taken into burette, and mixed with 80 c.c. of air; hence—

Volume of water in burette before explosion............. = 10 c.c.
Volume of water in burette after explosion .... = 26 c.c.
Therefore total contraction in volume was .... 16 c.c.
Volume of water in burette before absorbing CO_2 formed by explosion .... = 26 c.c.
Volume of water in burette after absorbing CO_2 formed by explosion .... = 30.7 c.c.
Therefore CO_2 = 4.7—that is, volume of CH_4 in 10 c.c. of residue .... = 4.7 c.c.

But if 100 c.c. of coal gas had been taken into burette, then the total residue of CH_4 and hydrogen would have been—

$$100 - (0.11 + 2.77 + 8.22)$$
$$= 100 - 11.10$$
$$= 88.9 \text{ residue of } CH_4 \text{ and H.}$$

Therefore the total CH_4 will be

$$4.7 \times \frac{88.9}{10} = 41.78 \text{ c.c.}$$

Now, we have seen that one volume of CH_4 combines with two volumes of O_2 to form one volume of CO_2 and two volumes of H_2O. The two volumes of H_2O condense to water, and are quite negligible. Therefore we see that the diminution in volume due to CH_4 in the exploded gases is equal to twice the volume of CO_2 formed by the combustion.

Volume of CO_2 absorbed from products of combustion
= 4·7 c.c.
Total contraction of volume after explosion = 16 c.c.
Therefore contraction due to free hydrogen
= total contraction − contraction due to CH_4
= 16 − 4·7 × 2 = 16 − 9·4 = 6·6 c.c.

Now, two volumes of hydrogen combine with one volume of oxygen, and all three volumes disappear after the steam formed by combustion is condensed. It is evident, therefore, that out of the 6·6 c.c. of contracted volume only two-thirds was free hydrogen.

The volume of hydrogen in 10 c.c. of residue

$$= 6·6 \times \tfrac{2}{3} = 4·4.$$

Therefore the volume of hydrogen in total residue, namely,

$$88·9 \text{ c.c.} = 4·4 \times \frac{88·9}{10} = 39·11.$$

Out of 10 c.c. of residue we have obtained 4·4 hydrogen and 4·7 CH_4, which together make up 9·1 c.c.; the remaining 0·9 c.c. should be the volume of nitrogen in the coal gas. Therefore, by difference, the nitrogen amounts to

$$0·9 \times \frac{88·9}{10} = 8·0 \text{ c.c. (nearly).}$$

But our analysis ought to be further checked, and we will proceed to estimate the nitrogen by direct measurement.

Our residue now consists of nitrogen due to coal gas + nitrogen due to air taken in for the explosion + excess of oxygen in the air not required to complete the combustion.

If we absorb the excess of oxygen, we shall at once obtain the whole volume of nitrogen present.

Referring to last reading of burette, we find—

Volume of water in burette before absorbing oxygen, 30·7 c.c.

Volume of water in burette after absorbing oxygen, 35·9 c.c.

Therefore excess of oxygen = 5·2 c.c.

Therefore the total nitrogen left in burette = 100 − 35·9 = 64·1 c.c.

The percentage of nitrogen in air is approximately 79 per cent; therefore out of 80 c.c. taken into burette the nitrogen

$$= 80 \times \frac{79}{100} = 63\cdot 2 \text{ c.c.}$$

Therefore the volume of nitrogen due to the coal gas

= 64·1 − 63·2 = 0·9 c.c. (nearly).

This agrees with our determination by difference; hence we know our analysis to be very approximately correct.

Collecting our results, we get—

Volume per cent of CO_2 = 0·11
,, ,, C_2H_4 = 2·77
,, ,, O = 0·00
,, ,, CO = 8·22
,, ,, H = 39·11
,, ,, CH_4 = 41·78
,, ,, N = 8·00 (by direct measurement)

99·99 error 0·01.*

The various producer gases may be analysed by Hempel's apparatus in the manner described. The following tables give the composition of coal and producer gases analysed in

---

* The author regards this near approximation to accuracy as the result of rather larger *compensating* errors in the work. Nothing less than 0·1 c c. can be read with certainty upon the burette scale; hence an error of 0·01 on the analysis may give a false impression of the accuracy obtainable with this apparatus.

connection with gas-engine trials. It will be understood that the figures given below refer to particular samples of town gases, and that the daily variation in the composition always necessitates an analysis when the constituents of the gas are required with accuracy.

Composition of Coal Gas in Various Cities.

Percentage by volume. Constituents in gas.	Leeds, 1895 (Grover).	London Society of Arts trial.	Kilmarnock (Professor Kennedy).	Paris (Witz).
Marsh gas CH_4	41·78	37·34	42·80	32·30
Olefines C_2H_4	2·77	3·77	5·55	5·50
Hydrogen H	39·11	50·44	43·60	52·80
Carbon-monoxide	8·22	3·96	4·30	5·60
Nitrogen	8·00	3·98	2·70	3·80
Carbon-dioxide and oxygen (Chiefly CO_2 with traces of O.)	0·12	0·51	5·35	0·00

Composition of Poor Gases.*

Name of gas.	Oxygen. Vol. %	Hydrogen. Vol. %	Marsh gas. Vol. %	Olefiant gas. Vol. %	Carbon-monoxide. Vol. %	Carbon-dioxide. Vol. %	Nitrogen. Vol. %
Siemens producer gas	..	8·60	2·40		24·40	5·20	59·40
Water gas	0·10	50·50	0·60	..	44·40	1·60	..
Strong gas		53·00	..	..	35·00	4·00	8·00
Lowe gas	..	30·00	..	..	28·00	34·00	8·00
Dowson gas	0·03	18·73	0·31	0·31	25·07	6·57	48·98
Dowson gas	0·23	24·36	1·16	0·15	17·55	6·07	50·48
Lenchanchez	0·50	20·00	..	4·0	21·00	5·00	49·50

* From "Donkin on Gas, Oil, and Air Engines."

CHAPTER XIV.
CALCULATIONS REQUIRED IN WORKING OUT RESULTS OF ENGINE TRIALS.

THE most important deductions to be made from the analysis of the gases used are—(1) The quantity of air required for complete combustion; (2) to obtain the calorific value of the gas; (3) to calculate the specific heat of the waste gases. Of these the two first mentioned are of the greatest importance from a commercial standpoint. The loss of heat in the waste gases is difficult to determine with accuracy, and where the temperature of the gases is only approximately known it is an absurd refinement to calculate the specific heat of the gases to three places of decimals.

For the complete explanation of the reactions which take place between the constituents of coal gas and oxygen, the reader is referred to any modern elementary text-book on chemistry. A knowledge of the facts set forth in the following table enables us to work out the theoretical quantity of air required for combustion.

The nitrogen, carbon-dioxide, and oxygen are not combustible. Strictly, the oxygen contained in the coal gas should be deducted from that quantity given in column (h), but the oxygen is usually in such small quantities as to be quite negligible.

Air is composed of 23 per cent of oxygen and 77 per cent of nitrogen by weight; therefore the weight of air required per pound of coal gas will be

$$2{\cdot}89 \times \frac{100}{23} = 12{\cdot}5.$$

In other words, the proportion of air to gas by weight for complete combustion is equal to 12·5 to 1. One cubic foot of air weighs 0·08082 lb. Hence the proportion of air to gas by volume equals 5·72 to 1. It must be remembered that all these figures are worked out for a temperature of 32 deg.

Fah. and a pressure of 14·7 lb. per square inch absolute. Any increase of pressure causes an increase in density—that is, an increase in weight per unit volume. Conversely, any increase in temperature causes a decrease in density when the pressure remains constant—that is, decrease in the weight per unit volume.

Constituents.	(a) Volume per cent.	(b) Weight of one cubic foot.	(c) Calorific value per pound.	(d) Proportion of weight of oxygen required.	(e) Weight in one cubic foot of coal gas.	(f) Proportion by weight.	(g) Calorific value per cubic foot of coal gas.	(h) Weight of oxygen required.
		Lbs.	B. T. U.		Lbs.		B. T. U.	Lbs.
Marsh gas........	41·78	0·0447	21,690	4	0·01867	0·506	404·9	2·024
Olefines	2·77	0·1174	20,260	3½	0·00325	0·088	65·8	0·302
Hydrogen ,.......	39·11	0·00559	52,500	8	0·00218	0·059	114·4	0·472
Carbon monoxide.	8·22	0·0783	4,300	½	0·00643	0·174	27·7	0·099
Nitrogen.........	8·00	0·0783	..	..	0·00626	0·170	..	..
Carbon · dioxide and oxygen...	0·12	0·1060	..	..	0·00012	0·003	..	..
	..	..	..	..	0·03691	1·000	612·8	2·897

Column (a) gives the volumes per cent of the constituents as furnished by analysis.

Column (b) gives the known weights of each constituent per cubic foot at 32 deg. Fah. and at 14·7 lb. per square inch in absolute pressure.

Column (c) gives the known heating value of 1 lb. of each constituent at 32 deg. Fah. and 14·7 lb. square inch absolute.

Column (d) gives the proportion of weight of oxygen required to combine with a given weight of gas. Thus one cubic foot of marsh gas weighs 0·0447 lb., and will require for its combustion four times that weight of oxygen: 0·0447 × 4 = 0·1788 lb. oxygen.

From these data the remaining columns may be filled in.

Column (e).—Multiply figures in column (a) by those in column (b).

Column (f).—This gives the proportion of weight of constituents in 1 lb. of coal gas. These figures are found by dividing the weight of each constituent in column (e) by the total weight of one cubic foot of coal gas.

Column (g).—These figures are the products of (c) × (e).

Column (h).—These figures are the product of (d) × (f).

SPECIFIC HEATS OF GASES AT CONSTANT VOLUME.

The calorific value of the gas, as given in column (g), should agree with the experimental determination by Junker's calorimeter when both are reduced to the same standard. The calorific value for hydrogen is given minus the latent heat taken up in the formation of steam; therefore no correction need be made, as described in the text relating to Junker's calorimeter.

It is sometimes of interest to calculate the maximum temperature possible during the combustion of the mixture in the cylinder. To do this we require to know the thermal value of the charge of gas, the specific heat at constant volume, and the weight of the whole charge. The volume of gas entering the cylinder per cycle is easily obtained from the gas-meter readings. We will now proceed to find the specific heats of various mixtures of coal gas and air for the sample tabulated in the above table. First, to find the specific heat of the coal gas. The following table gives the data required:—

	(a) Proportion by weight.	(b) Specific heat of constituent at constant volume.	(c)
Marsh gas	0·506	0·470	0·2378
Olefines	0·088	0·332	0·0292
Hydrogen	0·059	2·406	0·1419
Carbon-monoxide	0·174	0·173	0·0301
Nitrogen	0·170	0·173	0·0294
Carbon-dioxide	0·003	0·171	0·0048
Oxygen	....	0·155	
			0·4732

Column (a) gives the proportion by weight of the constituents of the coal gas. These figures are copied from the previous table.

Column (b) gives the specific heats of the constituents at a constant volume.

Column (c).—These figures are the result of the product of the figures in column (a) by column (b), and the total is the specific heat of the gas. This equals 0·473.

Taking the specific heat of air as 0·168 at constant volume, we will next work out the specific heats of the following mixtures of air and gas :—

Volume of air to gas.	Specific heat of mixture at constant volume.	Proportion of air to gas by weight.
6—1	0·189	13·13 to 1
7—1	0·186	15·32 to 1
8—1	0·184	17·51 to 1
9—1	0·183	19·70 to 1
10—1	0·181	21·89 to 1
11—1	0·180	24·07 to 1
12—1	0·179	26·26 to 1
13—1	0·178	28·45 to 1
14—1	0·178	30·64 to 1
15—1	0·177	32·83 to 1

First find the proportion of air to gas by weight. The ratio of the weight of one cubic foot of air to one of gas

$$= \frac{0·0808}{0·0369} = 2·189.$$

Therefore proportion of 6 to 1 mixture by weight = 6 × 2·189 to 1 = 13·134 to 1. The other figures are similarly calculated.

Proceeding now to obtain the specific heat of a 6 to 1 mixture, we have (proportion by weight of air) × (specific heat of air) + (proportion by weight of gas) × (specific heat of gas) ÷ (total weight of air + gas). This, in figures,

$$= \frac{(13·13 \times 0·168) + (1 \times 0·473)}{13·13 + 1} = \frac{2·205 + 0·473}{14·13} = \frac{2·678}{14·13} = 0·189.$$

Similarly the remaining figures in the above table are arrived at.

The specific heat of any mixture may be determined approximately by a formula known as Grashof's formula.

SPECIFIC HEATS OF GASES AT CONSTANT VOLUME. 143

The formula is based upon a mean specific heat for coal gas, assuming that its constituents never vary in their proportion one to the other.

Let c_v = specific heat of mixture at a constant volume.
R = ratio of vols. of air to gas in the mixture;

then
$$c_v = \frac{R \times 0\cdot168 + 0\cdot226}{R + 0\cdot415}.$$

Putting in values for the above case, already worked out from the exact data, we obtain,

$$c_v = \frac{6 \times 0\cdot168 + 0\cdot226}{6 + 0\cdot415}$$
$$= \frac{1\cdot234}{6\cdot415}$$
$$= 0\cdot192,$$

the error in this instance amounting to about $1\frac{1}{2}$ per cent.

The following will serve as an example of the use of these figures, until we come to consideration of the indicator diagram.

Suppose 6 cubic feet of air to be mixed with 1 cubic foot of the coal gas given in the previous analysis. What would be the maximum temperature possible when the explosion takes place at 32 deg. Fah. and 14·7 lb. pressure?

Data required.—(1) Specific heat of mixture; (2) weight of mixture; (3) calorific value of the gas.

Then temperature
$$= 32 + \frac{\text{total heat present}}{\text{weight of mixture} \times \text{specific heat}}$$
$$= 32 + \frac{612}{0\cdot521 \times 0\cdot189}$$
$$= 32 + 6320 \text{ (nearly)}$$
$$= 6352 \text{ deg. Fah.}$$

In a gas engine the theoretical temperature is never recorded by the indicator card, as there is a very rapid transmission of heat through the walls of the cylinder.

CHAPTER XV.

CALCULATIONS ON THE INDICATOR DIAGRAM.

The Indicator Diagram.—We have already considered the means and method of actually taking an indicator diagram. It now remains to be shown what results may be obtained from it by simple calculations. The indicator diagram furnishes information upon the following points, which we will consider in order : (1) The indicated horse power ; (2) the valve setting ; (3) the initial, maximum, and exhaust temperatures ; (4) the nature of the expansion and compression curves.

Although the indicated horse power of a gas engine is never a very certain quantity, it is always calculated in gas-engine trials. The inertia of the indicator levers, the effects of high temperature upon the indicator spring, and the difficulty in obtaining a true average from a number of diagrams when the engine is running below its full load, all contribute towards inaccuracy. For these reasons the ratio of brake horse power to indicated horse power cannot always be relied upon as correct. High mechanical efficiencies of gas engines must, therefore, be regarded with suspicion unless we have complete access to all the details of the test.

The indicated horse power is found as follows :—

Let I = the indicated horse power.
    P = mean pressure per square inch on the piston.
    L = length of stroke in feet.
    E = number of explosions per minute.
    A = area of cylinder in square inches.

Then
$$I = \frac{L\,E\,A\,P}{33000}.$$

In working out a number of diagrams from one engine, it will be found convenient to work out in decimal form the fraction $\frac{LA}{33000}$, and record this once for all as the engine constant.

The factor we require to determine from the diagram is the mean pressure per square inch. Vertical measurements give pressures, and horizontal measurements distances; hence the length of an ordinate measured with the scale of pressures gives the pressure per square inch at a particular point of the stroke. If the pressure remained constant throughout the whole stroke, the diagram would become a rectangle, and the product of pressure and distance would give the work done. From this we see that the length × breadth, or area of the diagram, represents to some scale the work done per stroke. We may therefore find the mean pressure upon the piston, either by getting the average height of a set of equidistant ordinates, or by dividing the area of the diagram by the length.

To facilitate the work of finding the mean height, instruments commonly known as averagers are used. Before illustrating these we will briefly describe the most expeditious way of calculating the mean height without special instruments.

Divide the diagram into ten equal vertical strips. Subdivide each of these by a dotted line passing through their centres. It is required to find the average height of these dotted lines. Take a strip of paper, and mark off upon its edge the length of the first ordinate, then add to this the length of the second by applying the paper to the second ordinate. In this way we obtain the sum of the lengths of the ordinates. Measure this with a rule divided into inches and tenths. Suppose this gives us 5·08 in., we know that the average height will be 0·508 in. If the diagram be taken with a 100 spring, our mean pressure becomes 50·8 lb. per square inch. When a number of diagrams are to be dealt with, it will be found convenient to construct a set of ten converging lines upon tracing paper. By applying this to the indicator diagrams, the ten ordinates may readily be pricked off.

Where a great deal of testing is done, the work will be much facilitated by the use of an averager for obtaining mean pressures. Of these we shall describe very briefly the two most commonly used, viz., the Goodman and Coffin averagers.

Fig. 82.

Goodman's averager is shown in fig. 82, and is supplied by Messrs. Jackson Brothers, Leeds. The tracing point is fixed to the horizontal bar. The other leg of the instrument is carefully ground to a knife edge in such a way that the edge, if produced, would pass through the tracing point. The distance between the knife edge and the tracing point is adjustable by sliding the former along the horizontal bar, by means of which the instrument is set to the exact length of the diagram to be measured. Suppose the diagram, fig. 83, is to be measured. Choose a point A somewhere about the centre of the figure, and draw any line A B to meet the boundary. The tracing point is placed upon A, and the the hatchet end put so that the mean position of the instrument is roughly square with A B, as shown at X. The position of X is marked by pressing the knife edge upon the paper. Now take the tracing point lightly in the fingers, so that the movement of the hatchet end is not controlled by the pressure of the hand. Travel from A to B, then follow the direction of the arrows round the boundary of the figure, say in a clockwise direction, returning to the point B, thence back to A. The knife edge will then occupy a new position at Y, which is marked as before. The indicator diagram should now be turned about the point A through 180 deg. The figure is again traced by the point, but this time in a contra-clockwise direction, following the dotted outline, fig. 83. When the point returns again to A the hatchet will have travelled back towards X, say to X_1. The mean side movement of the hatchet end gives at once the average height of the diagram. Thus, suppose the distance from Y to the dot between X and X_1 is measured off as 0·56 in.; then this is the average height of the diagram, and multiplying 0·56 by the scale of pressures gives the mean pressure upon the piston.

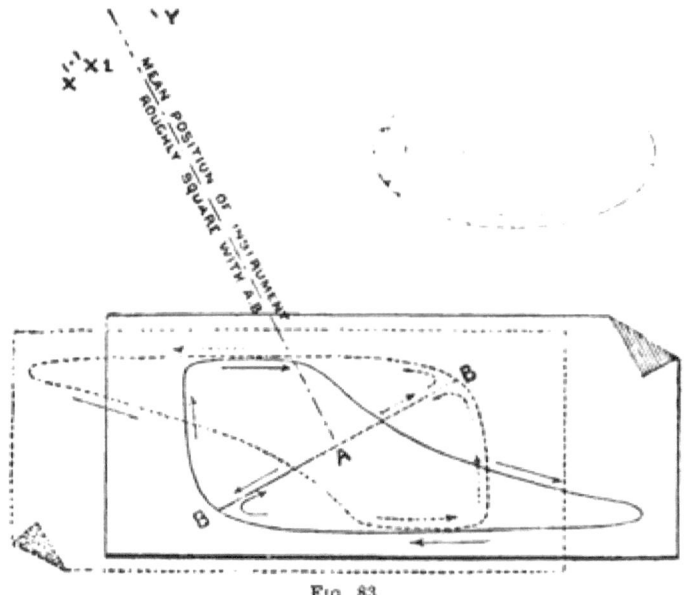

Fig. 83.

The ordinary hatchet planimeter was invented by Captain Prytz, of Copenhagen, but its use involved calculations far too tedious for practical men. Professor Goodman has embodied these calculations on a scale marked upon his hatchet planimeter, which enables an area to be measured by reading off the side travel of the hatchet end as so many square inches marked upon the scale. The averager described is so arranged that the area of the figure traversed by the boundary is equal to the side travel of the hatchet multiplied by the length of the diagram. The complete theory of these instruments is beyond the province of this work; we may, however, refer those interested to the pages of *Engineering*, vol. lvii., page 687, also vol. lxii., page 225.

Before leaving the subject, it is is well to point out that accuracy can only be obtained by careful manipulation. The instrument should be carefully set to the total length of the diagram to be measured. The hatchet end should travel on a good surface, such as drawing or blotting paper, and, finally, the diagram should always be reversed so that the *mean* travel of the instrument may be read off. With these precautions Goodman's averager will be found valuable in quickly determining the average pressures. It further possesses the important advantages that it is not liable to derangement by rough usage, and it is procurable at a price far below that of any other instrument used for the same purpose.

The Coffin averager supplied by the Globe Engineering Company, Manchester, is illustrated in fig. 84. This instrument consists of a bar, carrying a recording wheel, having a tracing point at one end, and a pin at the other end, moving in a vertical slot. The only movable parts are the bar, with its wheel and the vertical sliding piece, marked K. The diagram to be measured is placed upon the instrument as shown in the illustration. The atmospheric line should be parallel with the edge of the square marked B. The vertical edges, marked C and K, should nearly touch the extremities of the diagram. The tracing point D, when moved down the inner edge of K, should then coincide with the extremity of the diagram. The weight W is intended to keep the instrument from lifting out of the slot when in use. The recording wheel runs upon a piece of paper fastened to the board upon which the other parts are mounted.

Having placed the diagram in position, make an indentation at its extreme end, as at E, with the tracing point D, at the same time setting the wheel to zero. Then trace out

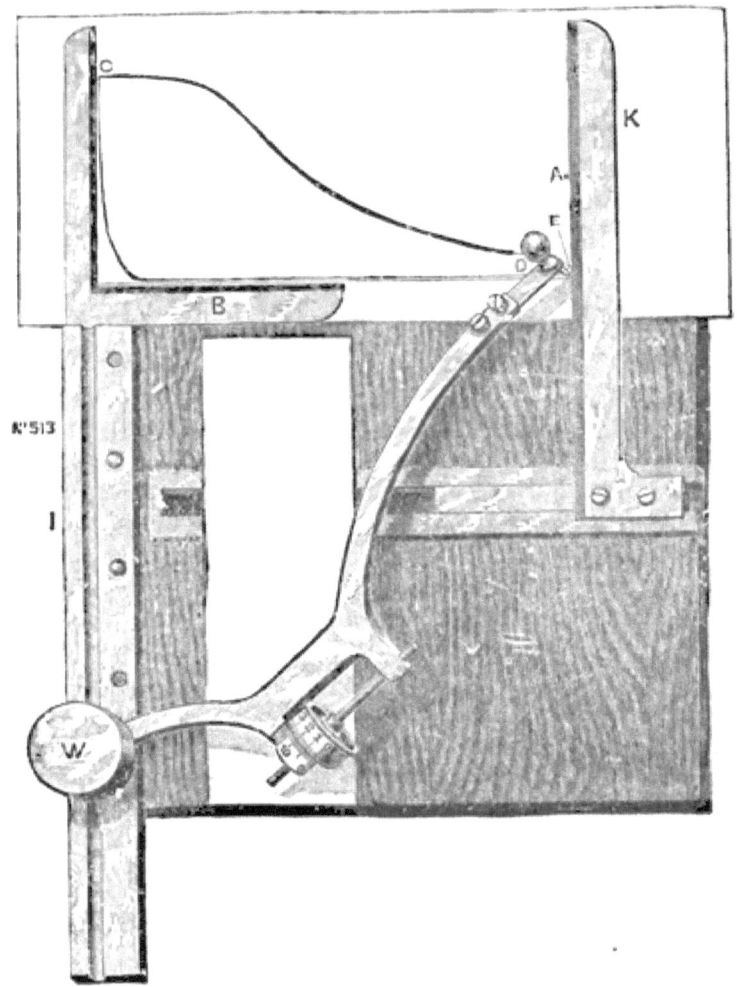

Fig. 84.

the diagram by moving in a *clockwise direction*, until returning to the point E. The *area* of the diagram may now be read off in square inches upon the wheel and its vernier scale. We, however, require the mean height of the diagram; hence, if we move the pointer D upwards along the inner edge of K until the wheel returns to zero, this vertical distance E A will give the mean height. This distance should be measured with the scale of pressures corresponding to the spring used in taking the diagram. The distance A E, as found by this instrument, would be the same as the mean-side travel of the Goodman averager, and might be measured in inches, and then multiplied by the scale of the spring.

The well-known Amsler's planimeter is often used for determining the area of indicator diagrams. It is, however, much more convenient to use one of the instruments above described, as they are specially designed for the purpose, whereas Amsler's planimeter is designed for measuring much larger areas than usually obtained on indicator diagrams.

We have already incidentally touched upon the defects of diagrams occasioned by bad valve setting. A weak-spring diagram is necessary to show the action of the inlet valves. These valves, being too small or not having sufficient lift, will cause the suction line of the diagram to fall below the atmospheric line. Late admission of the inlet valves would, of course, be shown by a marked depression of the suction line at the early part of the stroke. When the valves opened the suction line would rise towards the atmospheric.

With respect to the exhaust, a frequent fault is its late opening. This is invariably caused by the wear of the spindle. An adjusting screw is provided on the lifting lever, so that the lead of the exhaust valve may be increased. The effect on the diagram is to give a sharp point to the toe, with a falling exhaust line.

The next point to be considered is the temperature of the gases in the cylinder during the working stroke. We have already stated that without very special apparatus the temperature of the exhaust gases cannot be measured experimentally. It is, however, customary to furnish in reports of engine trials an account of the heat distribution. For this reason we require to know the temperature of the exhaust gases, so that we may determine approximately the heat thrown away as the exhaust gases pass into the atmosphere.

It is usually assumed that the following law holds under the conditions in a gas-engine cylinder. When $P =$ absolute pressure, $V =$ volume, and $T =$ absolute temperature, we have

$$\frac{P V}{T} = \text{constant.}$$

If, therefore, we determine one set of values for P, V, and T, we can calculate corresponding values for any point on the diagram. The values of P and V are easily measured from the diagram, but at no time is the value of T actually known. We do know, however, the temperature of the jacket water, and it is certain that the inner walls of the cylinder will be hotter than the jacket water. Then, again, exhaust gases left in the clearance volume of the cylinder will help to raise the temperature of the cold incoming mixture. As a compromise, it may be assumed that the temperature of the incoming mixture, before compression commences, is 5 deg. Fah. above that of the jacket water.

Suppose the following data obtained: Engine clearance, 30 per cent; length of indicator diagram, 3·5 in.; pressure during the instroke obtained from weak-spring diagram, 13·5 lb. absolute per square inch; temperature of jacket water, 150 deg. Fah. Let the exhaust take place at 0·9 of the stroke, and let the pressure measured off from the atmospheric line at the moment of exhaust be 25 lb.

Horizontal measurements on the indicator diagram represent distances travelled by the piston; but the piston diameter being constant, these same measurements may also be taken to represent volumes swept out by the piston; 3·5 in. therefore represents the working volume of the cylinder. The clearance volume is known to be 30 per cent of this.; thus the whole volume is represented by a length of

$$3\cdot 5 + 3\cdot 5 \times \frac{30}{100} = 4\cdot 55 \text{ in.}$$

$\frac{PV}{*T}$ then $= \frac{13\cdot 5 \times 4\cdot 55}{150 + 5 + 460} = 0\cdot 0982.$

Value of V when exhaust valve opens may be measured from the diagram. In our data it becomes

$$(3\cdot 5 \times 0\cdot 9) + \left(3\cdot 5 \times \frac{30}{100}\right),$$

which equals 4·15. The value of P in pounds per square inch absolute $= 25 + 14\cdot 7 = 39\cdot 7$;

therefore
$$T = \frac{39\cdot 7 \times 4\cdot 15}{0\cdot 0982}$$
$$= 1677 \text{ absolute}$$
$$= 1217 \text{ deg. Fah.}$$

The heat thrown away in the exhaust gases per minute will therefore be (temperature Fah.) × (weight of products of combustion per minute) × (specific heat at a constant volume of products of combustion).

The specific heat at a constant volume, and at constant pressure, may be found by Grashoff's formulæ. When $R =$ ratio of air to gas by volume,

specific heat of products at constant pressure

$$= \frac{0\cdot 2375 \times R + 0\cdot 343}{R + 0\cdot 48};$$

specific heat of products at constant volume

$$= \frac{0\cdot 1684 \times R + 0\cdot 286}{R \times 0\cdot 48}.$$

The temperature at any point on the indicator diagram may be found as above. In calculating the maximum temperature, as shown on the indicator diagram, a correction

---

* Absolute temperature = temperature in deg. Fah. plus 460.

for an increase of volume should be made if the explosion line be other than perpendicular.

The maximum temperature of the gases as shown on the indicator diagram is little more than half the theoretical temperature possible. This is partly owing to the rapid transmission of heat through the walls of the cylinder to the jacket, and partly to the fact that the whole of the heat is not evolved when the highest pressure is reached. From certain characteristics of the expansion curves it is probable that the burning of the gases continues after the maximum pressure is arrived at.

We have now discussed the deductions which are usually required to be made from the indicator diagram when reporting a gas-engine trial. There are many other points of scientific interest. These are, however, rather beyond the scope of the present work, but are completely discussed in a book recently published upon "Heat and Heat Engines," by Mr. W. C. Popplewell.

Before leaving the subject of the indicator diagram, it may be well, for the sake of completeness, to state certain facts with respect to the expansion and compression curves, leaving those interested to pursue the question further.

The equation to the expansion and compression curves is of the form $PV^n =$ constant. When the value of n is equal to

$$\frac{\text{specific heat of products of combustion at constant pressure}}{\text{specific heat of products of combustion at constant volume}}$$

the expansion is adiabatic—that is, without loss or gain of heat through the cylinder walls. In a gas engine the water jacket is constantly abstracting heat from the walls; hence we should expect to find the expansion curve much below the adiabatic. This, however, is not the case; indeed, in practice it is found that the expansion curve is sometimes above the adiabatic, though usually slightly below. In view of the fact that the maximum temperature of the explosion is little more than half the theoretical temperature possible, and yet the expansion curve so nearly follows the adiabatic line, notwithstanding the rapid loss of heat to the cylinder walls, it must be concluded that burning continues long after the maximum pressure has been reached.

The compression curve, as might be expected, is very nearly adiabatic.

CHAPTER XVI.

Gas-engine Trial, Otto Cycle: Coal Gas Used.

We have now explained the apparatus required for a complete test of a gas engine, and we have discussed various calculations in detail. It now remains for us to go through the figures of a complete trial, which may be taken as a typical example of modern practice.

Measurements of Engine.—

    Diameter of cylinder, 9 in. ; stroke, 18 in.
    Clearance volume of cylinder, 490 cubic inches.
    Diameter of brake wheel, 4 ft.
    Diameter of brake rope, 0·75 in.
    Weight of unbalanced part of brake rope, including hook, 5 lb.

Note.—Spring balance tested by dead weights, and found to be reading 2 lb. in excess of real weight.

Mean Results of Observations taken during a Two Hours' Test.—

Brake readings { Spring balance (uncorrected), 17·5 lb.
                 { Load on brake (excluding hook), 255 lb.

Mean revolutions of engine by counter per minute, 160.
Explosions per minute, 80.

Gas-meter readings { Total gas in cubic feet, 815.
                   { Temperature of meter, 65 deg. Fah.
                   { Pressure in mains, 0·9 in. water.

GAS-ENGINE TRIAL.   155

Jacket water { Quantity (total), 1,860 lb.
               Inlet temperature, 58 deg. Fah.
               Outlet temperature, 155 deg. Fah.

Mean pressure on piston derived from indicator diagrams, 80·5 lb. per square inch.
Pressure when exhaust valve opens, 41 lb. per square inch.
Pressure at end of suction stroke, 13·8 lb. per sq. inch absolute.
Exhaust commences at 88 per cent of working stroke.
Barometric pressure, 15 lb. per square inch.
Calorific value of gas per cubic foot obtained by Junker's calorimeter at a pressure of 0·9 in. water = 615 B.T.U.
Temperature of calorimeter meter, 65 deg. Fah.

Calculation of Results from above Data.

I.H.P. $= \dfrac{9^2 \times 0.7854 \times 1.5 \times 80.5 \times 80}{33000} = 18.6$.

B.H.P. Corrected spring balance reading $= 17.5 - 2$
$= 15.5$ lb.
Total load on brake $= 255 + 5 = 260$ lb.
Net load on brake $= 244.5$ lb.
Effective diameter of brake wheel $= 4 + \dfrac{0.75}{12}$ ft.
$= 4.062$ ft.

B.H.P. $= \dfrac{4.062 \times 3.14 \times 160 \times 244.5}{33000} = 15.1$.

Mechanical efficiency $= \dfrac{\text{B.H.P.}}{\text{I.H.P.}} = \dfrac{15.1}{18.6} = 0.812$.
$= 81.2$ per cent.

Gas Used per I.H.P. Hour.—Total consumption of gas uncorrected for pressure and temperature = 815 cubic feet. Consumption reduced to 32 deg. Fah. and 14·7 lb. per square inch,

$= 815 \times \dfrac{32 + 460}{65 + 460} \times \dfrac{15 + (0.434 \times 0.075)}{14.7}$

$= 781$ cubic feet (corrected).

Gas used per I.H.P. hour (reduced to 32 deg. and 14·7 lb.)

$$= \frac{781}{2 \times 18\cdot6} = 21 \text{ cubic feet.}$$

Gas used per B.H.P. hour (reduced to 32 deg. and 14·7 lb.)

$$= \frac{781}{2 \times 15\cdot1} = 25\cdot9.$$

The ratio of air to gas should be determined from analysis of the products of combustion. When not done this way, account must be taken of the temperature and pressure of the gas at the end of the suction stroke. The temperature is difficult to determine with precision, but usually assumed to be equal to that of the outlet jacket water. Under this assumption the following figures for the ratio of air to gas by volume.

Volume of gas per cycle (corrected for temperature and pressure at end of suction stroke)

$$= \frac{781}{80 \times 2 \times 60} \times \frac{14\cdot7}{13\cdot8} \times \frac{155 + 460}{32 + 460} = 0\cdot108 \text{ cubic feet}$$

Working volume of cylinder + clearance volume = 0·947
Volume of air per cycle = 0·947 − 0·108 = 0·839 cubic

Ratio of air to gas = 7·7 to 1.

NOTE.—When the engine is worked without a scavenging device the working volume only is considered.

(by Grashof's formula)

$$= \frac{0\cdot168 \times 7\cdot2 + 0\cdot286}{7\cdot2 + 0\cdot48} = 0\cdot196.$$

Temperature of Exhaust Gases, by Calculation from Indicator Diagram.—Temperature of gases before compression commences, assumed as temperature of jacket water + 5 deg.,

$$= 155 + 5 = 160.$$

Total volume of cylinder = clearance volume + working volume

$$= 490 + 1145 = 1635 \text{ cubic inches,}$$
$$= 0\cdot948 \text{ cubic feet.}$$

$$\frac{PV}{T} = \frac{P^1 V^1}{T^1} \text{ when } P = \text{pressure (absolute).}$$
$$V = \text{volume (total).}$$
$$T = \text{temperature (absolute).}$$

Filling in values—

$P = 13.8$ lb. per square inch absolute.
$V = 0.948$ cubic feet.
$T = 160 + 460 = 520$.
$P^1 = $ pressure when exhaust valve opens $= 14.7 + 41$.
$V^1 = (1145 \times 0.88) + 490 = 0.867$ cubic feet.

Then
$$T^1 = \frac{T P^1 V^1}{PV} = \frac{55.7 \times 0.867 \times 520}{13.8 \times 0.948} = 1920.$$

Temperature $= 1920 - 460 = 1460$ deg. Fah.

Heat Lost in Exhaust Gases.—Weight of 1 cubic foot of coal gas $= 0.0369$. Air weighs 2.63 more than coal gas. Therefore weight of charge per cycle

$$= 0.948 \left\{ \frac{0.0369 \times 2.63 \times 7.2}{8.2} + \frac{0.0369}{8.2} \right\} = 0.081 \text{ lb.}$$

Heat lost in exhaust gases per cycle
$$= 0.081 \times 1460 \times 0.196 = 231 \text{ B.T.U.}$$

Heat lost in exhaust gases per minute
$$= 231 \times 80 = 1848 \text{ B.T.U.}$$

Heat lost in jacket water per minute
$$= (155 - 58) \times \frac{1860}{2 \times 60} = 1503 \text{ B.T.U.}$$

Heat equivalent of work done in the cylinder
$$= \frac{18.6 \times 33000}{772} = 793 \text{ B.T.U.}$$

Heat equivalent of work done on brake
$$= \frac{15.6 \times 33000}{772} = 644 \text{ B.T.U.}$$

Heat Received by Engine per Minute.—Calorific value of gas, as given by calorimeter, and corrected for hydrogen only = 615 B.T.U. Correcting for pressure and temperature, we have—

Calorific value at 32 deg. Fah. and 14·7

$$= 615 \times \frac{525}{492} \times \frac{14\cdot7}{15\cdot03} = 640 \text{ B.T.U.}$$

Heat received per minute by engine

$$= 640 \times \frac{781}{2 \times 60} = 4165 \text{ B.T.U.}$$

Heat efficiency, as calculated on equivalent of work done in cylinder,

$$= \frac{793}{4165} = 0\cdot186 = 19 \text{ per cent.}$$

Heat efficiency, as calculated on work done on brake,

$$= \frac{644}{4165} = 0\cdot151 = 15\cdot4 \text{ per cent.}$$

HEAT ACCOUNT.

Heat received by engine per minute................	4,165	Thermal equivalent of work done	793
		Heat lost in jackets...	1,503
		Heat lost in exhaust gases	1,848
	4,165		4,144

It is not unusual to find that the heat account gives a slight *excess* of heat accounted for. The temperature of the exhaust has been calculated at the point of opening of the valve—that is, at 88 per cent of the working stroke. Some of this heat is transmitted to the jacket water, and is therefore measured twice. On the other hand, large losses due to radiation are not measured. As before stated, the temperature of the exhaust gases is a rather uncertain quantity. It therefore not infrequently works out that a percentage of heat is unaccounted for on one or other side of the heat account.

During the progress of a trial it is extremely useful to plot all quantities as they are observed upon a large sheet of squared paper. Errors of observation are thus easily discovered in time to be rectified. A break in the plotted curves will indicate either a mistake in the readings or fluctuations in the conditions of the trial. It is important that either should be checked. The person responsible for the trial will learn more from a casual glance at these curves than by attempting to check each observer individually.

CHAPTER XVII.

GAS-ENGINE DESIGN.

IN writing upon the subject of gas-engine design, it will be assumed that the general arrangements of a gas engine are already familiar to the reader. Hitherto the calculations required to determine the sizes of the various essential parts have been entirely excluded from the literature upon the subject. Considering the difference existing between the gas engine and the steam engine, it is important that calculations determining the proportions of the former should be dealt with quite independently. We propose, therefore, to work out, from data already established, the leading dimensions of a gas engine to develop 20 horse power on the brake.

The mechanical efficiency of a gas engine may reasonably be supposed to reach 80 per cent. This is, of course, sometimes exceeded, but it is wise to underestimate, as no engine will develop its highest efficiency unless perfectly adjusted, and in the exigencies of practice this should not be relied upon. If, therefore, we assume 80 per cent mechanical efficiency, we shall require a cylinder capable of developing $\frac{20}{0\cdot 8} = 25$ indicated horse power.

In steam-engine design, our next subject for consideration would be the maximum boiler pressure at our disposal. From this, with due regard to the number of expansions permissible, we should ultimately draw a prospective indicator diagram, and so obtain the mean effective pressure per square inch of piston area. Now, the pressure obtained in a gas-engine cylinder depends upon three factors : (1) the mixture of air and gas ; (2) the quality of the gas ; (3) the density of the mixture before ignition takes place. A fourth factor — namely, the mean working temperature of the cylinder—would, if variable, greatly affect the pressure. The temperature is, however, necessarily reduced by the presence of the jacket water to an almost constant limit. Early designers of gas engines did not attempt high compression ; thus, up to the year 1890, the compression seldom exceeded 40 lb. per square inch. This, however, has been gradually raised, until now the compression on small engines amounts to over 90 lb. per square inch. It is inadvisable to exceed, or even approach, this figure in designing large power gas engines, say over 50 I.H.P., on account of the liability to ignition during the compression stroke.

This risk is, however, much reduced when a scavenging arrangement clears the hot gases from the combustion chamber, and replaces them with cooler air. In round numbers, we may take it that the maximum pressure obtained will be 3·5 times the pressure before ignition. Thus, compressing up to 60 lb. per square inch, we may expect, with the usual proportions of air to gas, a maximum pressure of 210 lb. Although this is the maximum pressure obtainable when running at full power, it must not be forgotten that when the governor cuts out the gas supply for one or perhaps more cycles, a particularly dense mixture may be drawn into the cylinder. The ignition of a strong mixture may thus produce a maximum pressure far in excess of that calculated. For this reason a large margin is necessary.

There is a marked similarity between all indicator diagrams from gas engines, and from a comparison of a large number of diagrams it will be found that the mean effective pressure produced is roughly equal to $2C - 0.01 C^2$ when $C =$ compression in pounds per square inch above atmospheric pressure. These figures may be varied one way or other by the valve setting and cylinder proportions.*

The expansion curve of an indicator diagram may be raised by decreasing the time of expansion and by reducing the cylinder surface to a minimum. The first mentioned condition reduces the *time* during which heat may be transferred from the burning gases to the jacket water, and the second condition reduces the surface by means of which the transmission of heat is facilitated. Let us first consider the effects of cylinder proportions, and engine speed, upon the rate of expansion, and in so doing we will assume that the diameter of the cylinder and power developed remain constant, whilst the revolutions per minute and the length of stroke are variable.

The number of feet travelled by the piston per minute is limited. For practical reasons it is unadvisable to exceed 700 ft. per minute. When L = length of stroke in feet, and R = revolutions per minute, then we have the limiting value of piston speed

$$2 L R = 700 \text{ ft.}$$

---

* It will be observed that this formula gives a maximum mean pressure of 100 lb. per square inch when the compression reaches 100 lb. It has been shown by Messrs. Mallard and Le Chatelier that the rate of cooling follows the law expressed by $a \theta + \beta \theta^2$ where a and β are constants, and $\theta =$ temperature. It is interesting to note that the above formula, deduced from actual indicator diagrams, shows that the mean effective pressure follows a similar law. The formula holds *only up to 100 lb.* compression, and must only be regarded as giving approximate values, for neither the mixture nor quality of gas form factors of the expression.

It is evident that a variety of dimensions might be chosen for L and R. As R is increased, L is diminished. As R is increased the number of impulses per minute may be increased, and, consequently, the time of each expansion is diminished. The volume of gas used per cycle is diminished, but the maximum pressure obtained need not be, if the same compression be given to the mixture. Thus we see that a smaller volume of gas gives the same maximum pressure per square inch as a larger volume, and, further, it is expanded in very much less time. If R be increased continuously, and L correspondingly diminished, then at some value of R the outstroke of the piston will take place in less time than the charge can be effectually ignited. Let us investigate the limit of speed of any engine in which the *connecting rod is five times the crank* length.

Let T = time required for explosion pressure to arrive at its maximum;

C = length of crank radius in feet;

R = revolutions per minute of engine;

then mean speed of crank pin

$$= \frac{2 \pi C R}{60} \text{ ft. per second.}$$

The mean velocity of the piston during the first one-tenth of its forward stroke will be very nearly

$$= \frac{2 \pi C R}{60} \times 0.32 \text{ ft. per second.}$$

The distance travelled

$$= \frac{\text{stroke}}{10} = \frac{2 C}{10} = 0.2 \, C \text{ feet.}$$

Therefore time taken by piston in travelling one-tenth stroke

$$= \frac{0.2 \, C}{\frac{2 \pi C R \times 0.32}{60}}$$

$$= \frac{5.9}{R} \text{ (nearly) seconds.}$$

Now, in order that the engine may fully expand the hot gases, the maximum pressure should not be reached at a point later than one-tenth of the stroke. Even so late as this is disadvantageous. Hence the lowest value of

$$\frac{5\cdot 9}{R} \text{ must equal T.}$$

Mr. Dugald Clerk ascertained that the time required to reach the maximum pressure, with a mixture of coal gas and air in the proportion of 1 to 5 by volume, was 0·05 second. In his experiments the initial temperature of the mixture was low, and the initial pressure was atmospheric. The author has found that the time of explosion is greatly diminished by raising the initial pressure, but has not yet succeeded in measuring accurately by how much. Witz found that the duration of explosion of a mixture of 1 to 6·3, behind a freely-moving piston, to be 0·06 second. As the ignition took place at atmospheric pressure, these results can hardly be applied to modern gas engines. It is probable that the maximum number of revolutions approaches the limit at 500 per minute. Putting this value for R in the equation,

$$\frac{5\cdot 9}{R} = T,$$

we find T = 0·0118 second. We might here appropriately consider the effect of *lead* on the igniting valve. The total time of rise of pressure in a gas-engine cylinder may be divided into two distinct parts. Firstly, the time taken for the flame to strike back into the mixture, and, secondly, the time during which the pressure rises after this has been accomplished. The former effect may be largely compensated for by giving lead to the ignition valve, but the latter cannot be dealt with in this way without seriously increasing the liability to what is known as "back explosion." The severe strains occasioned by such back explosion should, of course, be avoided. In the absence of experimental data with regard to the values of T, we shall do well to accept the limiting speed of revolutions as approaching 500. In practice it is found advisable to run large engines at a speed much below 500 (about 160) revolutions, because of the excessive vibration due to the rapid movements of reciprocating parts, and the consequent stresses brought to bear upon them. It is also probable that the value of T is much increased when large cylinders are used. A large number of smaller engines run at from 250 to 300 revolutions.

The result of our investigation has, so far, led to the conclusion that the speed approaches a limit at 500 revolutions per minute, and it has been further shown that this is independent of the length of stroke, on the assumption that the maximum pressure shall be reached during the first tenth of the stroke. We have now to consider the ratio of length of stroke to diameter of cylinder.

It is certain that the loss of heat increases in a greater proportion than the difference in temperature between the burning gases and the cylinder walls. Also the loss of heat is greater, the greater the density of the charge. In other words, the loss of heat is very much greater during the beginning of the stroke than at any other time. If it be true that the loss of heat varies directly as the density, and directly as the surface, and roughly as the difference in temperature, then we may express the loss of heat in a time t_x as

$$A \int_0^{t_x} (\text{surface} \times \text{difference in temperature} \times \text{density})\, dt.$$

As, however, the density varies inversely as the volume, we may write the expression thus—

$$B \int_0^{t_z} \left(\frac{\text{surface} \times \text{difference in temperature}}{\text{volume}} \right) dt,$$

A and B being constants.

From this it is evident that the ratio of surface to volume should be a minimum near the beginning of the stroke. To investigate the subject further, by attempting to evaluate the quantities in the above expression, would be rather begging the question, inasmuch as the temperature differences must be estimated by references to the diagrams taken from existing engines. Experiments might be devised to furnish data upon this subject, but the author is not aware that such independent data at present exists.

It is the opinion of Mr. Hamilton, the patentee of the Premier gas engine, that the ratio $\frac{\text{surface}}{\text{volume}}$ should be a minimum at about one-third of the stroke. Supposing, therefore, that the combustion chamber were one-third the length of the stroke, then we should require a minimum ratio of $\frac{\text{surface}}{\text{volume}}$ when the volume is actually equal to (area of piston × two-thirds stroke). Now, it is easily shown that the ratio $\frac{\text{surface}}{\text{volume}}$ is a minimum when the diameter of a cylinder is equal to its length.* Thus we see that a minimum ratio of

---

* Let x = diameter, c = volume (constant). Then, length
$$= \frac{4c}{x^2 \pi}.$$

Surface
$$= \frac{x^2 \pi}{2} + \frac{4c}{x^2 \pi} \cdot x \pi$$

$$= \frac{\pi}{2} x^2 + 4c \frac{1}{x}.$$

$$dS = \frac{\pi}{2} d(x^2) + 4c \, d\left(\frac{1}{x}\right) = \frac{\pi}{2} 2x \, dx - \frac{4c}{x^2} dx$$

$$\frac{dS}{dx} = \pi x - \frac{4c}{x^2}.$$

When surface is a minimum $\frac{dS}{dx} = 0$.

$$\therefore \pi x^3 - 4c = 0 \therefore 4c = x^3 \pi.$$

But length
$$= \frac{4c}{x^2 \pi},$$

and, by putting $4c$ in terms of x, we have length
$$= \frac{x^3 \pi}{x^2 \pi} = x.$$

Hence length = diameter when surface is a minimum.

$\dfrac{\text{surface}}{\text{volume}}$ is given when the diameter is = two-thirds stroke. This, as may be supposed, is a favourite proportion. The author is convinced that the effect of large cylinder surface is very marked.

Cylinders of large dimensions have a much larger proportion of volume to surface than those of small dimensions, even though the proportions be chosen to favour a minimum of surface in both cases. It is therefore to be expected that large size gas engines will give greater economy than smaller ones. This has been fully realised in practice.

We have discussed very briefly the controlling factors determining the size of cylinder for a gas engine, and we now proceed to apply the conclusions arrived at. We shall base our calculated size upon the following data :—

1. Piston speed, 500 ft. per minute.
2. Compression before ignition, 80 lb. per square inch.
3. Stroke of engine, $1\frac{1}{2}$ times diameter of cylinder.

Let D = diameter of cylinder. Then stroke = $1\cdot5\ D$
Revolutions per minute

$$= \frac{\text{piston speed}}{2 \times \text{stroke}} = \frac{500}{3D}$$

Explosions per minute (on Otto cycle)

$$= \frac{\text{revolutions}}{2} = \frac{500}{6D}.$$

Mean effective pressure may be taken approximately as

$$= 2C - 0\cdot01\ C^2 \text{ (when } C = \text{compression pressure)}$$
$$= 160 - 0\cdot01 \times 6400$$
$$= 96 \text{ lb. per square inch.}$$

The indicated horse power is to equal 25. Hence we have

$$25 = 1\cdot5\ D \times \frac{500}{6D} \times \frac{D^2 \pi}{4} \times 96 \times \frac{1}{33000},$$

whence $\quad D^2 = 87\cdot5$ (nearly);

$\therefore D = 9\cdot35$ in., say $9\tfrac{3}{8}$ in. diameter of cylinder.

Stroke therefore equals $1\cdot5 \times 9\cdot35 = 14$ in., nearly.

Size of Combustion Chamber to give 80 lb. Compression (above Atmosphere).

Let V = whole volume,
= volume of combustion chamber + volume swept out by piston.

P = absolute pressure in pounds per square inch.

Then the following equation holds good for the compression curve—

$$P V^{1\cdot3} = \text{constant.}$$

To simplify the figures, the numerical value of V may be represented by linear inches, for, when the combustion chamber is the same diameter as the cylinder, the movement of the piston is proportional to the volume swept out. Hence the volume of the combustion chamber may be represented by

V − stroke,
= V − 14.

At the commencement of the compression stroke the value of P will equal about 14 lb. per square inch absolute.

At the end of the compression stroke the pressure required is equal to $80 + 15 = 95$ lb., absolute. We have therefore

$$P V^{1\cdot3} = P_1 V_1^{1\cdot3}$$

Taking $P = 14$ lb. per square inch, $P_1 = 95$ lb. per square inch, and $V_1 = (V - 14)$, we have

$$14\, V^{1\cdot3} = 95\, (V - 14)^{1\cdot3}$$

then $\quad V^{1\cdot3} = 6\cdot78\, (V - 14)^{1\cdot3}$

and $\quad V = \sqrt[1\cdot3]{} = 6\cdot78\, (V - 14)^{1\cdot3}$

$\quad\quad\quad = (V - 14)\, \sqrt[1\cdot3]{6\cdot78}$

$\quad\quad\quad = (V - 14)\, 4\cdot36,$ nearly,

from which $\quad 3\cdot36\, V = 61$;

$\therefore V = 18\cdot1.$

Thus the actual volume of the combustion chamber, of any shape whatever, must

$$= (18\cdot 1 - \text{stroke of piston}) \times \text{area of cylinder}$$
$$= (18\cdot 1 - 14)\frac{D^2 \pi}{4}$$
$$= 283 \text{ cubic inches.}$$

With respect to the arrangement of valves, it must be pointed out that the surface of all passages leading into the cylinder should be reduced as much as possible. The size of valves should be such that the velocity of the gases, as calculated upon the mean piston speed, is not more than 100 ft. per second. Although it is not possible to fully discuss all the details of cylinder design in the space at our disposal, it is hoped that we have sufficiently indicated how to determine the leading dimensions of a cylinder to develop a given horse power. By reference to the illustrations and descriptions of engines already given, there should be no difficulty in setting out the leading dimensions of an engine cylinder. It must not be forgotten, however, that the success of an engine depends upon minor details, a knowledge of which can only be acquired by practical experience in the working of gas engines. We make no attempt at describing the thousand and one minor details which will be readily supplied by the practical draughtsman, our object being rather to place before the reader those facts and figures which are not acquired in the erecting shop.

The Crank Shaft.

A gas-engine crank shaft should be made from the very best mild steel procurable. The severe stresses upon the shaft render it imperative that a large margin for strength be allowed. The author has known cases of gas-engine crank shafts of large diameter working successfully for many months, but which have suddenly failed, without apparent cause.

It is desirable that the crank webs be balanced by weight on the crank rather than on the flywheels. When the speed is high, and the flywheels of large diameter, balance weights fitted or cast on the wheels cause considerable oscillation of the whole engine. The bearings should be as close together as possible, and have ample surface.

To ascertain the true maximum twisting moment on a crank shaft when under normal conditions of working, it is necessary to correct the indicator diagram for the inertia of the reciprocating parts. This done, a polar diagram of twisting moment may be plotted for various positions of the crank. We have already stated that the maximum pressure upon the piston will be approximately $= 3.5$ times the compression pressure. Thus, in the example under consideration, we should expect a pressure of $80 \times 3.5 = 280$ lb. per square inch. This pressure occurs almost on the dead centre of the crank, and decreases as the tangential effort increases. We shall not be far wrong in taking 70 per cent of the maximum pressure as the load producing maximum twisting moment. Thus the maximum tangential effort may be taken as compression pressure $\times 2.5$. When the bearings are close up to the crank webs, bending stresses may be neglected.

If $D =$ diameter of shaft required, skin stress on the shaft 8,000 lb., then we have—

$$\frac{\pi}{16} D^3 \cdot 8000 = 80 \times 2.5 \times 7 \times 69 ;$$

$$D^3 = \frac{16 \times 80 \times 2.5 \times 7 \times 69}{3.14 \times 8000} ;$$

from which $D = 3.95$, say 4 in. diameter.

We are aware that this rule gives an exceptionally large diameter of shaft. We are, however, inclined to believe that the wisdom of an engine builder may be measured in terms of his crank-shaft dimensions, and we are therefore inclined to favour maximum dimensions.

The crank webs should be of ample size to give rigidity. The depth of the webs is, of course, largely determined by the diameter of the shaft. A good rule is to make the depth of web equal to

$$D + \frac{D}{3};$$

whilst the thickness of each web should be

$$= D - \frac{D}{8},$$

where D = diameter of shaft.

The crank pin should not be less in diameter than $1\cdot2\,D$, the length being determined by the pressure upon the crank pin. In a gas engine (unlike a steam engine) the pressure upon the piston falls very rapidly; hence the maximum load per square inch may exceed that of steam-engine practice. The maximum pressure on a gas-engine crank pin should not exceed 1,000 lb. per square inch; but, with due regard to this, the load per square inch, as calculated upon the *average* piston pressure, may reach 400 lb.

Applying the rules given, our crank-shaft dimensions for the case under discussion will be as follow :—

Depth of web

$$= 3\cdot95 + \frac{3\cdot95}{3} = 5\cdot26, \text{ say } 5\tfrac{1}{4}\text{ in.}$$

Thickness of each web

$$= 3\cdot95 + \frac{3\cdot95}{8} = 3\cdot46, \text{ say } 3\tfrac{1}{2}\text{ in.}$$

The diameter of crank pin

$$= 3\cdot95 \times 1\cdot2 = 4\cdot74, \text{ say } 4\tfrac{3}{4}\text{ in.}$$

Then length of crank pin *(calculated on maximum pressure)*

$$= \frac{69 \times 280}{1000 \times 4\cdot75} = 4\cdot06.$$

Then length of crank pin *(calculated on average pressure)*

$$= \frac{69 \times 96}{400 \times 4\cdot75} = 3\cdot48.$$

Hence the length should be (say) $4\frac{1}{5}$ in., to satisfy the worst condition.

The main bearing pressures are largely affected by the weight of the flywheels, for the maximum pressure upon the bearings is the resultant of a thrust upon the crank and a vertically applied load due to the flywheels. A safe rule, which comprehends all conditions, is to allow 100 lb. per square inch, as calculated upon the mean piston pressure. Thus, in the example before us, we should have ample bearing surface by making the *total* lengh of bearings

$$= \frac{69 \times 96}{100 \times 4} = 16\tfrac{1}{2} \text{ in.}$$

Dimensions of Flywheels Required for Gas Engines.

In calculating the weight of gas-engine flywheels, we shall neglect the effect of inertia of reciprocating parts. Having regard to the fact that the wheels must drive for three strokes out of every four without undue fluctuation of speed, the effect of inertia becomes insignificant.

Let R_1 = maximum velocity, expressed as revolutions per minute;

R_2 = minimum velocity, expressed as revolutions per minute;

V_1 = maximum velocity in feet per second at the mean diameter of the wheels;

V_2 = minimum velocity in feet per second at the mean diameter of the wheels;

W = weight of flywheel in pounds.

Then mean revolutions per minute

$$= \frac{R_1 + R_2}{2}.$$

Average work done per stroke

$$= \frac{\text{H.P.} \times 33,000}{2 \times \frac{R_1 + R_2}{2}} = \frac{\text{H.P.} \times 33000}{R_1 + R_2}.$$

Let n = number of strokes the engine runs without impulse. (It may here be noted that no allowance need be made for the work done in compression during the idle strokes, for the energy thus absorbed is always given back again during the out strokes.)

The energy to be stored in flywheels

$$= \frac{\text{H.P.} \times 33000 \times n}{R_1 + R_2}.$$

Let the fluctuations in speed be represented as

$$\frac{V_2}{V_1} = C = \frac{R_2}{R_1};$$

then $\qquad V_2 = C V_1,$
and $\qquad R_2 = C R_1.$

Now, the energy absorbed during n revolutions, without impulse to the flywheels, must not reduce the speed below R_2 or V_2. Hence energy absorbed must equal

$$\frac{W}{2g}(V_1^2 - V_2^2) = \frac{W}{2g}(V_1^2 - C^2 V_1^2) = \frac{W V_1^2}{2g}(1 - C^2).$$

Let D = mean diameter of wheels, then

$$V_1^2 = \left(\frac{D \pi R_1}{60}\right)^2$$

Hence, by substituting this value of V_1^2, we have work done per n stroke = energy derived from flywheels—that is,

$$\frac{\text{H.P.} \times 33000 \times n}{R_1 + R_2} = \frac{W}{2g} \cdot \frac{D^2 \pi^2 R_1^2}{3600}(1 - C^2),$$

and putting $R_2 = C R_1$, we have—

$$W = \frac{\text{H.P.} \times 33000 \times n \times 2g \times 3600}{R_1 (1 + C) D^2 \pi^2 R_1^2 (1 - C^2)},$$

and, reducing the weight to tons, we have—

$$W \text{ (in tons)} = 343900 \frac{\text{H.P.} \times n}{R_1^3 \times D^2 (1 - C^2)(1 + C)}.$$

We have here taken D as the mean diameter, instead of twice the radius of gyration; the error is, however, insignificant, and is more than compensated for by the absence of complications in the formula. The value of c for electric light work should be taken as 0·98, thus allowing a total variation of speed of 2 per cent. It is, of course, desirable to keep the flywheels as light as possible, not only on account of cost, but with the object of increasing the mechanical efficiency. For this latter reason, wheels of large diameter are to be preferred, inasmuch as the required weight varies inversely as the square of the diameter. Although not usual in gas-engine practice, it might be desirable to box in the arms of large wheels, to prevent losses due to air resistance. If flywheels are made too large, they become dangerous on account of centrifugal action on the rim of the wheel. For safety, the outside of the wheel should be limited to a speed of 100 ft. per second.

With respect to the value of n, we may say that it is undesirable to work a gas engine missing fire oftener than alternate cycles. This is indeed highly important with large engines, because small leakages of unburnt gas pass through the cylinder, and if not fired frequently, serious explosions are thereby liable to occur in the exhaust pipes. It is much safer, even though accompanied by loss in efficiency, to set the governor and gas valves to fire the engine every cycle at half load. We may take the value of n, therefore, as being equal to seven strokes.

Taking the following values for the symbols, we can find the weight of flywheels for a 25 indicated horse power engine.

$$\text{Weight in tons} = \frac{343900 \times 25 \times 7}{R_1^3 \times D^2 (1 - 0.98^2)(1 + 0.98)};$$

putting

$$D = 5 \text{ ft., and } R_1 = \frac{\text{piston speed}}{2 \text{ stroke}} = \frac{500}{2 \cdot 33} = 215,$$

we have—
$$W = \frac{343900 \times 25 \times 7}{215^3 \times 5^2 \times 0.04 \times 1.98} = 3.05 \text{ tons.}$$

Thus, if two flywheels be used, they should weigh a little more than $1\frac{1}{2}$ tons each. We have neglected the weight of the spokes and boss, but as the error favours steady running, there is no necessity for further complications.

Connecting Rods.—The determination of connecting-rod sizes for high-speed engines has already been fully dealt with in books on engine design. We may refer the reader to the chapter on connecting rods in Professor Unwin's treatise on machine design. Regarding gas engines as high-speed engines, we shall quote a formula from the above-mentioned work, which we think gives a result in agreement with practice. We are quite aware that many connecting rods will be found working satisfactorily which are nevertheless under the size given by the formula. Considering the complexity of the conditions, it is impossible, without devoting much space and re-writing much that has already been written, to deduce a formula embracing all conditions. The value obtained by the following rule may be excessive for slow-speed engines, but it may be regarded as safe for all cases.

Let d = mean diameter of connecting rod;
  D = diameter of cylinder;
  l = length of connecting rod;
  p = initial pressure on the piston in lbs. per square inch;

then $\qquad d = 0.038 \sqrt{\{D\, l\, \sqrt{p}\}}.$

Having obtained a mean diameter, the rod may, if more convenient, be made of oval section. The mean diameter may be increased by about $\frac{1}{8}$ in. towards the crank-pin end of the rod, and diminished by the same amount at the piston end. The length of rod may be from five to six times the crank length.

For the example under consideration—

$$d = 0.038 \sqrt{\{9.35 \times 35 \sqrt{280}\}}$$
$$= 2.8 \text{ in.}$$

Hence the diameters may be, say, $2\frac{3}{8}$ in. and $3\frac{3}{8}$ in.

The Piston Pin.

The pressure on the piston pin may be much more than upon the crank pin, on account of the small relative movement of the rod at this end. A pressure of 600 lb. per square inch, as calculated upon the mean effective pressure, will give suitable proportions to the pin. The length of the pin may be about $1.4 \times$ diameter. It must here be noted that the design of any part should be carried out with due regard to the facilities in machining. For this reason it might be convenient to have the small end of the connecting rod the same width as the larger end, thus avoiding troublesome packings to set the rod level when machining.

The size of pin required will be as follows :—

Total mean pressure

$$= 69 \times 96 \text{ lb.}$$

Bearing area in square inches

$$= \frac{69 \times 96}{600} = 11.05.$$

Diameter of cylinder is $9\frac{3}{8}$ in. Allowing $5\frac{1}{2}$ in. for the total length of boss to receive the pin, we may take the length as

$$9\frac{3}{8} - 5\frac{1}{2} = 3\frac{7}{8}.$$

Then diameter of pin

$$= \frac{11.05}{3.87} = 2.6, \text{ say } 2\frac{5}{8} \text{ in. pin.}$$

The pin should be secured in the bosses of the trunk piston by set screws, to prevent rotation therein. A drip lubricator should be arranged to supply oil to the pin when working.

The piston should carry from three to six cast-iron packing rings, according to the pressure, of about $\frac{5}{8} \times \frac{1}{2}$ section.

The side shaft should be driven by screw gearing, the designs for which may be taken from any treatise upon gearing. The governor should be driven by bevel gearing from the side shaft, if requiring rotary motion.

We have already given data required for sizes of pipes, tanks, and fittings external to the engine itself. Let us conclude these few notes on gas-engine design with one word of warning. Never rely upon lock nuts *without* split pins to prevent them working completely off. We have known serious accidents to result from overlooking this apparently small detail. The vibration of all combustion engines renders it absolutely necessary that steady pins and positive lock nuts should be freely used in connecting the parts.

CHAPTER XVIII.

PRODUCER GAS, AND ITS APPLICATION TO GAS ENGINES.

IN the early days of the gas engine, one of the chief points in favour of its extended use was the convenience with which the ordinary coal gas of town supplies could be utilised as its motive power. So long as the power developed by gas engines was small, the commercial advantages resulting from their use would have been seriously minimised by the necessity of a large capital outlay. Thus, in the early days of the gas-engine industry, the motive power was entirely supplied from the ordinary town mains. Gas engines had been established as a commercial success for some four or five years before any other means of supplying them with motive power was recognised as practicable or economical. Nor was this state of things entirely due to lack of invention. It is indeed surprising how many names are associated with the development of a practical gas generator, suitable not only for gas engines, but for many industrial processes, and especially for metallurgical purposes. In view of this, we shall merely explain the broad principles upon which all gas producers work ; but we shall refer specially to the work of Mr. Emerson Dowson, whose name has for many years been associated with the practical application of gas-producing plant for the supply of motive power to gas engines.

Any combustible substance when heated to a high temperature, either by the process of its own combustion or by the application of external heat, will be partially or wholly gasified. The most familiar example of this process is the ordinary household fireplace. The sudden blaze which so often results from stirring the fire is merely the burning of those gases which are rising continually through the red-hot fuel, but which are prevented from burning when passing through the hot fuel because of the inferior supply of oxygen. When, however, these gases mingle with the fresh air passing above the surface of the fuel, the oxygen renders them combustible. If the fire be dull, the heat at this point is insufficient to ignite the gases, and much of the gaseous fuel passes away unburnt. If, however, the fire be stirred to allow more air to enter its upper strata, then the gases are kindled by the heat, and the flame, thus started, rapidly spreads.

It will be seen from this that a simple gas producer might be made by charging a vessel with red-hot coke, then passing through it a stream of oxygen sufficient to form a combustible gas, but insufficient to allow complete combustion while passing through the red-hot fuel. This gas might be collected in a suitable reservoir, and burnt at will by the addition of a further supply of oxygen. The process of manufacture of the gas is represented symbolically by

$$CO_2 + C = 2\,CO.$$

The resulting gas, carbon-monoxide, has a calorific value of about 340 B.T.U. per cubic foot. For commercial consumption the oxygen is supplied to the hot coke or carbon by passing air through the containing vessel. The resulting gas is therefore very largely diluted with nitrogen, which reduces its calorific value per cubic foot to about 112 B.T.U., or about one-sixth that of coal gas.

It is clear that, so long as atmospheric air alone is used as a vehicle for the oxygen necessary for combination with the carbon, a very inferior gas will be produced. In order to avoid this, another method has been resorted to, the result of which is the production of a gas known as water gas. The bare outline of the operation is as follows : Atmospheric air is passed through a chamber containing coke or anthracite until the whole mass of fuel is at a bright red heat. The gases formed during this process are not collected. The air supply is then entirely cut off, and superheated steam is passed through the incandescent fuel. This steam is decomposed into its elements, oxygen and hydrogen, and the process may continue until the temperature of the fuel falls to a point below which no further decomposition is possible. By this process as much as 50 per cent of free hydrogen is obtained, whilst the liberated oxygen re-combines with the carbon to form about 44 per cent of carbon-monoxide, together with traces of free oxygen, carbon-dioxide, and marsh gas. The calorific value of this gas is about 240 B.T.U. per cubic foot, and, moreover, the percentage of combustibles approaches 100. Hence this gas is eminently suited for gas-engine purposes, and would be largely used excepting for the intermittent action of the apparatus. In generators of this gas the production can only continue for periods of about 15 minutes. After this time steam must be turned off, and air again passed through the fuel, in order to raise it to the incandescent state. Some success has been attained by duplicating this apparatus, but the additional capital outlay required, and the introduction of simpler methods of equal efficiency as regards gas production, has prevented the general adoption of intermittent producers.

The method so successfully carried out by Mr. Emerson Dowson embraces a combination of the above-described processes. From a specially-constructed nozzle a jet of steam is blown into the incandescent fuel. The steam induces a current of air to enter the fuel at the same time. The oxygen thus continuously supplied to the fire maintains it at a proper temperature, whilst the resulting gas is greatly enriched by the decomposition of the steam; and, moreover, by the judicious regulation of the weight of air and steam passing through the fuel, the process is continuously carried on.

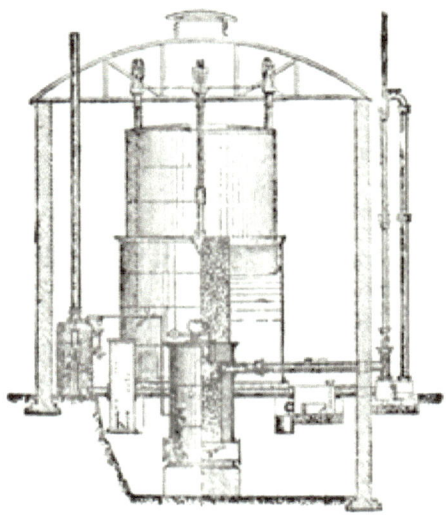

FIG. 85.—Dowson gas plant.

Figs. 85 and 86 show an elevation and plan of Dowson gas plant, of which the following is a brief description.

Referring to fig. 85, the boiler for generating the steam is shown at A. This boiler is kept at a pressure of from 30 lb. to 60 lb. per square inch, according to the size of the generator. Superheated steam passes over from the boiler through the pipe O to the gas generator shown at C. Beneath the firebars of the generator the steam passes through a nozzle of special construction, and so draws air with it into the closed ashpit

E. The gases resulting from the contact of the air and steam with the incandescent fuel in C pass up through the delivery pipes to the stand pipes F. The gases are here cooled, and are afterwards cleansed by passing through water in the box H. From H the gases pass to the scrubber J, and afterwards through the coke scrubber K placed inside the gasholder L, where they remain until conducted to the gas engine. The pressure in the gasholder is allowed to remain at about 1½ in. of water, and the pressure produced

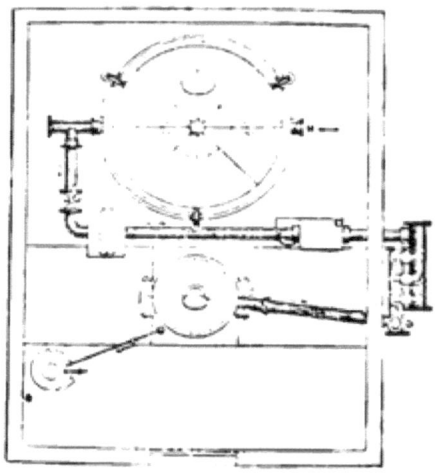

FIG. 86.—Plan of Dowson gas plant.

in the closed ashpit by the action of the steam jet is sufficient to maintain proper circulation of the gases from the producer to the gasholder. The supply of steam to the generator is regulated by a cock at O, the handle of which is attached to the upper moving portion of the gasholder L, thus automatically preventing the generation of gas when the holder becomes fully charged.

The fuel most suitable for consumption in the generator is anthracite, because of the absence of sulphur, smoke, and other impurities. Its cost may be taken at from 12s. to 15s. per ton delivered, and the fuel required per 1,000 cubic feet of gas equals about 13·5 lb. Hence the cost of fuel in the generator per thousand cubic feet may be taken as about one penny. Including all charges, depreciation, wages, &c., upon a small plant capable of delivering 1,000 cubic feet per hour, the cost is worked out at $4\frac{3}{4}$d. per 1,000 cubic feet.* A larger plant, producing 3,000 cubic feet per hour, works out to about $2\frac{3}{4}$d. per 1,000 cubic feet. It must here be remembered, however, that about five volumes of Dowson gas are required to evolve the same heat as one volume of coal gas. Hence the cost per 1,000 cubic feet must be multiplied by five before a comparison can be made between Dowson and coal gas. Thus we see that with large producers a saving of 67 per cent is effected, and with small producers a saving of 41 per cent, when coal gas is taken at 3s. per 1,000.

The lowest fuel consumption obtained with Dowson plant, working a twin-cylinder Crossley engine, indicating 118 horse power, was 0·76 lb. per indicated horse power hour during a working test of eight hours. When the losses in the generator due to clinkering and standing all night were added, the total consumption was 0·873 lb. per indicated horse power hour. The cost per indicated horse power hour, exclusive of wages and incidental expenses, is therefore 0·06d. This exceptionally low consumption of fuel can hardly be expected under ordinary working conditions. The average consumption may be taken as $1\frac{1}{2}$ lb. of anthracite per indicated horse power hour.

Referring to analyses previously given of Dowson gas, it will be seen that it consists largely of carbon-monoxide, which gas is very poisonous. It is therefore important that all fittings should be tight, and that there should be good ventilation in the engine-room.

* Inst. Civil Engineers, Proceedings, vol. lxxiii.

It has already been mentioned that the calorific value of producer gas is much lower than that of coal gas; also that the air volume required for its combustion is less than for coal gas. Although some difficulty is found in practice in keeping the composition of the gas quite uniform, owing to choking up of the firebars, &c., yet an average composition of Dowson gas will be found to require, theoretically, 1·01 volumes of air to 1 of gas. In gas engines, 1·5 volumes of air to 1 of gas are usually adopted.

The following table, worked out similarly to that given previously for coal gas, will be found useful in working out the results of trials. For the purposes of these calculations, an average analysis is quoted:—

	Volume per cent.	Weight in one cubic foot of gas.	Proportion by weight.	Calorific value due to each constituent per cubic ft at 32° and 14·7.	Weight of oxygen required per pound of gas.	Specific heat at constant volume.
Hydrogen	20	0·00111	0·008	58·27	0·064	0·01924
Carbon-monoxide ..	23	0·01890	0·136	77·40	0·077	0·02352
Carbon-dioxide	7	0·07420	0·561		....	0·09593
Nitrogen	50	0·03915	0·295	....	....	0·05103
	100	0·13246	1·00	135·67	0·141	0·18972

From the above table we see that 0·141 lb. of oxygen is required to combine with 1 lb. of Dowson gas. Hence

$$\frac{0·141}{0·23} = 0·613 \text{ lb.}$$

of air will be required to supply this weight of oxygen. 1 lb. of air occupies (at 32 deg. Fah. and 14·7 lb.) 0·08059 cubic feet. Volume of air required therefore

$$= \frac{0·613}{0·08059} = 7·61 \text{ cubic feet (nearly).}$$

1 lb. of Dowson gas occupies

$$\frac{1}{0\cdot 13246} = 7\cdot 56 \text{ cubic feet (nearly).}$$

The ratio of air to gas theoretically required is, therefore,

$$\frac{7\cdot 61}{7\cdot 56} = 1\cdot 01 \text{ (nearly).}$$

CHAPTER XIX.

The Effects of the Products of Combustion upon Explosive Mixtures of Coal Gas and Air

EXPERIMENTS previously made upon gaseous mixtures have been directed towards the investigation of the actual pressures produced by the combustion of an inflammable gas, in the presence of oxygen or pure air only. Thirty years ago such experiments were conducted in chemical laboratories on a very small scale quite incomparable with the volumes of the cylinders which are used in practical work. The practical difficulties which beset the development of the gas engine retarded, rather than stimulated, any very complete research upon the behaviour of explosive mixtures. Practical men were satisfied with an approximation to the maximum pressure which might be expected with any given mixture; this information was amply provided by Hirn, Bunsen, and later by Berthelot. As the mechanical arrangements became more efficient, the need was felt for further data regarding the comparative economy of various mixtures.

The most complete practical contribution upon this subject has been afforded by the experiments of Mr. Dugald Clerk, which enabled him to estimate the most economical mixture to be used in a non-compression engine, but no account was taken of the effects of the products of combustion which are present in the cylinder of a gas engine, notwithstanding that the early engines were constructed with a clearance volume of 60 per cent. To obtain some definite data upon this important subject the author has recently carried out a series of experiments in the Engineering Laboratory of the Yorkshire College, Leeds.

It has been generally inferred that the products of combustion, when mixed with a fresh charge of coal gas and air, will decrease the maximum pressure and thereby reduce the efficiency of the charge; if this inference be correct, it would justify the efforts of gas-engine manufacturers in introducing a scavenger stroke, in order to minimise the evils of the presence of residual gases. The experiments carried out by the author show that the presence of the products of combustion in certain mixtures actually raise, rather than diminish, the maximum pressure obtained. It is, however, incontestible that the expulsion of the products of combustion has effected an increase in the economy of gas consumption; but, in the author's opinion, the reduced consumption per horse power is due to the increase in the effective cylinder capacity of any given engine when the products of combustion are replaced by explosive mixture, as well as to the cooling effects of the scavenging stroke. Following the example of previous experimenters upon gaseous mixtures, the author made use of a closed vessel of constant volume, and ignited the charges at atmospheric pressure. The use of such apparatus is considered by some to detract from the practical value of the results obtained, but if the presence of certain constituents affects the rise of pressure in a vessel of constant volume, it may be asked, Why should it not also affect the rise of pressure in the expanding chamber of a gas engine? The author is now continuing this series of experiments with compressed mixtures, the result of which he hopes shortly to publish.

The apparatus used for the explosion of the gases consisted of a thick cast-iron cylinder, flanged at both ends, of

1 cubic foot capacity. The cylinder (A, fig. 87) was bolted vertically to the column B.

FIG. 87.

Igniting Arrangements. — The charge was ignited by passing an electric spark in the mixture by means of a secondary battery and induction coil, the wires from which passed through the insulated brass plug C on the top cover.

The insulation at first gave a great deal of trouble through moisture collecting on the under surface of the insulating material at the point where the wires penetrated (see fig. 88, *a*). The difficulty was ultimately overcome by adopting the arrangement shown in fig. 88, *b*. The brass casing, by projecting beyond the surface of the insulation,

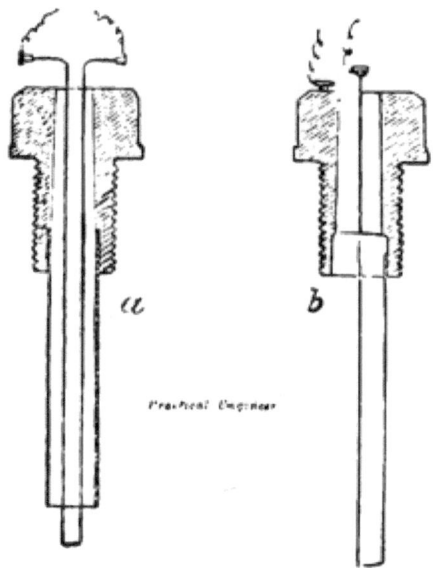

FIG. 88.—The Igniter.

prevented the water, during the filling of the cylinder, from rising to within the cup thus formed. By thoroughly drying, then oiling the surface of the insulation, the sparking was made certain. If any mixture failed to explode, the igniting gear was carefully tested, and the inflammatory nature of the gas ascertained by applying flame as it was gently driven from the experimental cylinder.

Temperatures.—The temperatures were measured, before ignition, by means of a thermometer enclosed in a wrought-iron case, containing mercury, which penetrated into the gas chamber.

Recording Gear.—The pressures were recorded by means of a Crosby indicator, the pencil of which was arranged to scribe upon a continuously-revolving drum, 8 in. diameter, driven by clockwork. The exact speed of this drum was checked by the vibrating spring, fig. 89, adjusted to make four complete oscillations per second, the dimensions of the spring being such that the inertia enabled it to overcome the slight friction of the pen during one experiment. By allowing this pen to remain stationary during one revolution of the drum, a zero line was traced, which was crossed at every eighth of a second by the wave line produced by the vibrating spring. This period of time is represented by a linear distance of 0·3 in., and thus further sub-divisions may be made if desired. It was inconvenient to arrange the pen of the time recorder immediately over

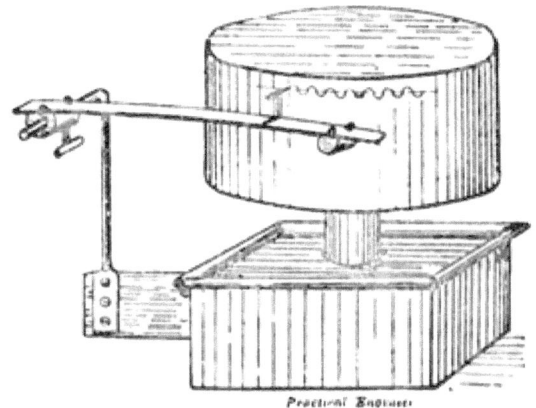

FIG. 89.—The Recorder.

the indicator pencil, but due correction has been made by transferring the required portion of the time wave to its proper position on the diagram.

In all the experiments the volumes were measured by filling the cylinder with water, and afterwards allowing the gas to enter as a measured quantity of water flowed out. After firing the charge, a known volume of water was injected into the cylinder (care being taken that no air was inhaled by the partial vacuum formed by the condensation of the previous charge), thus expelling all but the required volume of residual gas; this, together with a fresh supply of air, and the same volume of coal gas as before, formed the next charge. It need hardly be pointed out that the presence of products of combustion reduced the proportion of gas to pure air, for if this ratio had remained constant during the whole series, it would have necessitated a reduction in the quantity of coal gas, and consequently a reduction of the maximum explosion pressure. Undoubtedly the best arrangement would have been one in which the cylinder

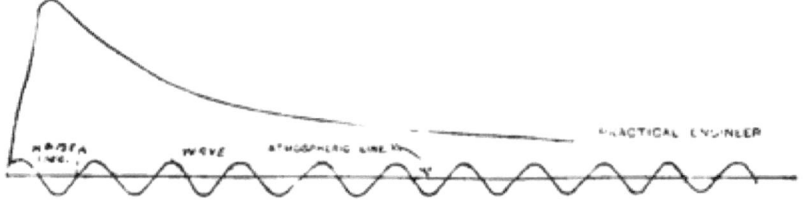

FIG. 90.—Indicator diagram, one volume coal gas, eight volumes air.

itself could have been subject to alteration in volume, for each experiment, sufficient to contain the quantity of products which might be present. The conclusions which may be deduced from these experiments involve the careful consideration of this point. The gases for each experiment were taken into the cylinder in the following order:—

1. The products of the previous combustion, if any.
2. Half the volume of pure air.
3. The coal gas.
4. The remaining air required to complete the charge.

No appreciable time was allowed for the diffusion of the mixture, it having been fired immediately after taking the temperature. It is impossible to estimate how the diffusion of the gases in a working gas-engine cylinder is assisted by the rapid motion of the piston, though it is probable that the coal gas and air are more intimately mixed with one another than with the residual gases. In all experiments great care was taken to obtain atmospheric pressure in the cylinder, special precaution being taken to allow the excess of pressure of the coal gas to escape after uncoupling the supply.

The coal gas used throughout the experiments was taken from the service pipes of the Leeds gas supply. From analyses of three samples made by the author after the experiments, the composition was found to be as follows:—

Analysis of Leeds Coal Gas.

Constituents.	Volume per cent.	Weight of 1 cubic foot.	Weight in 1 cubic foot of coal gas.	Proportion by weight.	Calorific value per pound.	Ditto, per pound of coal gas.	Proportion by weight of oxygen required for combustion.	Weight of oxygen required.
		Lbs.	Lbs.		B.T.U.			Lbs.
Marsh gas	35·2	0·0447	·01573	0·514	21,690	11,148	4	2·056
Olefines	4·2	0·1174	·00493	0·161	20,260	3,261	3½	0·532
Hydrogen	52·9	0·00559	·00295	0·096	52,500	5,040	8	0·768
Carbon monoxide	6·5	0·0783	·00508	0·166	4,300	713	½	0·094
Nitrogen	0·1	0·0783	·00078	0·025	..	..	..	..
Carbon dioxide and oxygen	1·1	0·1060	·00116	0·038	..	..	..	..
	100·0	..	·03063	1·000	..	20,162	..	3·47

The mixtures experimented upon were as follow:—

Volume of coal gas.	Volumes of air.	Volume of coal gas.	Volumes of air.
*1	*16	1	12
1	15	1	10
1	14	1	8
1	13	1	6

* Failed repeatedly to explode.

Referring to Table I. (Appendix), it will be seen that after igniting a mixture of 1 volume of coal gas and 15 volumes of air, the residue was added to the next charge in the proportion of 5 per cent of the cylinder volume. Column 5 gives the actual pressure above the atmosphere as recorded by the indicator. In calculating the calorific values of the volumes of coal gas present in the experiments, the original temperatures and barometric pressures were allowed for; in other cases, the slight variations in initial temperature and barometric pressures have been neglected.

In Column VI. is recorded the rise of pressure above, or fall below, that obtained with a pure mixture, when the various percentages of residue were added. The greatest rise of pressure, namely, 19 lb. per square inch, took place when the products of combustion amounted to about 30 per cent of the whole cylinder volume, which left a proportion of coal gas to pure air of about 1 to $9\frac{1}{2}$ by volume. The air was again decreased by the addition of residual gases until, in the proportion of 1 volume of gas to 6 of air, the rise in pressure was only 8 lb. per square inch above that recorded for the pure mixture. Fifty-five per cent of products was found to be the greatest quantity that might be introduced without preventing ignition. The results given in Table II. show that when the mixture was originally in the proportion of 1 volume of gas to 14 of air the explosions were somewhat less regular than in the previous cases, and the maximum rise of pressure was greatest when the residual gases were present in the proportion of from 10 to 30 per cent, but only 12 lb. per square inch rise above the normal was recorded in this series.

The accompanying diagram, fig. 91, has been prepared from the figures in Column VI. of the tables. The ordinates above the line AB represent the excess of pressure above that recorded when mixtures of pure air and gas were exploded. Below the line the fall in pressure is plotted.

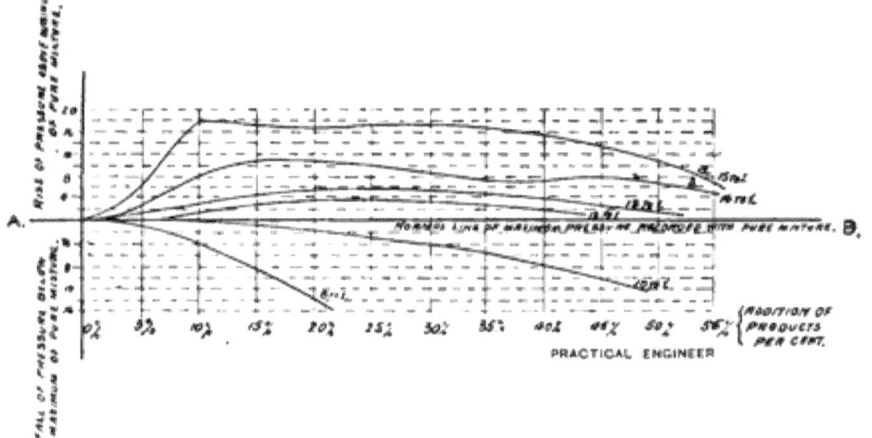

Fig. 91.—Diagram showing rise and fall of maximum pressure due to the addition of products of combustion.

The abscissæ represent the percentages of residue present. The curve marked a represents the rise of pressure with a mixture of 15 to 1. Similarly, the curve marked b, with a mixture of 14 to 1. When the volume of coal gas is as great as one-tenth of the cylinder volume, the addition of residual gases immediately reduces the pressure below that of a pure mixture. The general conclusions which may be be drawn from this diagram are as follow : That with weak mixtures the maximum pressure is least when the excess of pure air is greatest. That the maximum pressure, obtained from a given quantity of coal gas, rises as the excess of air is diminished by the addition of products of combustion; but this no longer holds when the volume of pure air to coal gas approaches the proportion of 10 to 1.

From an examination of fig. 92 it is seen that the explosion becomes more rapid as the excess of air is replaced by neutral gases. If the time is short compared with that of the outstroke of the motor, then the expansion line of an indicator diagram, taken under ordinary conditions, would be below the adiabatic curve. If, on the contrary, the burning continues during the whole of the outstroke, the expansion curve would probably be above the adiabatic, and would consequently give a greater mean effective pressure. Although in the diagrams before us we have only the curve due to cooling, we may still estimate the relative economy of a charge by measuring the area enclosed by the curve of pressure from its commencement to a point determined by an ordinate of time, which shall be chosen equal to that of the outstroke of a motor. Assuming the

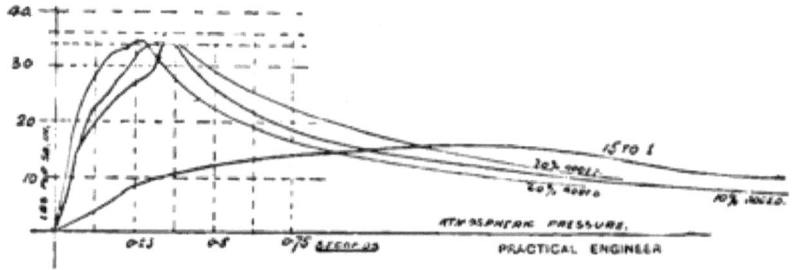

Fig. 92.—Diagram showing increase in the rate of combustion due to the addition of neutral gases.

rather slow speed of 0·25 second as being the duration of the outstroke, we obtain the following mean pressures derived from the areas of the pressure-time diagrams up to 0·25 second. It appears from the following calculations that the mean pressure is not influenced by the quantity of the products of combustion present, but it is always a maximum when pure air is present in the proportion of about 10 to 1 of gas.

TABLE OF GREATEST MEAN PRESSURES, CALCULATED FROM PRESSURE-TIME DIAGRAMS, UP TO 0·25 SECONDS FROM COMMENCEMENT OF EXPLOSION.

Proportion of volume of coal gas to volume of cylinder.	Greatest mean pressure recorded. Pounds per square inch.	when	The percentage of products (estimated as clearance in an engine) was—	which gives—	The proportion of pure air to coal gas, of—
1/9	9 / 20		None / 30		15 to 1 / 11 to 1
1/8	11 / 23		None / 20		14 to 1 / 11 to 1
1/7	11 / 24		None / 18		13 to 1 / 11 to 1
1/6	16 / 21		None / 18		12 to 1 / 10 to 1
1/5	22 / 33		None / 17·8		11 to 1 / 8·3 to 1
1/4	42 / 40		None / 11		8 to 1 / 7 to 1
1/3	30 / 26		None / 5·2		6 to 1 / 5·6 to 1

From the composition of the coal gas used, it has been calculated that 5·7 volumes of air are required for complete combustion; and the experiments show that, as long as this ratio is not widely departed from, the mixture is explosive, notwithstanding the presence of 55 per cent of inert gases.

The results of all the experiments point conclusively to the fact that the ratio of air to gas alone determines the possibility of an explosion, and that the explosion pressure depends chiefly upon a suitable ratio being chosen.

The total heat evolved in each of the experiments was as follows:—

Heat values of the volumes of coal gas used.	Proportion of volume of gas to volume of cylinder.	Volume of air to volume of gas.
B.T.U.	Per cent.	
37	6·2	15 to 1
39	6·6	14 to 1
42	7·1	13 to 1
45	7·7	12 to 1
53	9·1	10 to 1
63	11·1	8 to 1
86	14·2	6 to 1

It was found, as might be anticipated, that the explosion pressures varied directly as the number of thermal units generated from the combustion of the gas. In fig. 93, the explosion pressures have been plotted as ordinates, and the number of British thermal units as abscissæ.

The diagrams in all cases show an alteration in the rate of combustion, in two places, but in no instance is there any sign of an actual reduction in pressure—merely an alteration in the rate of increase. Mr. Dugald Clerk, in his work upon the "Explosion of Gaseous Mixtures," produces an indicator diagram taken during the explosion of a mixture of one volume of gas to five volumes of air, in which the pressure curve distinctly falls after having reached a pressure of 60 lb. per square inch; it then rises to its maximum of nearly 100 lb. In none of the diagrams taken by the author, or in any single instance, out of some hundreds of experiments made by the Students of the College, has any such fall been recorded. It is therefore impossible to believe in a theory which attempts to explain it. Mr. Clerk's theory supposes that, after complete inflammation has taken place the pressure is further raised as the constituents of the coal gas comb'ne with oxygen, only at a much slower rate than during inflammation. So far this may be satisfactory, but to believe that this explains the momentary fall in pressure is, in the author's opinion, carrying the theory beyond its legitimate application.

It is found from an examination of the diagrams taken during the explosions of pure mixtures of air and coal gas, that the first alteration in the slope of the rising pressure curve occurs at 0·4 of the maximum height of the diagram. Whatever may be the real cause of this characteristic of all

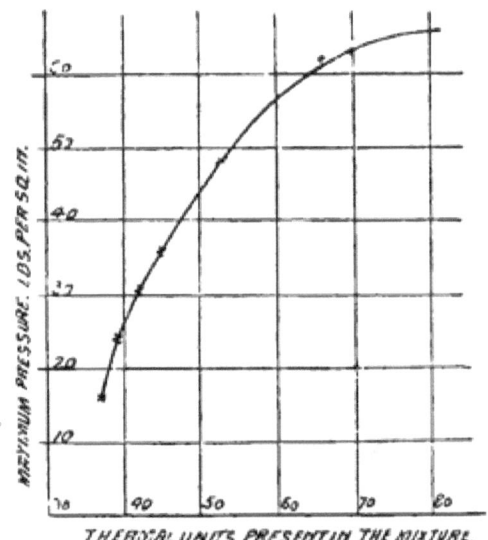

Fig. 93.—Diagram showing relation between maximum pressure obtained and thermal units present in the charge.

coal-gas explosion diagrams, it is interesting to note that the heat generated by the combustion of the hydrogen and the olefines combined is found to be just 0·4 of the total heat of the whole of the constituents of the coal gas experimented upon. Experiments have been made by Messrs. V. Meyer and F. Fryer, to determine the temperature at which each of the constituents of coal gas combine with oxygen. The results of their experiments are as follow :—

Ignition Temperatures of Explosive Gaseous Mixtures Burnt in a Closed Bulb.

Hydrogen combined with oxygen at............. 1,124 deg. Fah.
Olefines combined with oxygen at................ 1,124 deg. Fah.
Marsh gas combined with oxygen at............ 1,201 deg. Fah.
Carbon monoxide combined with oxygen at 1,347 deg. Fah.

It will here be noted that the hydrogen and olefines burn at the lowest temperature, namely, 1,124 deg. Fah., that the marsh gas burns next in order, and lastly the carbon monoxide at the highest temperature. From the calorific values of the constituents of the gas, which are given in a previous table, 1 lb. of coal gas is found to contain—

    8,301 thermal units due to hydrogen and olefines.
   11,148 thermal units due to marsh gas.
     713 thermal units due to carbon monoxide.
   ―――――
   20,162 total.

The total heat may, therefore, be divided into three parts, the proportion of each to the whole being—

   0·417 of total heat due to hydrogen and olefines.
   0·548 of total heat due to marsh gas.
   0·035 of total heat due to carbon monoxide.

The annexed diagram (fig. 94) shows the application of these figures to the results. This diagram was taken during the explosion of 1 volume of gas mixed with 12 volumes of air. If horizontal lines are drawn through the points A, B, C, the figure is divided into three bands. If the specific heat be sensibly constant, then the pressures produced will be proportional to the heat developed at a given time. If, then, 0·41 of the total heat were developed first, we should expect to find the height of the first band to be 0·41 of the total height of the diagram. From several diagrams taken with pure mixtures the mean height of this band was found to be 0·403 of the total height. In the shaded diagram illustrating this point, the heights of the bands are not quite in agreement with the previous figures, but very nearly so. The diagrams, taken when the residual gases are present in large volumes, show the point A is very much raised, probably on account of the hydrogen and olefines combining with the greater part of the oxygen present, the remainder being insufficient to completely burn the marsh gas and carbon monoxide. In other words, the total height of the diagram is not what it would have been had the heat due to the marsh gas and carbon monoxide been wholly developed.

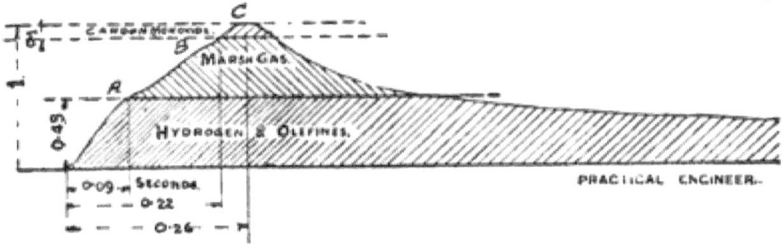

Fig. 94.

In every experiment the pressures recorded were low compared with those obtained by Clerk. Fig. 94 shows a maximum pressure of 38 lb. per square inch above the atmosphere, from which the maximum temperature works out to 1,350 deg. Fah. The maximum temperature possible was 3,250 deg. Fah., showing a loss of heat of 58·5 per cent, or 41·5 per cent accounted for, and the maximum pressure correspondingly higher. The difference is no doubt due to the fact that water was present on the walls of the cylinder, much of the heat thereby rendered latent in converting it into vapour. The pressure at the point A on fig. 6 is about 18 lb. per square inch above the atmosphere, and the heat accounted for at this point is found to be 49 per cent of that due to the hydrogen and olefines. That the heat accounted for at points on the pressure line near the atmospheric is more than at the maximum is what we should anticipate, for the cooling curves are all much steeper at the top than lower, showing that the rate of transmission of heat is greatest at the highest temperature.

A summary of the whole series of these experiments is shown by fig. 95. Plotted to a scale of 20 lb. = 1 in. are the pressures recorded during each experiment. The dotted line passes through all the points of pressure; the full line shows the mean rise and fall of pressure throughout.

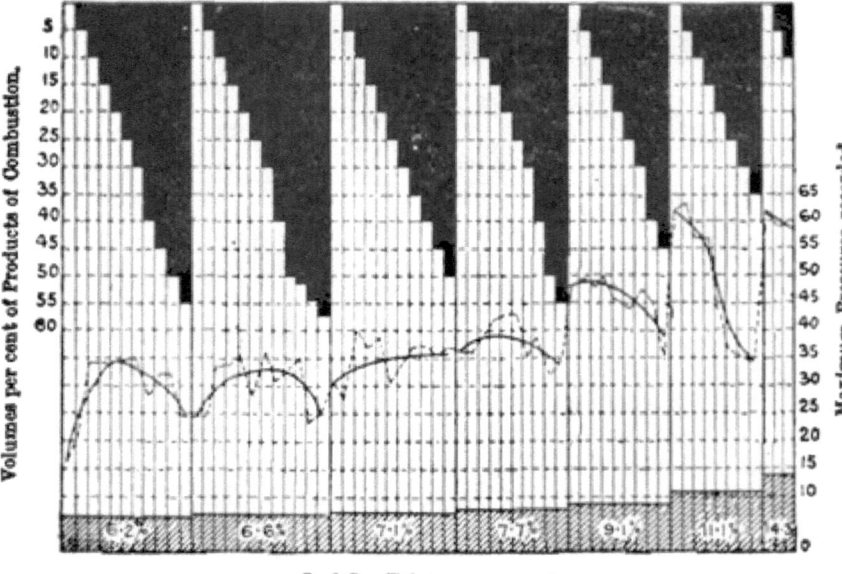

Diagram showing Volumes of Coal Gas, Air, and Neutral Gases, with Maximum Pressures in pounds per square inch for each mixture.

Fig. 95.

CONCLUSIONS.

From these combined results the following conclusions may be drawn:—

1. That the highest pressures are obtained when the volume of air present is only slightly in excess of the amount required for complete combustion.

2. That higher pressures are recorded when residual gases take the place of an *excess* of air.

3. That when the volume of the products of combustion does not exceed 58 per cent of the mixture, then it is explosive, provided the volume of air is not less than 5·5 times the volume of coal gas.

4. That the time of an explosion is much reduced when excess of air is replaced by products of combustion.

APPENDICES TO PART I.

TABLES OF RESULTS OF EXPERIMENTS ON THE EFFECTS OF THE PRODUCTS OF COMBUSTION UPON EXPLOSIVE MIXTURES OF COAL GAS AND AIR. (REFERRED TO IN CHAPTER XIX.)

TABLE I.

Col. I.		Col. II.		Col. III.		Col. IV.		Col. V.	Col. VI.
Ratio of volume of coal gas to volume of cylinder.		Ratio of volume of coal gas to volume of air.		Ratio of volume of products to volume of cylinder.		Ratio of volume of products to volume of air+coal gas.		Maximum pressures, pounds per square inch.	Rise of pressure above (+) or fall below (−) maximum for pure mixture.
Actu'l	Per cent	Actual	Per cent	Actu'l	Per cent	Actu'l	Per cent		
1/16	6·2	1/15	6·6	0	0	0	0	16	..
,,	,,	1/14·2	7·0	1/20	5	1/19	5·2	22	+ 6
,,	,,	1/13·2	7·4	1/10	10	1/9	11·1	34	+ 18
,,	,,	1/12·6	7·9	1/6·6	15	1/5·6	17·8	34	+ 18
,,	,,	1/11·8	8·4	1/5	20	1/4	25	34	+ 18
,,	,,	1/11	9·0	1/4	25	1/3·3	30	34	+ 18
,,	,,	1/10·2	9·8	1/3·3	30	1/2·3	45	35	+ 19
,,	,,	1/8·6	11·6	1/2·5	40	1/1·5	66	28	+ 12
,,	,,	1/7·8	12·8	1/2·2	45	1/1·2	89	32	+ 16
,,	,,	1/7	14·3	1/2	50	1/1	100	32	+ 16
,,	,,	1/6·1	16·2	1/1·8	55	..	..	24	+ 8
,,	,,	1/5·3	18·6	1/1·6	60	..	..	Failed.	..

TABLE II.

1/15	6·6	1/14	7·1	0	0	0	0	24	..
,,	,,	1/13·3	7·5	1/20	5	1/19	5·2	24	0
,,	,,	1/12·5	8	1/10	10	1/9	11·1	33	+ 9
,,	,,	1/11·8	8·4	1/6·6	15	1/5·6	17·8	34	+ 10
,,	,,	1/11	9·1	1/5·0	20	1/4	25	36	+ 12
,,	,,	1/9·7	10·3	1/4	25	1/3·3	30	28	+ 4
,,	,,	1/9·5	10·4	1/3·3	30	1/2·3	45	36	+ 12
,,	,,	1/8	12·4	1/2·5	40	1/1·5	66	31	+ 7
,,	,,	1/6·6	15·1	1/2	50	1·1	100	33	+ 9
,,	,,	1/6·2	16·1	1/1·9	52	..	..	35	+ 11
,,	,,	1/5·7	17·3	1/1·8	55	..	..	23	− 1
,,	,,	1/5·2	19·2	1/1·7	58	..	..	25	+ 1
,,	,,	1/5	19·9	1/1·6	60	..	..	Failed.	

APPENDICES TO PART I.   201

Table III.

Col. I.		Col. II.		Col. III.		Col. IV.		Col. V.	Vol. VI.
Ratio of volume of coal gas to volume of cylinder.		Ratio of volume of coal gas to volume of air.		Ratio of volume of products to volume of cylinder.		Ratio of volume of products to volume of air+coal gas.		Maximum pressures, pounds per square inch.	Rise of pressure above (+) or fall below (−) maximum for pure mixture.
Actu'l	Per cent	Actual	Per cent	Actu'l	Per cent	Actu'l	Per cent		
1/14	7·1	1/13	7·7	0	0	0	0	31	..
,,	,,	1/12·3	8·1	1/20	5	1/19	5·2	27	− 4
,,	,,	1/11·6	8·6	1/10	10	1/9	11·1	40	+ 9
,,	,,	1/11	9·1	1/6·6	15	1/5·6	17·8	37	+ 6
,,	,,	1/10·2	9·8	1/5	20	1/4	25	39	+ 8
,,	,,	1/9·5	10·5	1/4	25	1/3·3	30	30	− 1
,,	,,	1/8·8	11·3	1/3·3	30	1/2·3	45	34	+ 3
,,	,,	1/8·1	12·3	1/2·8	35	1/1·8	54	37	+ 6
,,	,,	1/7·4	13·5	1/2·5	40	1/1·5	66	37	+ 6
,,	,,	1/6·7	14·9	1/2·2	45	1/1·2	89	36	+ 5
,,	,,	1/6	16·9	1/2	50	1/1	100	37	+ 6
,,	,,	1/5·3	18·9	1/1·8	55	1/	..	Failed.	..

Table IV.

1/13	7·7	1/12	8·3	0	0	0	0	36	..
,,	,,	1/11·3	8·8	1/20	5	1/19	5·2	36	0
,,	,,	1/10·7	9·3	1/10	10	1/9	11·1	40	+ 4
,,	,,	1/10	9·9	1/6·6	15	1/5·6	17·8	42	+ 6
,,	,,	1/9·4	10·6	1/5	20	1/4	25	41	+ 5
,,	,,	1/8·7	11·4	1/4	25	1/3·3	30	43	+ 7
,,	,,	1/8·1	12·3	1/3·3	30	1/2·3	45	35	− 1
,,	,,	1/6·8	14·7	1/2·5	40	1/1·5	66·7	39	+ 3
,,	,,	1/5·5	18·3	1/2	50	1/1	100	32	− 4
,,	,,	1/4·8	20·8	1/1·8	55	..	..	34	− 2
,,	,,	1/4·4	22·7	1/1·7	58	..	..	Failed.	..
,,	,,	1/4·1	24·3	1/1·6	60	..	..	Failed.	..

TABLE V.

Col. I.		Col. II.		Col. III.		Col. IV.		Col. V.	Col. VI.
Ratio of volume of coal gas to volume of cylinder.		Ratio of volume of coal gas to volume of air.		Ratio of volume of products to volume of cylinder.		Ratio of volume of products to volume of air+coal gas.		Maximum pressures, pounds per square inch.	Rise of pressure above (+) or fall below (−) maximum for pure mixture.
Actu'l	Per cent	Actual	Per cent	Actu'l	Per cent	Actu'l	Per cent		
1/11	9·1	1/10	10	0	0	0	0	48	..
,,	,,	1/9·4	10·6	1/20	5	1/19	5·2	49	+ 1
,,	,,	1/8·9	11·2	1/10	10	1/9	11·1	48	0
,,	,,	1/8·3	12	1/6·6	15	1/5·6	17·8	50	+ 2
,,	,,	1/7·8	12·8	1/5	20	1/4	25	45	− 3
,,	,,	1/7·2	13·8	1/4	25	1/3·3	30	44	− 4
,,	,,	1/6·7	14·9	1/3·3	30	1/2·3	45	47	− 1
,,	,,	1/5·6	17·9	1/2·5	40	1/1·5	66·7	45	− 3
,,	,,	1/5	19·8	1/2·2	45	1/1·2	82	35	− 13
,,	,,	1/4·9	20·2	1/2·1	46	1/1·7	85	0	..
,,	,,	1/4·7	21·3	1/2·08	48	1/1·1	92	0	..
,,	,,	1/4·5	22·2	1/2	50	1/1	100	0	..

TABLE VI.

1/9	11·1	1/8	12·5	0	0	0	0	62	..
,,	,,	1/7·5	13·4	1/20	5	1/19	5·2	63	+ 1
,,	,,	1/7·1	14·2	1/10	10	1/9	11·1	57	− 5
,,	,,	1/6·6	15·2	1/6·6	15	1/5·6	17·8	57	− 5
,,	,,	1/6·2	16·1	1/5	20	1/4	25	43	− 19
,,	,,	1/5·7	17·4	1/4	25	1/3·3	30	36	− 26
,,	,,	1/5·3	18·8	1/3·3	30	1/2·3	45	35	− 27
,,	,,	1/4·8	20·6	1/2·8	35	1/1·8	54	35	− 27
,,	,,	1/4·6	21·8	1/2·6	38	1/1·6	61	Failed	..

TABLE VII.

1/7	14·3	1/6	16·6	0	0	0	0	62	..
,,	,,	1/5·8	17·7	1/20	5	1/19	5·2	59	− 3
,,	,,	1/5·3	18·6	1/10	10	1/9	11·1	60	− 2
,,	,,	1/4·9	20·2	1/6·6	15	1/5·6	17·8	Failed	..

Results of Gas-engine Trials. Town Gas Used.

Name of engine.	I.H.P.	B.H.P.	Mechanical efficiency.	Cubic feet of gas per I.H.P. hour.	Cubic feet of gas per B.H.P. hour.	Authority and remarks.
Otto-Crossley	17·1	14·7	0·86	20·7	24·1	Society of Arts Report.
Clerk's engine	9·05	7·23	0·8	24·3	30·4	Clerk's "Gas Engines," page 141.
Atkinson's Differential	..	2·6	..	..	25·7	Robinson's "Gas and petroleum engines."
Atkinson's Cycle	5·56	4·80	0·88	19·78	22·5	Professor Unwin.
Griffin	15·47	12·51	0·8	23·1	28·5	Professors Kennedy and Jamieson.
Forward engine	5·54	4·8	0·86	20·79	23·97	Professor Smith.
Simplex	..	8·79	..	..	20·38	Witz.
Wells Brothers small gas engine	8·5	11·9	0·71	20	27·8	At half load. Professor Goodman.
Wells Brothers small gas engine	13·5	17·6	0·76	16·3	21·2	Nearly full load. Professor Goodman.
Ditto ditto Premier Cycle	47	61	·77	15·27	..	Full load. Professor Goodman.

Trials in which Dowson Gas was Used.

Name of engine.	I.H.P.	B.H.P.	Anthracite consumed in producer per I.H.P. Pounds.	Ditto B.H.P. Pounds.	Authority.
Crossley Otto	27·5	..	1·4	..	Inst. Civil Engineers. Proc., vol. lxxiii.
Crossley Otto	119·7	..	0·762	..	The *Engineer*, February 12, 1892.
Atkinson's Cycle engine	21·9	..	1·06	..	The *Engineer*, February 12, 1892.
Simplex	110	75·86	..	1·31	
Stockport	70	..	0·86	..	Mr. H. Robb.

*TABLE SHOWING THEORETICAL INDICATED EFFICIENCY OF CROSSLEY OTTO ENGINES WITH DIFFERENT COMPRESSIONS, COMPARED WITH ACTUAL INDICATED EFFICIENCES WITH THE SAME COMPRESSIONS.

Calculated efficiency for perfect Otto cycle engine from compression space volume.	Actual indicated efficiency from diagram and gas consumption.	Ratio of actual to ideal efficiency.	Cylinder diameter in inches.	Piston stroke in inches.	Ratio of compression space to space swept by piston.	Pressure of compression in pounds.	Gas consumption per I.H.P. per hour in cubic feet.
0·33	0·15	$\frac{0·15}{0·33} = 0·45$	9	18	0·6	38·0	21·0
0·4	0·189	$\frac{0·189}{0·40} = 0·47$	9¼	18	0·4	61·6	20·5
0·393	0·19	$\frac{0·19}{0·393} = 0·48$	6½	18	0·418	53·0	20·3
0·428	0·25	$\frac{0·25}{0·428} = 0·58$	7	15	0·34	87·5	14·8

*TABLE SHOWING COMPARISON OF THE ACTUAL AND THEORETICAL EFFICIENCIES OF OTTO ENGINES OF DIFFERENT DIMENSIONS.

	Engine cylinder.	Relative capacity.	Theoretical efficiency.	Actual indicated efficiency	Rates of actual and ideal efficiency.
	7 in. diameter by 15 in. stroke	1·00	0·428	0·250	$\frac{0·25}{0·428} = 0·58$
Nearly equal compression	11½ in. diameter by 15 in. stroke	3·77	0·428	0·275	$\frac{0·275}{0·428} = 0·64$
	9¼ in. diameter by 18 in. stroke	1·00	0·40	0·210	$\frac{0·21}{0·41} = 0·53$
	14 in. diameter by 25 in. stroke	2·97	0·41	0·277	$\frac{0·277}{0·41} = 0·67$

* Clerk on "Gas Engines." Proc. Inst. C.E.

PART II.

PETROLEUM ENGINES.

CHAPTER XX.

The discovery of petroleum in large quantities in Russia and America has materially stimulated inventors to devise means of utilising this enormous latent energy. Before dealing with the oil engines which have attained success, it will be well to discuss the physical properties of the substance known generally as petroleum. The chemistry and the commercial production of petroleum are subjects beyond the scope of this work. Those physical properties, however, which more directly affect the design of oil engines should be carefully studied.

Petroleum has been found at various times in nearly all parts of the world, and has received a variety of names. The most productive American area lies within the boundaries of New York and Pennsylvania. In Canada there has been a large production, and the famous Baku wells of Russia are well known. Petroleum consists chemically of hydrogen and carbon. It is probably of vegetable origin, though this point is vigorously contested by geologists supporting other theories. Crude petroleum is usually of a dark green hue by reflected light, showing red by transmitted light.

An idea of the commercial value of petroleum and the variety of its uses will be gathered from the following table :—

ONE HUNDRED GALLONS OF CRUDE PETROLEUM WILL YIELD UPON FRACTIONAL DISTILLATION:—

	Gallons.	Specific gravity.	Flashing point.
Benzene light oil ⎫	1	0·725	− 10 deg. Cen.
Gasolene ⎬ oil engines	3	0·775	+ 0 ,, ,,
Kerosene ⎭	27	0·822	25 ,, ,,
Saliarovi ⎫	12	0·870	100 ,, ,,
Veregenni ⎬ lubricating	10	0·880	150 ,, ,,
Lubricating oil	17	0·905	175 ,, ,,
Cylinder oil ⎭	5	0·915	200 ,, ,,
Vaseline	1	0·925	....
Residuum .... liquid fuel	14		....
Loss	10	..	....

The oils used in oil engines are benzene, gasolene, and kerosene, the two former of which are generally known as light oils. They are extremely volatile at ordinary atmospheric temperatures, and are consequently dangerous when carelessly handled. In order that these light oils may be used by owners of oil engines without the inconvenient restrictions imposed by the Petroleum Acts of 1871-9, regulations were issued on November 3rd, 1896, by the Secretary of State. For the purposes of these regulations a light oil is defined as having a *flashing point** of less than 73 deg. Fah. When the flashing point exceeds 73 deg. Fah. the oil is said to be *heavy*, and to this class the above regulations do not apply. Moreover, engines driven by the heavy oils are regarded as safe, and for this reason they will no doubt in time supersede the light oil motors which are at the present time used for driving vehicles. Such oils may be stored in air-tight tanks, all openings from which

---

* The temperature at which oil commences to give off inflammable vapour, when under ordinary atmospheric pressure, is termed the flashing point.

must be covered with gauze of 400 mesh. No tank may exceed 20 gallons capacity; they must be kept in well-ventilated places. When used in connection with motors for driving vehicles the quantity carried by each vehicle must not exceed 40 gallons.

A rough test of the flashing point may be made in the following way: Take a small quantity of the oil to be tested

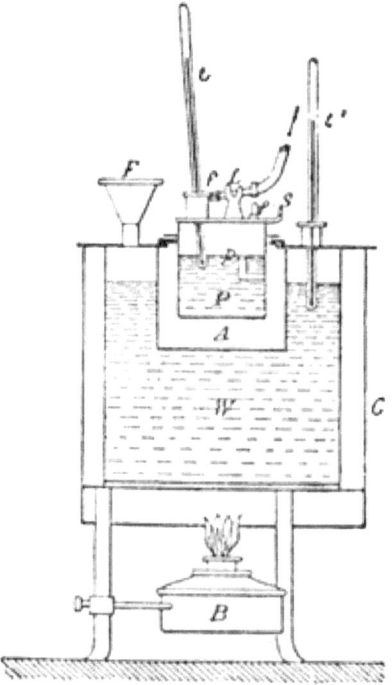

FIG. 96.—Abel tester.

in a metal vessel. Heat the vessel gradually by means of a lighted taper. Apply the light occasionally to the surface of the oil. When the oil ignites immediately put out the flame and take the temperature of the oil with a Fahrenheit thermometer. This will give the flashing point approximately.

In England and Canada an instrument known as the Abel Tester is legally recognised as giving the flashing point. This instrument is shown in fig. 96. The copper vessel W contains water, which is heated by the lamp B to 130 deg. Fah. The oil to be tested is placed in the chamber P, which is surrounded by an air jacket A. A gas flame f, outside the chamber P, is arranged to swing round until the flame shoots through a small hole in the cover of the oil chamber, when the hole is uncovered by the moving of the slide S. To test a sample of oil, it should first be cooled to about 60 deg. Fah.; a quantity is then placed in the chamber P, until the pointer p is just covered. Light the gas at the nozzle f. For each degree rise of the thermometer t, the slide s is opened, and the flame gently tilted into the oil chamber. A pendulum is usually provided to time this operation to four oscillations, the slide being closed on the fourth swing. When a blue flash is obtained on the application of the test flame, the flashing point of the oil is read from the thermometer t.

The specific gravity of shale oils, as sold in Britain, varies 0·78 to 0·85, and the flashing point varies with the density from 76 deg. Fah. to 225 deg. Fah. The following table has been obtained by Professor Robinson, who has carried out an interesting series of experiments, the results of which may be more fully referred to in *The Engineer*, September 11th, 1891.

The chief difficulty in the construction of oil engines is the design of the vaporiser, and in this connection the figures given in the latter columns of the above table are particularly interesting. We see that American Royal Daylight oil boils at a temperature of 144 deg. Cen., but at 215 deg. Cen. only one quarter of the volume of oil treated is vaporised. At a temperature of 230 deg. Cen. 65 per cent by volume still remains. Thus it appears the temperature must be raised far beyond this point in order that the whole volume may be distilled. But it is just here that the designer meets with fresh difficulties, owing to the fact that if the temperature be raised too much decomposition

PROPERTIES OF PETROLEUM AND SHALE OILS USED IN BRITAIN (ROBINSON)

Name of oil	Colour	Wholesale price delivered in London and Liverpool per gallon.	Specific gravity at 60 deg. Fah.	Specific heat.	Flashing point.		Boiling Point. Cen.	Distillation.				
								Liquid.				
					Fah.	Cen.		Volume distilled under 250 deg. Cen. Per cent.	Highest temp. Deg. Cen.	Volume distilled. Per cent.	Time. Hrs.
Burning oils.		Pence					Deg.					
American Royal Daylight	Light straw.	4	0·811	0·47	76	24·5	144	25	230	35	3
American ordinary	Light straw.	3½	0·791	...	75	24	143	29	223	36	3
American Water-white	Colourless	5	0·780	...	108	42	150	55	216	55	4
American Tea Rose	Light straw.	4½	0·797	...	83	28·3	150	22	213	37	3
Russian ordinary (Russoline)	Light straw.	3½	0·824	0·45	82	27·8	151	30	224	56	3
Russian Lustre	Light straw.	4	0·825	0·45	...	...	...	...	...	...	...
Broxbourne Lighthouse	Light straw.	5½	0·810	0·44	152	66·7	165	First drop	(243, 270, 300)	(55, 90, 100)	(2, 2, 3)
Intermediate oils.												
American mineral sperm	Straw.	...	0·833	...	...	...	195	...	300	5	3
Storrar's Scotch gas oil	Reddish brown.	2½	0·843	...	...	...	195	...	293	5	3
Scotch intermediate shale oil	Clear brown.	2½	0·846	...	...	...	195	...	291	15	2
Light lubricating oil	Clear brown.	2½	0·853	...	225	107	195	...	285	16	2

takes place, and a carbon residue remains, which, if present in large quantities, is quite fatal to the successful action of a vaporiser. The best method of dealing with this class of oils is to raise the temperature to a safe limit, then allow hot air to pass over the oil. In the description of the various methods of vaporising we shall see how this is practically carried into effect. Suffice it to say that in the

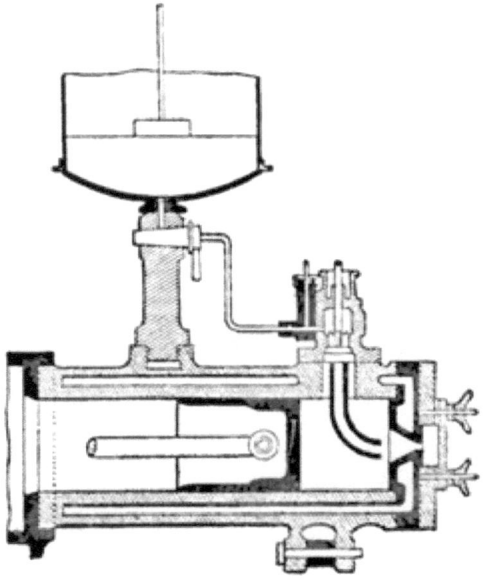

Fig. 97.—Longitudinal section of Spiel engine.

design of any oil engine the brand of oil to be used must be the first consideration of the designer.

The earliest oil engines worked with the light oils, such as gasolene, which vaporise at ordinary atmospheric temperatures. The method of working was to cause air to pass through scattered particles of the oil, and thus become saturated with oil vapour. It is said that the Lenoir oil engine developed 1 horse power hour by the consumption of 0·9 lb. of oil of 0·65 density.

SPIEL'S ENGINE.

In 1873 Brayton constructed an engine driven by a safe oil of 0·85 density, the consumption of which is stated to be 2 lb. per horse power hour. In this engine air was mixed with petroleum vapour by forcing the air at considerable pressure through the liquid. The mixture then passed to the cylinder through a network of wire gauze, the latter being kept hot by the exhaust products.

The Spiel engine, a longitudinal section of which is shown at fig. 97, is worked with light oil of specific gravity about

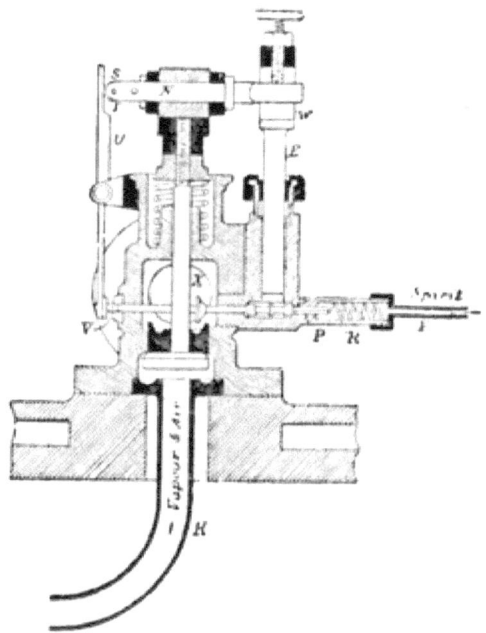

FIG. 98.—Supply valves of Spiel engine.

0·7. The liquid is contained in the upper chamber, from which it runs down the pipe F to the supply valves shown in detail in fig. 98. These valves act in the following way : A spiral spring R forces a double seated valve P towards the end V. Spirit, therefore, passes through the open valve and remains beneath the plunger E. A cam shown at M, fig. 99, gives a vertical motion to the crosshead N, fig. 98. Upon the down stroke of N, the roller S forces the upper end of the lever U outwards, thereby forcing the spindle V inwards, closing

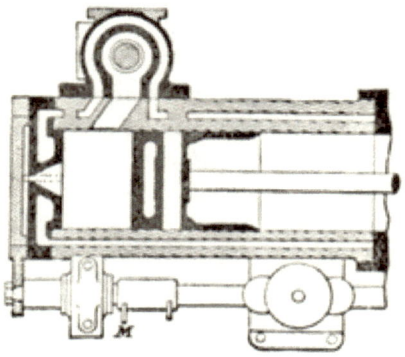

FIG. 99.—Sectional plan of Spiel engine.

the spirit valve P, and compressing the spiral spring R. The down stroke is prolonged until the spirit is discharged by the plunger E against a cone-shaped disc in the chamber X. The

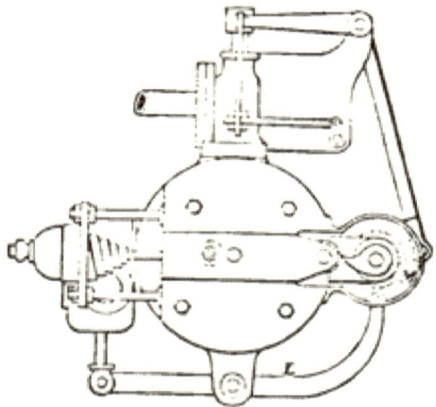

FIG. 100.—End view of Spiel engine.

function of this cone is to spray the spirit and to cause it to mix with air. During the downward movement of the plunger E the admission valve to the cylinder is opened, and the piston, on its outward stroke draws the spirit vapour and air down the pipe H. Ignition is caused by a moving slide, shown in figs. 97, 99, 100. The action of the slide is very similar to that of the early Otto slide ignition engines.

Simplex Carburator.—Messrs. Delamare-Devoutteville and Malandin have adopted an arrangement for supplying gas

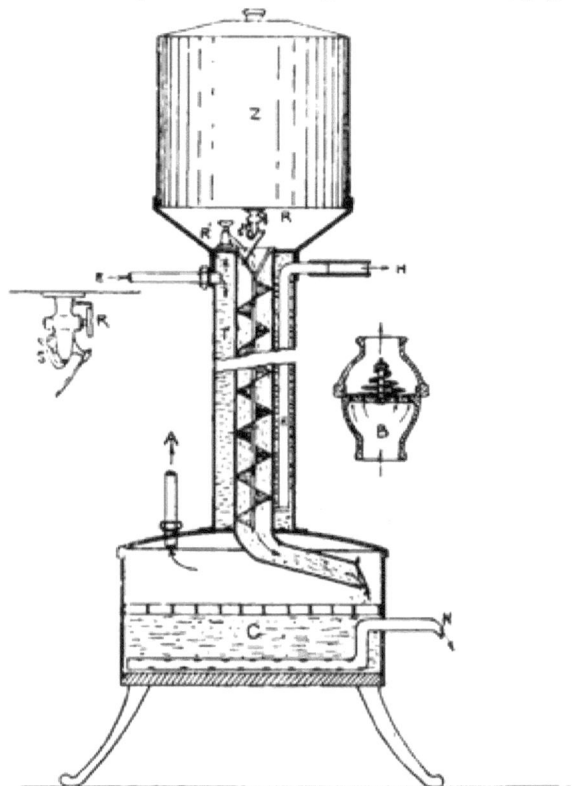

Fig. 101 —Simplex Carburator.

to their Simplex gas motors where a supply is otherwise unavailable. Fig. 101 shows a sectional elevation of this carburator. The spirit (density about 0·7) is contained in the tank Z. The pipe E conducts hot water from the engine jacket to a cylindrical casing T, whence it passes away through the pipe H. The central chamber contains a spiral wire brush, down which the spirit drops. Through the cock R a quantity of hot water is allowed to pass down the spiral; this assists in heating the spirit to completely vaporise it.

The water falls into the chamber C, whence it escapes through the pipe N. A perforated cork floats on the water, thus preventing the suction of water spray into the cylinder through the suction pipe A. The valve B is attached to the suction pipe A, and is used to prevent the return flow of high-pressure gases from the cylinder to the carburator. The supply of spirit is controlled by the action of the governor on the valve S.

The use of petroleum for firing boilers containing water has been successfully carried out, and economy has also been sought by evaporating spirit instead of water in the boiler. This arrangement is attended with considerable danger unless very carefully handled; at the same time it is true that certain thermal advantages result from the evaporation of spirit instead of water, on account of the smaller quantity of heat supplied to the spirit being rendered latent. These arrangements cannot be regarded as internal-combustion engines, and will not therefore be described.

CHAPTER XXI.

It is not our intention to traverse the early history of the oil engine. We shall at once, therefore, enter upon a description of the engines which have been made within the last few years. It will be understood that the main difference between the gas and oil engine is the addition to the former of some means of causing the oil to form an explosive mixture with air. This being so, our attention need only be directed to this matter; indeed, many makers are now building gas engines which may with very little trouble be converted into oil engines. This necessitates the addition of a vaporising chamber, which need be no encumbrance when the engine is worked by a supply of gas.

It has been the object of many inventors to construct an engine capable of working with heavy petroleum oils, instead of petroleum spirit. The inflammability of spirit, even when a light is applied at a distance of 2 in. or 3 in. from the spirit, renders its use highly dangerous; whereas petroleum oil will extinguish a lighted taper when, at ordinary atmospheric temperatures, the taper is plunged into the oil.

Although many attempts were made to utilise the heavy oils, none led to practical results until Messrs. Priestman, of Hull, having acquired Etève's patents, persevered with the constructive details, and were thus able to place a satisfactory engine upon the market in the year 1888.

In the Priestman engine the idea of spraying oil mingled with air into a heated chamber, called the vaporiser, was first brought forward.

Although it is now well known that oil may be vaporised without being finely divided into a spray and mixed with air, it is a noteworthy fact that the development of this class of motor proceeded on the lines indicated by Messrs. Priestman, and very great credit is due to this firm for their

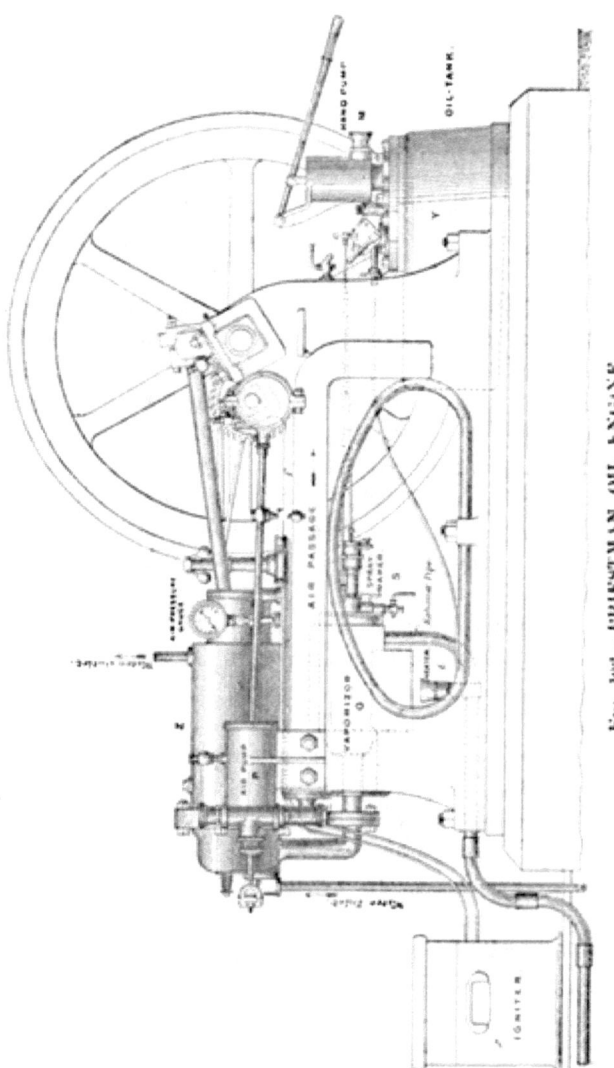

Fig. 102.—PRIESTMAN OIL ENGINE.

persevering efforts, which have resulted in the production of a motor of great economy and usefulness. The following description, together with the illustrations, will suffice to explain the working of the Priestman engine.

The oil is contained in a cast-iron tank Y, fig. 102, formed in the bed of the engine. The oil, with a supply of air under a pressure of about 8 lb. per square inch, is carried to the spray maker S; here they mix and break up into a fine vapour. This is then passed through a heating chamber, called the vaporiser (which latter is warmed by a lamp l

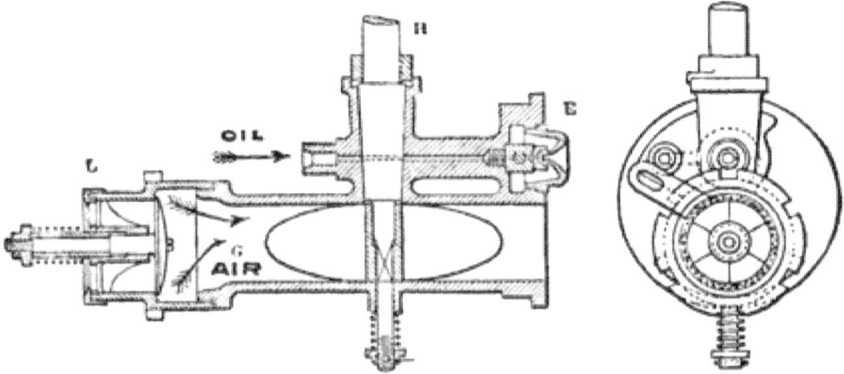

FIG. 103.—Section and End View of Spray Maker of Priestman Engine.

before starting, and is kept hot, when running, with the exhaust products). From this chamber the vapour is drawn into the engine cylinder, compressed by the piston, and ignited by an electric spark, or lamp and hot tube, as preferred. With the Edison L'alande system of creating the spark, an engine can be run for 500 to 1,000 hours without any attention being given to the two small cells. The governing is effected by regulating the quantity of oil, instead of by entirely stopping the supply. The piston is lubricated by the deposit of oil on the surface of the cylinder.

Fig. 103 shows a section of the spraying nozzle, and the wing valve for controlling the air supply. Oil is forced into the nozzle E by means of compressed air in the oil tank. On its way to the nozzle the oil passes through a tapered hole in the plug H, to the lower end of which the wing valve G is attached. The plug H is controlled by the governor, and it will be obvious that both the oil and air are simultaneously throttled, thus keeping the mixture uniform The nozzle E, a larger view of which is shown in fig. 104, is of special construction, and is the result of a long series of experiments. Oil enters the nozzle through the central opening, and the air is forced in through the annular space. It is an important feature in the construction of the nozzle that the air current is directed against the flow of oil. In the earlier

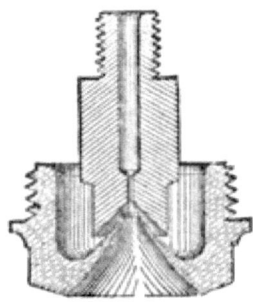

FIG. 104.—Spraying Nozzle, Priestman Oil Engine.

nozzles used by Messrs. Priestman the air and oil were made to flow in the same direction, where they mingled together. The form was, however, gradually altered, until it was found to give the best spray when made as in fig. 104.

For the ignition of the charge a simple bichromate cell may be used, with one induction coil.

The charge recommended for the battery is—

      8 parts by weight of bichromate of potash.
      6 parts by weight of sulphuric acid.
      80 parts by weight of water.

This charge will, if made up in ounces, last for about 30 hours, at a cost of about 6d.

PRIESTMAN OIL ENGINE.

The following figures have been obtained by Professor Unwin in a systematic test of a Priestman oil engine:

Loads.	I.H.P.	B.H.P.	Mechanical efficiency.	Oil per B.H.P. hour. Pounds.	Brand of oil used.	Mean effective pressure. Pounds sq. in.	Revolutions per minute.	Temperature of vaporising chamber.
Full load..	7·40	6·76	0·91	0·946	Russolene	41·38	207·73	264·5
Half load..	4·70	3·62	0·76	1·381	Russolene	25·48	214·29	254·0
No load...	0·889	..	..	I.H.P. 5·734	Russolene	5·51	187·3	260·5
Full load..	9·36	7·72	0·82	0·842	Royal Daylight	53·2	204·33	268·0

The dimensions of the engine from which these figures were obtained are as follow:

Diameter of cylinder	8·51 in.
Stroke	12·0 in.
Clearance in percentage of working volume	53 per cent.
Volume of air-compressing pump per stroke	0·0329 cu. ft.
Diameter	5·12 in.
Diameter of flywheel	4·61 ft.
Weight of engine without flywheel	26 cwt.
Weight of flywheel	10 cwt.

The oils used in the above trials yielded the following constituents:

	Russolene. Per cent.		Royal Daylight Per cent.
Carbon	85·88	....	84·62
Hydrogen	14·07	....	14·86
Oxygen, &c., by difference	0·05	....	0·52
	100·00		100·00

Density at 60 deg. Fah.	0·822	0·793
Flashing point (Abel test)	86 deg. Fah.	77 deg. Fah.
The calculated total calorific value	21,180	21,490
The calculated calorific value when steam formed is not condensed	19,957	20,198

The following is a résumé of the results of a trial conducted by Professor Unwin and Mr. D. Pidgeon, at the Royal Agricultural Show, Plymouth, in 1890:—

PRIESTMAN OIL-ENGINE TRIALS.

Loads.	I.H.P.	B.H.P.	Mechanical Efficiency	Oil per B.H.P. hour, Pounds.	Brand of oil used.	Mean effective pressure, Pounds sq. in.	Revolutions per minute.
Full load	5·24	4·49	0·85	1·066	Broxburn oil	33·96	179·5
Half load	3·21	2·36	0·73	1·460	Broxburn oil	20·65	180·8

ANALYSIS OF BROXBURN OIL.

Carbon	86·01	per cent.
Hydrogen	13·90	,,
Undetermined	0·09	,,

Calculated calorific value of Broxburn oil, when steam formed is not condensed, 19,700 British thermal units.

The Priestman oil engine has been successfully used for pumping, electric lighting, fog signalling, and for driving launches and barges. For the latter purpose Messrs. Priestman supply a patent reversible screw propeller, the blades of which can be inclined to drive ahead or astern without stopping the motor.

The Samuelson Oil Engine (Griffin's Patent).—This engine made by Messrs. Samuelson and Co. Limited, Banbury, and the Priestman engine, are the only two manufactured which work with the spray maker. The oil sprayer is shown in fig. 105. Its action is somewhat different from the Priestman nozzle, inasmuch as the oil is sucked up into the annular space surrounding the air nozzle by the action of the horizontal air jet; whereas in the Priestman engine the

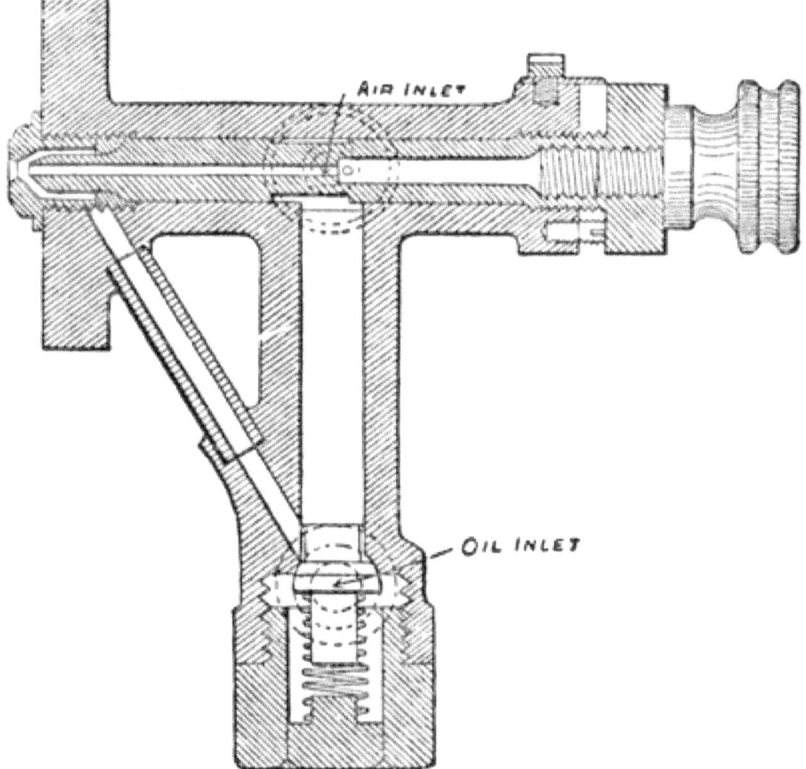

FIG. 105.—Griffin Patent Oil Sprayer.

oil occupies the central nozzle, and the air meets it at the orifice. The air pressure is maintained by an eccentric-driven pump, at about 12 lb. above atmosphere. The vaporiser is a long corrugated chamber, heated by the exhaust products. The governor is of the ordinary centrifugal pattern, and acts by cutting off the air supply, at the same time preventing the opening of the exhaust and admission valves. This method of governing has the advantage that the cylinder is not cooled by the admission of cold air when the engine is missing fire.

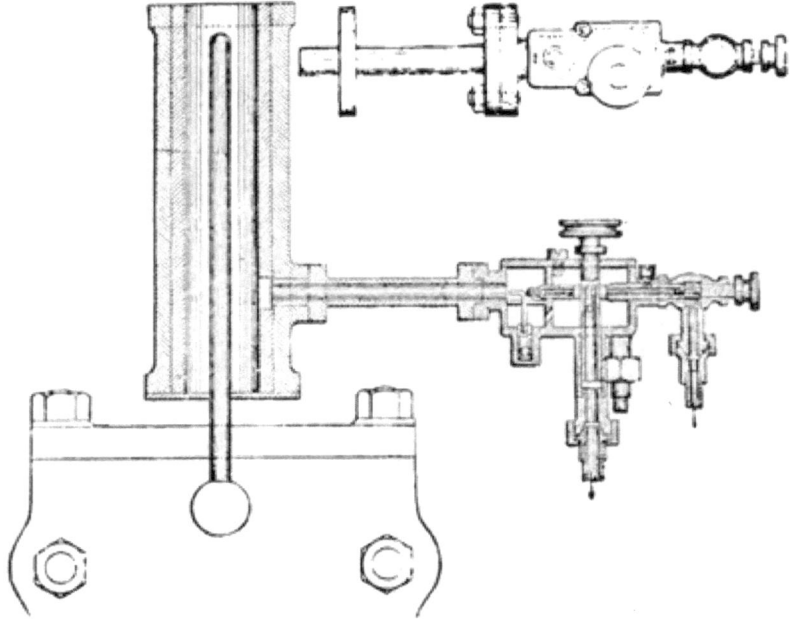

FIG. 106.—Samuelson's Igniting Arrangement.

The igniting arrangements are shown in fig. 106. An air jet plays upon a piece of bent wire, which latter dips into a chamber filled with oil to a constant level. The air jet draws a film of oil up the wire, carries the oil forward in the form of spray, and the mixture burns around the ignition tube. In starting this engine a hand pump is used to compress air for the ignition spray and for the vaporiser sprayer. Both are lighted, and the engine allowed to stand for about ten minutes, until the vaporiser is hot enough to work. The length of the ignition tube has apparently no little influence upon the form of card obtained, due no doubt to the fact that the charge does not get compressed into the hottest part of the tube when the latter is too short.

The Hornsby-Akroyd Oil Engine.—This engine is made by Messrs. Hornsby and Sons Limited, Grantham, and works upon an entirely different principle to those previously described. No sprayer is employed, neither is there an ignition tube to the engine. Fig. 107 shows a transverse section through the vaporiser. The action of the engine is extremely simple. A small quantity of oil is injected into the vaporiser, with a little air. The oil quickly spreads

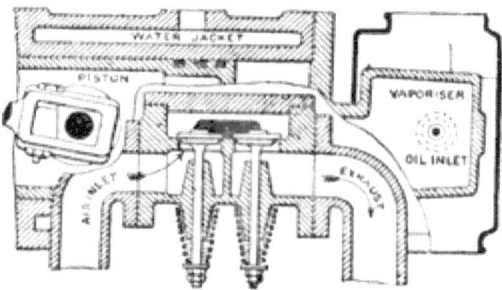

Fig. 107.—Section through Valves and Cylinder of Hornsby-Akroyd Oil Engine.

itself over a large surface of the hot walls of the vaporiser, and is consequently quickly evaporated. The vaporising chamber contains only the products of combustion of the previous charge at the moment the oil is injected. As the engine piston makes its outward stroke, fresh air is drawn into the cylinder through valves and passages which have no connection with the vaporising chamber; hence at the end of the outstroke of the piston the cylinder is filled with pure air, whilst the vaporiser is charged with oil vapour, mixed with the products of combustion of a previous charge. The charge in the vaporiser is not combustible until more fresh air is forced into it by the return stroke of the piston. During the instroke the piston drives the air from the cylinder into the vaporiser, thus rendering the charge in the latter highly explosive. When the compression is completed the temperature of the vaporising chamber is sufficiently high to cause ignition of the charge. It will be understood that correct proportion between the cylinder volume and that of the vaporising chamber is essential for the successful working of the engine. To determine this Messrs. Hornsby carried out numerous experiments. The area of the neck of the vaporising chamber is another important factor. This must be small enough to prevent the diffusion of the gases during the outstroke of the piston. Another rather important function of the small neck of the vaporising chamber is to control the flow of heat from the vaporiser

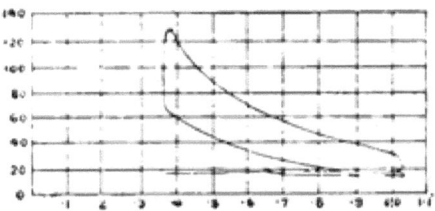

FIG. 108.—Indicator Diagram from Hornsby-Akroyd Oil Engine.

to the cylinder water jacket. By making the vaporiser without jacket, and suitably proportioning the area of metal at the neck, a proper temperature is maintained to ignite the charge every cycle. A lamp is provided to heat the vaporiser before starting the engine; afterwards the heat of combustion is sufficient to maintain it at a proper temperature.

The Hornsby engine was awarded the first prize in competition with nine other makers at the Royal Agricultural Show at Cambridge. According to the report of the trials, written by Professor Capper, this engine ran without hitch of any kind from start to finish. One attendant only was employed all through the trials, and he started the engine easily and with certainty, after working the hand blast to the lamp for eight minutes. The longest time taken to start was nine minutes, and the shortest seven. The revolutions were very constant, and the power developed did not vary one-quarter of a brake horse power from day to day. The oil consumption, reckoned on the average of the three days' run, was 0·919 lb. per brake horse power hour, including the oil used for the starting lamp. The oil used was Russolene, sold at Cambridge at that time for 3¾d. per gallon. The cost of oil per brake horse power hour is therefore about ¾d. At half-load the oil consumption was found to be 1·49 lb. per brake horse power hour.

The Hornsby engine is governed by the interception of the oil supply through a by-pass valve, thus decreasing the explosion pressures as the speed rises. It is important that the firing should take place regularly every cycle, as otherwise the temperature of the vaporiser is liable to become too low.

Fig. 108 shows a mean indicator diagram, taken from a Hornsby-Akroyd engine on full-power trial. The maximum explosion pressure was about 130 lb. per square inch, the mean pressure about 29 lb. per square inch.

Crossley Engine.—Fig. 109 shows a sectional elevation and plan of the Crossley vaporiser. The valve to the left of the plan view is held upon its seat by a spiral spring, but opens communication to the cylinder during the outstroke of the piston. The governor acts upon this valve by a hit-and-miss arrangement, so that as the speed of the engine rises the valve is not opened. During the outstroke of the piston air follows through a separate automatic valve, held upon its seat by a spring; consequently there is a considerable suction through the passages connected to the valve shown when the latter is opened. Through these passages hot air and oil are simultaneously drawn, the oil entering at the pipe shown in the plan. The air enters the annular space round the chimney shown in elevation, and passes downwards to meet the oil.

A lamp is continually burning beneath the vaporiser, and,

besides heating the latter, its flame plays upon the ignition tube, which is connected to the combustion chamber of the engine. The products of combustion of the heating lamp pass up through the square holes shown in the vaporiser. In this way the heating surface is largely increased. The

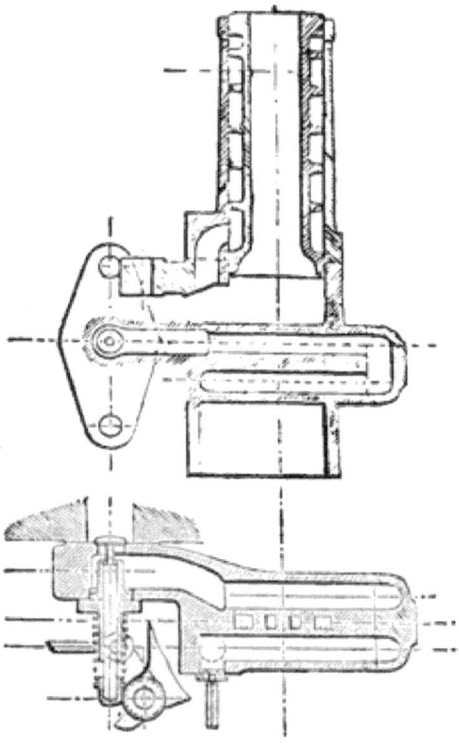

Fig. 109.—Sectional Elevation and Plan of Crossley's Vaporiser

average time taken to start the Crossley engine, at the Royal Agricultural Show trials at Cambridge, was, according to Professor Capper's report, 16 minutes. The engine ran without giving trouble, the governing was good, and the power developed was uniform throughout the trials.

The Wells Engine.—The oil feed to this engine is delivered by means of a rotating plug, driven by the link R, fig. 110

This plug allows a measured quantity of oil to drop on the inclined surface shown at V. Here it becomes vaporised by the high temperature maintained by an oil lamp and automatic air blast. The lever L is operated by a cam on the side shaft, and rocks upon a pin fixed in the boss E. The lower end of the lever opens the exhaust valve when pressed inwards against the tension of the spiral spring placed at its upper end. On the return stroke of the lever the oil plug is rotated, and oil emitted to the vaporiser at V; at the same time the air valve A is opened by the adjustable stud

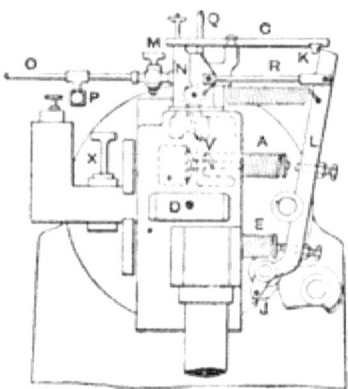

Fig. 110.—Arrangement of Valves and Levers in Wells' Oil Engine.

on the lever L. By this ingenious arrangement all the valves are controlled by the one lever.

The governing is effected by the horizontal link C. This link is balanced so that its position of equilibrium is such that the upper end of the lever L clears the point K when the former is moving from right to left. When the upper end of the lever L is moved outwards by the cam, the horizontal lever C is drawn downwards; when released it recovers its position of equilibrium in a definite time, depending upon the spring adjustment at M. If the speed of the engine be increased so that L moves inwards before K has risen, then the further movement of the lever is arrested by the catch K. In this way the exhaust valve is kept open, allowing the hot products of combustion to return into the cylinder; at the same time the oil and air valves are prevented from opening. The ignition of the charge is effected by means of a tube, heated by an auxiliary lamp.

Trusty Oil Engine.—Sectional views of this engine, which is made by Messrs. Weyman and Hitchcock, are shown at figs. 111 and 113, and an end view at fig. 112. The oil supply is pumped, together with a little air, into the tube C, fig. 111, and in falling to the bottom of the annular space

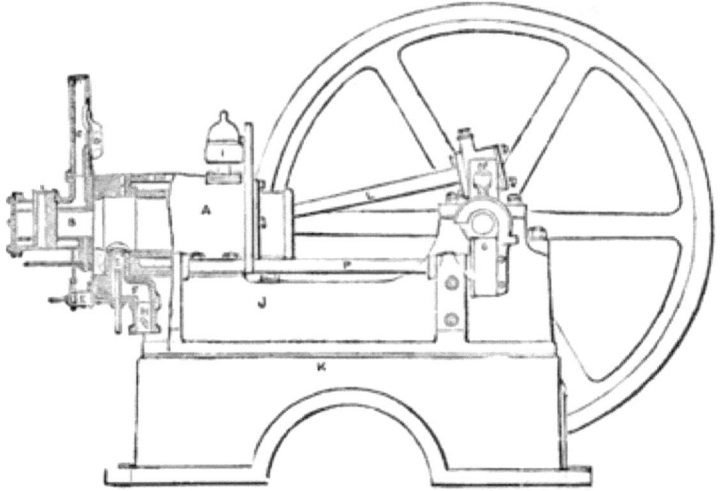

Fig. 111.—Section through Cylinder and Vaporiser of the Trusty Oil Engine.

becomes vaporised. The mixture then rises through the vapour valve, fig. 113, into the inner chamber, and passes away from there into the combustion chamber. Here it is mixed with more air, which enters the cylinder through valve F, fig. 111, on the outstroke of the piston. Ignition may be effected by contact with the hot chamber, though usually the ordinary hot tube igniter is used.

The following is an extract of a trial made by Mr. W. Worby Beaumont, M.Inst.C.E., on the Trusty engine, in 1893. The dimensions of the engine were as follow: Diameter of cylinder, 7·375 in.; length of stroke, 14 in.;

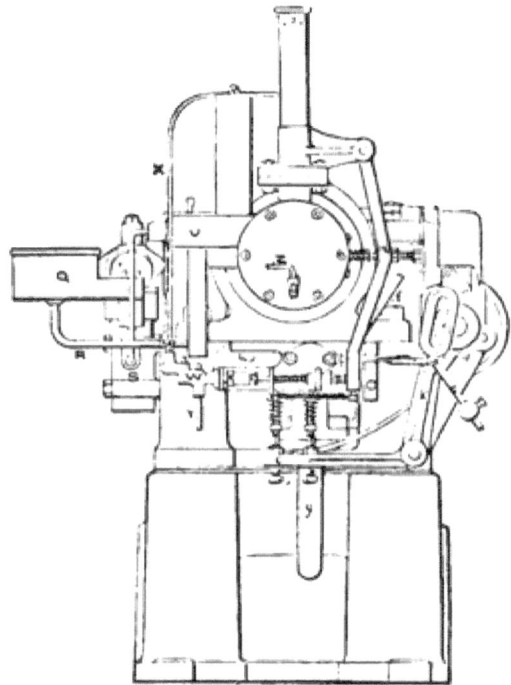

Fig. 112. - Arrangement of Valves, Levers, &c., in Weyman and Hitchcock's Trusty Oil Engine.

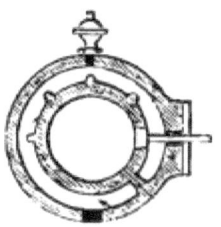

Fig. 113. — End Section of Trusty Vaporiser.

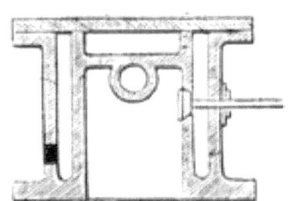

Fig. 113a.—Sectional Plan of Trusty Vaporiser.

revolutions per minute, 248; flywheel diameter, 5 ft. According to Mr. Beaumont's report, the engine works equally well with all kinds of lamp oil.

"The duration of the several trials was: Full power, four hours; half power, two hours; running light, one hour. The intended full-power load was 6 horse power, and the brake load was adjusted as nearly as possible to this. The running of the engine was very regular, and when at half power the speed was within 0·4 of 1 per cent of that of full power. The oil used in the trials was Royal Daylight, costing in quantities about 4d. per gallon. Its specific gravity was found to be 0·802, one pint thus weighing 1·0025 lb."

The general results of the trials are as follow:—

	Full power.	Half power.	Running light.
Brake horse power	5·98	3·32	..
Indicated horse power	7·04	5·48	2·72
Mechanical efficiency	84 %	61 %	..
Oil used per B.H.P. hour .... lbs	0·82	1·12	..
Oil used per I.H.P. hour .... lbs.	0·69	0·68	0·82

COST OF FUEL FOR TRUSTY OIL ENGINE WITH OIL AT FOURPENCE PER GALLON.

	Cost per I.H.P. hour.	Cost per B.H.P. hour.
Engine with full load	0·348d.	0·410d.
Engine with half load	0·342d.	0·565d.
Engine running light	0·406d.	....

The above figures do not include the cost of oil for heating the lamp. This is, however, small, and was found to be from 6 oz. to 7 oz. per hour. Thus, on the average, the total cost may be taken as not exceeding 0·4d. per I.H.P. hour.

CHAPTER XXII.

Campbell's Oil Engine.—The vaporiser of this engine is roughly shown in fig. 114. It is of simple construction, and acts in the following way: The automatic valve is held up to its seating by the spiral spring. Beneath the valve is a port communicating with the cylinder, and through this port the charge of vaporised oil and air is drawn. Oil is led through the small pipe into the annular passage surrounding the valve. When the piston moves outwards it

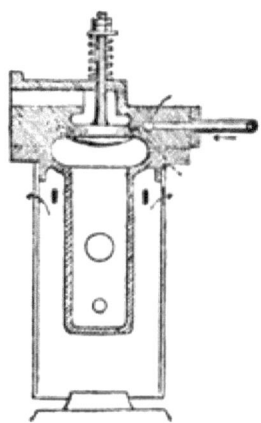

FIG. 114.—Campbell's Vaporiser

acts as a pump and draws air past the valve. At the same time the annular passage is thus opened for the admission of oil to the vaporiser. The oil drops upon the walls of the vaporiser, which is heated by a lamp beneath it. This lamp also heats the ignition tube. The governing is effected by intercepting the oil supply and by holding open the exhaust valve, thus allowing the exhaust products to return to the cylinder instead of drawing air through the automatic valve. The time taken to start the engine during the Royal Agricultural Society's trials was somewhat lengthened by attempting to start before the vaporiser was hot enough. With a larger lamp the time might have been reduced to about 10 minutes to heat the vaporiser.

The Britannia Company's Engine is the invention of Mr. Roots. Fig. 115 shows a section through the vaporiser of the Britannia oil engine made under Roots' patents. I is the ignition tube, which is surrounded by the casing H.

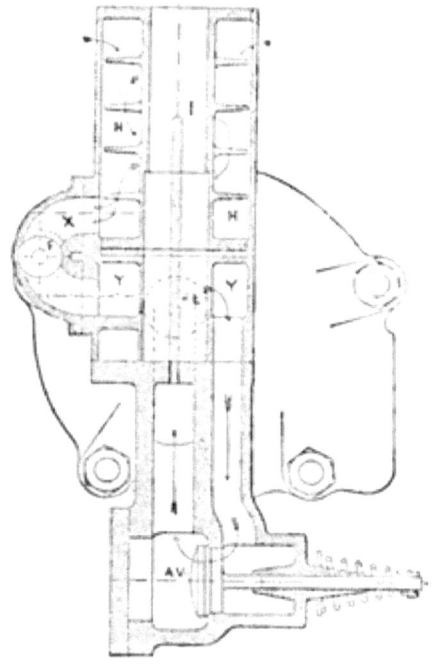

FIG. 115.—Section through the Vaporiser of the Britannia Oil Engine. The arrows show the direction of flow of the air.

Air enters the casing, and in passing round the spiral passages it becomes heated by the same lamp used to heat the ignition tube. During the outstroke of the piston the air is sucked from H, through the elbow at X, to Y, and so passes into the cylinder through the valve A V. As the air sweeps through the passages marked X, it carries away with it a certain quantity of oil from the grooves of a spindle which enters the chamber X at the point marked F. The oil is vaporised by contact with the hot walls of the chamber Y, and passes off with the air to the cylinder. On the return stroke of the piston the vapour is compressed into the ignition tube and ignited.

The way in which the oil is carried into the chamber, shown at X, fig. 115, is further illustrated in fig. 116. The spindle is here shown at A A, and the side view of the

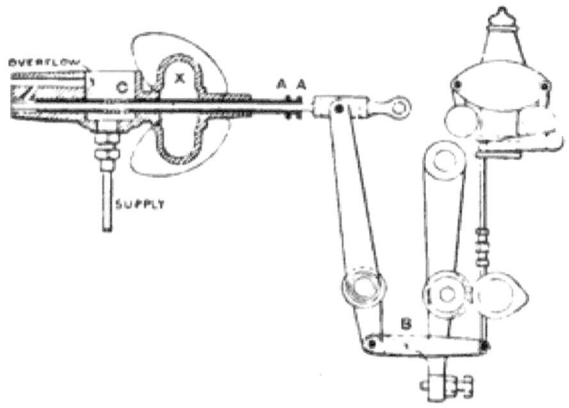

Fig. 116.—Arrangement of Oil Supply and Governor Gear of the Britannia Oil Engine.

chamber X shows the spindle A A passing through it. This spindle has grooves cut upon it, which are shown in the oil cavity C, fig. 116. The quantity of oil entering the chamber X is regulated by the governor. As the speed rises the piece B is lifted, so that all the grooves on the spindle do not enter the chamber X; thus the oil supply is reduced.

According to Professor Capper's report, from which we have produced the illustration, this engine gave no trouble in working. The average revolutions on each of the three days of the Cambridge trials did not vary, though there was some racing of the engine in spite of the ingenious method of governing.

The Capitaine Oil Engine is made by Messrs. Tolch and Co., of London, and its distinguishing features are shown in figs. 117 and 118. Fig. 117 shows the upper end of the vertical combustion chamber. On the outstroke of the piston air enters the automatic valve shown at B. The greater volume of air passes into the cylinder round the outside of the case D, whilst some air necessarily passes through the conical hole C. The part C is kept at a high temperature by the explosion, its heat being retained by the non-conducting substance surrounding it.

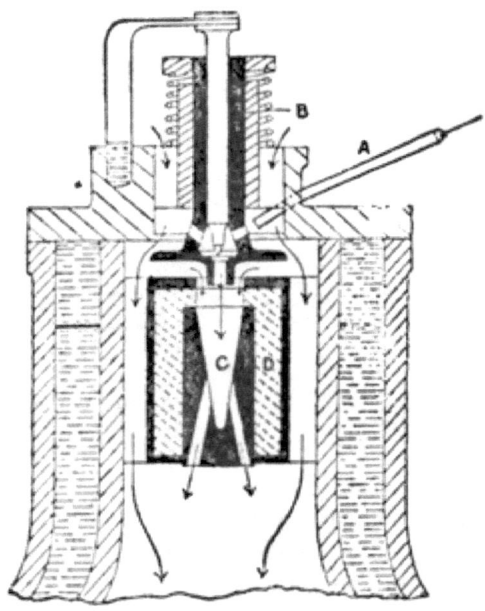

FIG. 117.—Section through Vaporiser and Combustion Chamber of Tolch and Co.'s Capitaine Engine.

Oil enters by the pipe A, and, passing through the hole in the air valve B, drops into C, and is vaporised. The central spindle within the valve B closes the oil passage to C, when the valve is in its uppermost position. The governing is effected by holding open the exhaust valve, so that B remains closed during the outstroke, and no air or oil is passed into the cylinder.

The delivery of oil to the pipe A is effected by the plunger pump B, shown in fig. 118. This pump works in a glycerine bath. Oil floats upon the surface of the glycerine and passes into the pipe A, fig. 117, through the slide valve A, fig. 118.

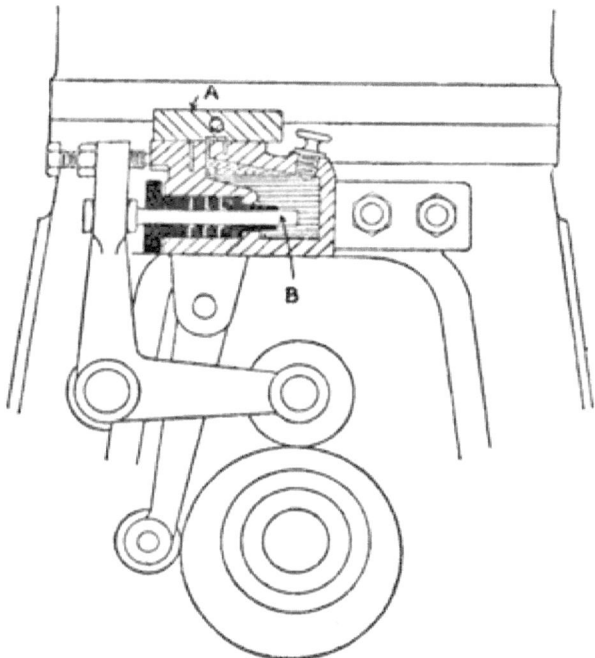

FIG. 118.—Glycerine Pump of Tolch and Co.'s Capitaine Engine.
A—Slide Valve.   B—Pump Plunger.

Professor Capper says: "The oil ordinarily used in this engine is Tea Rose, and some difficulty was experienced in keeping the vaporiser hot enough to work with Russolene. Experience with the use of Russolene oil may be expected to overcome these difficulties, and the engine certainly deserves praise for its particularly quiet running, and for the ingenuity as well as simplicity of its working parts."

Tangye's vaporiser, made under Pinkney's patents, is shown in fig. 119. The vaporising chamber is in direct communication with the cylinder. Air is drawn in through the mushroom valve, and meets oil fed by gravity from a tank to the hole on the valve seating. Thus, when the valve opens by the suction of the piston, oil drops through into the vaporiser. To govern the engine the exhaust valve

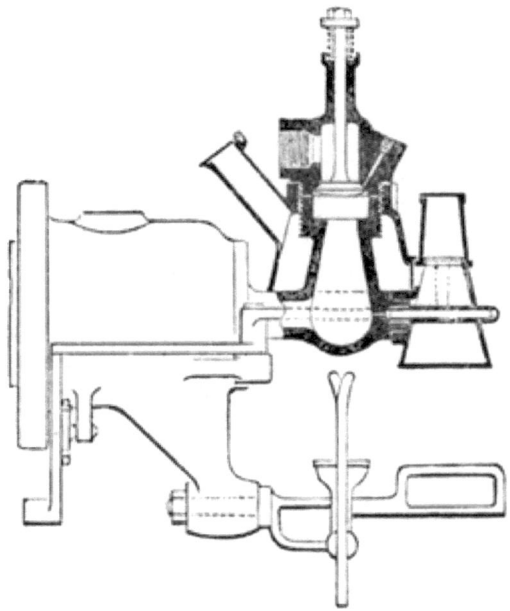

FIG. 119.—Tangye's Vaporiser.

is kept open and the automatic valve remains closed during the suction stroke, thus preventing the admission of fresh air or oil to the cylinder. A lamp placed beneath the ignition tube heats both the vaporiser and the tube. Before starting, the lamp is placed immediately beneath the vaporiser.

The Fielding Oil Engine is constructed by Messrs. Fielding and Platt Limited, of Gloucester. The engine works in a similar way to a gas engine, with the exception of the additional parts required to vaporise the oil. A longitudinal section of the vaporiser is shown in fig. 120. This vaporiser consists of two tubes, one above the other, the lower one being heated by the lamp to a bright red, whilst the upper one is kept at a lower temperature. Two copper tubes, at a high temperature, connect the air inlet shown to the upper vaporiser tube. V is an automatic valve, drawn open by the outstroke of the engine piston. The action of the engine

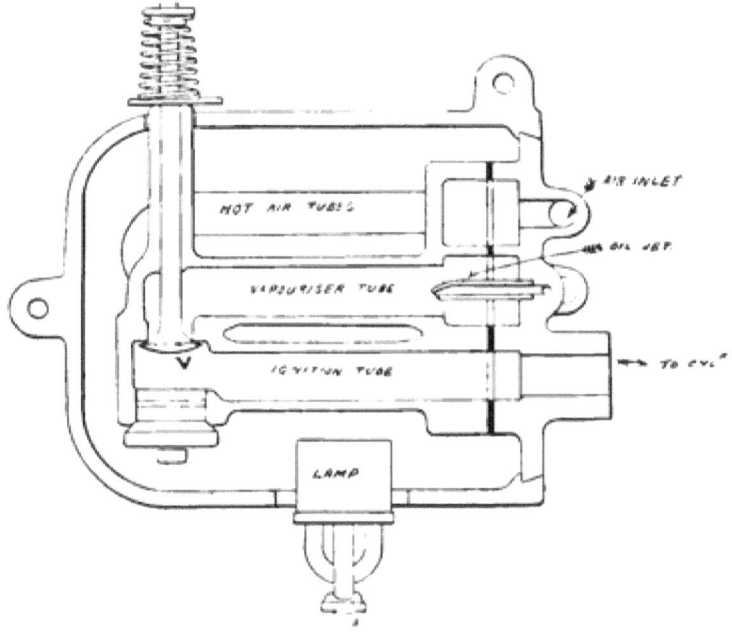

FIG. 120.—The Fielding Vaporiser.

is as follows : During the outstroke of the engine piston, air is drawn into the cylinder through a valve in the combustion chamber (not shown). The valve V also opens, and a current of hot air sweeps through the ignition tube into the cylinder. Oil vapour, which has been pumped into the vaporiser tube mixes with this air, but is not ignited by the ignition tube because of the inferior quantity of air drawn through the valve V. When the vapour charge enters the cylinder it mingles with the pure air entering by another valve, and thus forms an explosive mixture, which ignites when part of it is compressed back into the ignition tube. Fig. 121 shows an end view of the engine.

The speed is controlled by a centrifugal governor, which props up the exhaust valve lever and the oil pump rod. Hence no oil is injected into the vaporiser, nor is pure air

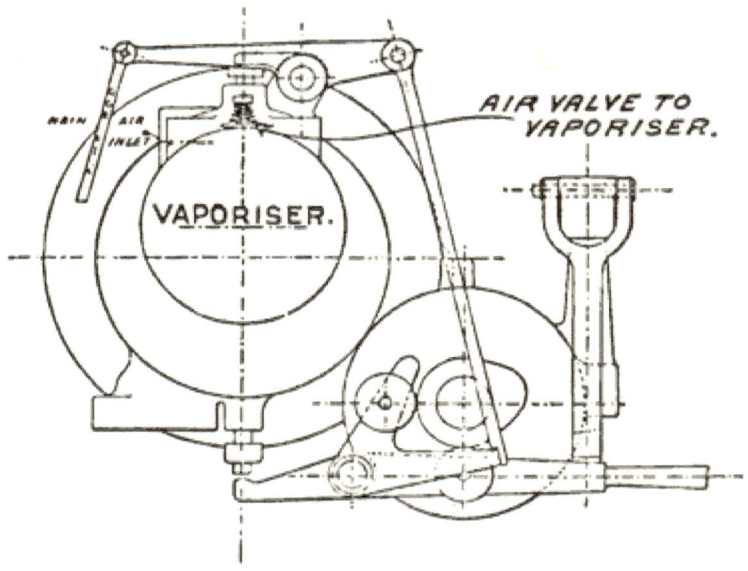

FIG. 121.—Elevation showing Arrangement of Valve Levers and Trip Gear of Fielding and Platt's Oil Engine.

drawn into the cylinder through either of the valves. This engine ran very steadily during the Cambridge trials, starting readily with one attendant after the vaporiser tubes were heated for about 20 minutes. This engine was, however, withdrawn from the competitive trials on account of slight defects in the heating lamp, which have since been remedied.

A section of Messrs. Clayton and Shuttleworth's method of igniting is shown in fig. 122. A steel needle projects into the combustion chamber. This needle is surrounded by a number of strips of asbestos millboard. The heat retained by this arrangement keeps the needle at a sufficiently high temperature to ignite the charge when it is compressed. A tube shown in the illustration serves for ignition when starting the engine. The igniter is said to work satisfactorily even at low loads.

As illustrating a class of oil engines working with light oil now upon the market, we reproduce a section of the

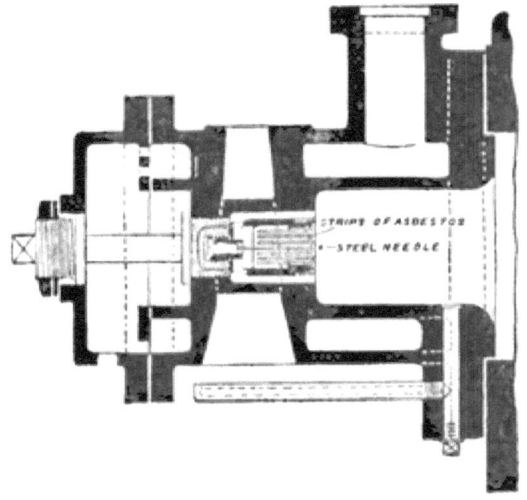

FIG. 122 —Section of Clayton and Stuttleworth's Oil Engine Igniter.

Daimler motor, fig. 123. This engine has been very successfully applied to motor cars, and works as follows: The small tank P is fed with benzolene. A float in the tank operates a check valve, which keeps the oil at a proper level in the tank. Upon the outstroke of the piston air enters the passage q, and, passing over the oil pipe v, induces a small quantity of benzolene to pass into q in the form of a fine spray. The air and benzolene pass into the cylinder through the automatic valve m. The piston returns, closes m, and compresses the charge into the igniting tube o. The exhaust takes place through the valve *n*, which is lifted by the rod X. The governing is effected by holding the

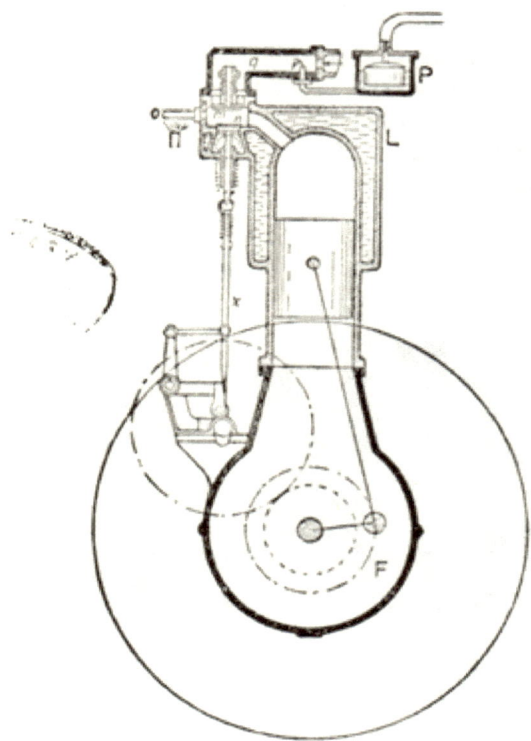

Fig. 123.—Daimler Motor (1895).

exhaust valve open, so that the burnt gases return to the cylinder, thereby destroying the partial vacuum, which would otherwise open the valve *m*.

CHAPTER XXIII.
OIL ENGINE TESTING.

IN a previous chapter we have described in great detail the method of testing gas engines. Much that has been said in reference thereto will readily be applied to the testing of oil engines. There are, however, some points arising in connection with oil-engine testing which require special consideration.

In the first place, it is convenient to arrange the oil supply in tanks calibrated to give the *weight* of oil. The calibration should be separately determined for each class of oil used, on account of the different density of the brands of oil now upon the market.

In testing gas engines the quantity of air per stroke is not difficult to obtain by difference, when the volume of gas in the cylinder is known. The measurement of the air supplied for combustion of the charge in an oil engine may present some difficulty, but unless this be determined the heat account cannot be ascertained. When air is supplied by a pump, an estimate of the volume may be made from the pump dimensions, though this is not satisfactory. It may, in some instances, be necessary to measure the air by arranging a suitable air trunk, and in it placing an anemometer. In the author's opinion this instrument is not reliable; nevertheless, if it be carefully tested, a correction curve may be plotted, by the application of which fairly accurate results may be obtained.

In dealing with gas-engine trials, a simple method of analysing the gases used was described. We shall now describe an equally simple method of making a determination of the carbon and hydrogen in a sample of petroleum. Although most engineers, in conducting trials, usually place samples for analysis in the hands of trained chemists, it is, nevertheless, a great advantage, when much testing is being done, to be able to perform these simple analyses oneself.

The various petroleum oils consist chiefly, as we have previously pointed out, of carbon and hydrogen. The sum of the weights of these two substances is found to be very nearly 100 per cent. The undetermined weight may amount to 0.5 per cent, and this may be neglected in engine trial calculations. The method about to be described is due to Liebig, who made use of the fact that if the substance to be analysed be mixed with an excess of copper oxide, and the whole be heated to redness, the carbon will reduce the oxide and pass off as carbon dioxide; at the same time the hydrogen will pass off as water vapour. The carbon dioxide is absorbed by caustic potash; the water is absorbed by calcium chloride. The additional weight of these substances after absorption has taken place gives the carbon and hydrogen.

The analysis may be done in the following way: A combustion tube of hard glass about $\frac{3}{4}$ in. bore and 2 ft. long, open at one end and drawn out to a point at the other, is supported upon a light iron stand. A row of Bunsen burners is placed beneath the tube, and a sheet of asbestos arranged round the tube and the flames, in order to concentrate the latter upon the tube. Take about 0.5 gram of petroleum, and place it in a small soft glass tube, the weight of which (empty) is known. Fill the tube, seal at both ends, and carefully weigh again. Subtract from the total weight, when full, the weight of the glass tube, and so obtain the net weight of petroleum. When heavy oil is being analysed the tube need not be sealed, but in the case of light volatile oils the evaporation constantly going on at atmospheric temperature renders it impossible to determine the weight accurately unless the tube is sealed. Place the sealed tube near the closed end of the combustion tube. Then fill the remainder of the combustion tube with copper oxide.

Attach to the open end of the combustion tube a bulb

containing porous calcium chloride, so that all the gas generated passes through this bulb first. From this bulb the gas must pass into another vessel, containing a concentrated solution of caustic potash. When the weights of these vessels are ascertained, and all the joints of the tubes carefully tested, the analysis may be made. First light the burners near the open end of the combustion tube until the copper oxide becomes heated. Gradually heat the tube towards the sealed end. When the petroleum sample becomes hot the soft glass vessel in which it is contained will burst by the expansion of the liquid, and the process of reduction will commence. To prevent a violent explosion, the liquid should completely fill the sealed vessel. The products of combustion will bubble through the bulbs until the petroleum is consumed. When the gases cease to pass through, break off the sealed end of the combustion tube, and inspire the gaseous contents of the latter into the absorption vessels by means of a rubber tube.

Weigh the absorption bulbs after the process is completed, and so obtain the weights of the carbon dioxide and water. The carbon dioxide is composed of 12 parts of carbon to 32 parts of oxygen ; hence $\frac{12}{44}$ or $\frac{3}{11}$ of the weight of carbon dioxide gives the weight of carbon in the petroleum sample. The weight of hydrogen will be found by multiplying the weight of water formed by $\frac{1}{9}$.

This method is satisfactory, provided you have a large excess of freshly ignited copper oxide in the combustion tube. There is, however, a liability to the formation of carbon in the combustion tube, in which case the analysis is incomplete. A modification of the above apparatus is as follows : Arrange the combustion tube with a free passage through both ends. To the end of the potash absorption bulb attach an aspirator tube, so that air or oxygen may be passed over to consume the petroleum. Whether air or oxygen be used, a calcium chloride drier should be attached to the combustion tube where the air enters, in order to absorb all moisture that might be otherwise carried over into the absorption bulb, and credited to the hydrogen. This method has the advantage that the reduced copper may be re-oxidised by passing over a large excess of oxygen while the analysis is being carried out.

With respect to the heat given to the engine, this may be calculated from the calorific value of the oil. To determine the calorific value of oil two methods may be adopted. The determination may be made by calculation from the analysis, or by the direct combustion of a known quantity of oil in some form of calorimeter. Neither method is in itself quite satisfactory. Calculated values are often found to be higher than those obtained by calorimetric tests. On the other hand, the calorimeters at present available are not perfectly satisfactory.

To calculate the heat value of oil from the analysis—
Let C = the percentage of carbon by weight;
H = the percentage of hydrogen by weight.
Then, $14500 \{C + 4\cdot28 H\}$ = *total* heat value per pound of oil.

This value includes the heat given up by cooling all the products of combustion to atmospheric temperature (60 deg. Fah.). For each pound of oil burnt about $1\frac{1}{4}$ lb. of water (according to the weight of hydrogen) is formed. If, therefore, this product passes off in the form of steam, as is inevitable in the case of internal combustion engines, the question arises, should the latent heat of the steam be deducted from the calorific value in working out the heat efficiency of the motor? The answer to the question is more a matter of opinion than of right. Both methods have been adopted in the treatment of trials. This point should, however, be referred to when reporting an engine trial, and the method adopted should be clearly stated. The author prefers to *deduct* from the calorific value of the oil the units of heat passing away with the steam.

The following example of this calculation will suffice: Upon analysis the oil yields—Carbon, 84·92 per cent; hydrogen, 15·03 per cent; undetermined, 0·05 per cent.

14,500 is taken as the calorific value of carbon, and 14,500 × 4·28 is the calorific value of hydrogen; hence the formula
$$14500 \{C + 4\cdot 28 \, H\} = \text{total heat}.$$

In the example given,
$$14500 \{0\cdot 8492 + 4\cdot 28 \times 0\cdot 1503\} = \text{total heat},$$
$$= 21641 \text{ B.T.U.}$$

But 1 lb. of oil will yield $9 \times 0\cdot 1503$ lb. of water. Each pound of water will carry away 966 units; therefore, the units to be deducted from the total value $= 9 \times 0\cdot 1503 \times 966 = 1306$.

Therefore effective calculated value
$$= 21641 - 1306,$$
$$= 20335 \text{ units}.$$

With respect to the indicating of oil engines, there is great difficulty in obtaining satisfactory diagrams with some engines, more especially when the engine is being forced by the use of excessive oil supply. Hence the indicated horse power is seldom reliable, and in all cases comparisons should be made on the brake power.

After reading the description of the vaporisers used by the leading makers of oil engines, it will be noticed that all engines working with heavy oils vaporise in one of the following ways: (1) Oil is injected, together with the whole of the air supply, into a large vaporising chamber, separate from the cylinder, or (2) oil is injected into a small vaporising chamber, together with some air, but the greater volume of air enters the cylinder through a separate air valve; (3) same as (2), but all the air goes through the vaporiser; (4) oil is injected into the combustion chamber, and is vaporised therein. Air is drawn into the cylinder through a separate air valve, and mingles with the oil vapour when compressed into the combustion chamber. The first method undoubtedly possesses the advantage that the mixture of the vapour with the air is more complete.

Detracting somewhat from this, there is the fact that a large volume of highly-explosive vapour is contained in the vaporiser, and back firing might occur with serious results. It will be observed that in this type of engine the whole of the air is heated before entering the cylinder; hence the weight of the charge is considerably reduced, and the mean pressure thereby reduced. It is sometimes suggested that difficulties in the governing are encountered by the use of this vaporiser. For if the explosions are discontinued by the cutting-out system of governing, then the vaporiser cools. Messrs. Priestman obviate this by their regulation of the oil and air supply, thus keeping the engine running even at light loads without missing fire. This method seems to be prejudicial to the economic consumption of oil at light loads. According to Professor Unwin's paper[*] on the Priestman oil engine, the consumption, when running with *no load*, was over 5 lb. of oil (Russolene) per hour whereas when the engine was doing nearly 7 brake horse power the oil consumption was only $3\frac{1}{2}$ lb. per hour—that is, 0·988 lb. per brake horse power. Thus it appears that the method of reducing the oil supply, even though the air is also reduced, is prejudicial to economy.

From an analysis of the trials (see table of oil engine dimensions and consumptions) there appears little to choose between the various classes of vaporisers. It is important, however, to note the difference existing between vaporisers working with all the air passing through and those with only a portion. The cooling effect of the air in the former case should be carefully considered in designing the vaporiser. Results show that either methods give excellent results, as far as consumption. The mean pressure in Crossley's and Fielding's engines exceed those of other types. The mean pressure in the Hornsby-Akroyd engine (of class 4) is lower than any other. A large size of cylinder is therefore required. This is, however, compensated for by simplicity of parts and general neatness.

---

[*] Inst. C.E. Proceedings. Vol. cix. 1892.

TABLE OF OIL ENGINE DIMENSIONS AND CONSUMPTIONS.

Name of engine.	Cylinder sizes.			Full load indicator diagrams.			Maximum.			Oil used.	Oil consumption at full load.		Oil consumption at half load.		Method of governing.	Class of vaporiser. (See definitions in text.)	Revolutions per minute.	Authority.
	Diameter.	Stroke.	Clearance volume.	Maximum pressure.	Mean pressure.	Compress'n pressure.	I.H.P.	B.H.P.	Mechanical efficiency.		Per I.H.P. hour.	B.H.P. hour.	Per I.H.P. hour.	B.H.P. hour.				
	in.	in.	c. in.	lbs. s. in.	lbs. sq. in.	lbs. s. in.			Per cent.		lbs.	lbs.	lbs.	lbs.				
Priestman	8½	12	363	151	53·2	35	9·37	7·72	82	Royal Daylight	0·694	0·842	1·063 Russolene	1·281 Russolene	Variable oil and air supply	No. 1	210	Professor Unwin
Hornsby-Akroyd.	10	15	638	130	28·9	65	10·3	8·57	83	Russolene	0·81	0·977	..	1·49	Variable oil supply	No. 4	239	Professor Capper
Crossley	7	15	2·6	238	72·2	82	7·9	7·01	88	Russolene	0·73	0·82	..	1·03	Intercepts oil supply	No. 3	200	Professor Capper
Wells' "Premier"	8½	15	360	..	40·6	..	7·3	6·46	89	Royal Daylight	0·93	1·04	..	1·39	Exhaust kept open. Oil intercepted	No. 3	169	Professor Capper
Weyman & Hitchcock's "Trusty"	7⅞	14	..	147	44·1	38	7·04	5·98	84	Russolene	0·69	0·82	0·69	1·12	Oil intercepted	No. 3	248	Mr. W.W. Beumo M.I.C.E.
Campbell	7⅞	12	..	218	65·3	58	5·9	4·81	80	Russolene	0·93	1·12	..	1·39	Exhaust kept open. Oil intercepted	No. 3	208	Professor Capper
Britannia	7⅞	13	250	175	47	60	8·4	6·21	74	Russolene	1·25	1·68	..	1·97	Oil variable	No. 3	213	Professor Capper
Clarke-Chapman	10½	16	..	..	..	..	..	..	..	Benzoline	..	1·25	..	1·56	Charge throttled in entering cylinder.	No. 3	..	Professor Capper
Fielding and Platt	8½	16	..	148	79	40	..	5·28	..	Russolene	..	0·90	..	1·25	Intercept oil		220	Messrs. Fielding and Platt

INDEX TO ILLUSTRATIONS.

A
	PAGE
Abel Oil Tester	207
Atkinson's Cycle Engine	20, 23
Atkinson's Differential Engine	21
Averager for Indicator Diagrams, Coffin	149
Averager for Indicator Diagrams, Goodman	146

B
Britannia Governor	233
Britannia Vaporiser	232

C
Calorimeter, Junker's	119, 121
Campbell Vaporiser	231
Capitaine Vaporiser	234
Carburator, Simplex	213
Clayton and Shuttleworth Igniter	239
Clerk-Lanchester Starter	76
Clerk Pressure Starter	75
Clerk Two-cycle Engine	83
Coffin Averager	149
Crosby Indicator	99, 100
Crossley Cylinder Section	35, 36
Crossley Double-cylinder Gas Engine	31
Crossley Tandem Gas Engine	29
Crossley Tube Igniter	32
Crossley Vaporiser	226
Crossley Weak-Spring Diagram	34
Cycles, Diagram of Gas Engine	26, 46

D
Daimler Oil Engine	240
Day Gas Engine	78
Diagrams of Combustion Experiments	198
Diagrams of Combustion, Stage	192
Diagrams of Combustion	188—191
Diagrams of Comparatives Cycles	26, 46
Diagrams of Heat and Pressure of Explosion	197
Diagrams, Indicator, from Dougill Engine	81
Diagrams, Indicator, from Fielding Gas Engine	60
Diagrams, Indicator, from Hornsby Oil Engine	224
Diagrams, Indicator, from Scavenging Engine	33, 34
Diagrams, Indicator, from Self-starters	57
Diagrams, Indicator, from Wayne Indicator	107
Diagrams, Indicator, from Wells Gas Engine	66
Diagrams showing Effects of Products of Combustion	188, 191, 192, 197, 198
Dougill Gas-engine Governor	80
Dowson Gas Plant	179, 180

INDEX TO ILLUSTRATIONS.

E
	PAGE
Electric Igniter	186
Explosion Apparatus, Experimental	183

F
Fielding Gas Engine	59
Fielding Oil Engine	237
Forward Gas Engine	68, 69

G
Gas Analysis, Hempel's Apparatus	127—131
Gas Engine, Crossley	29—36
Gas Engine, Day	78
Gas Engine, Dougill	80
Gas Engine, Fielding	59
Gas Engine, Forward	68, 69
Gas Engine, Griffin	47
Gas Engine, Kilmarnock	49, 51
Gas Engine, Koerting-Lieckfeldt	90
Gas Engine, Otto Early	9
Gas Engine, Stockport	38—44
Gas Engine, Tangye	55
Gas Engine, Wells Premier	66
Green Self-starter	73
Griffin Gas Engine	47
Griffin Oil Sprayer	221
Grover Indicator Gear	110—113

H
Hempel's Gas Analysis Apparatus	127
Hornsby Oil Engine	223

Indicator Diagrams from Crossley Engine	33, 34
Indicator Diagrams from Dougill Engine	81
Indicator Diagrams from Fielding Gas Engine	60
Indicator Diagrams from Hornsby Oil Engine	224
Indicator Diagrams from Self-starters	57
Indicator Diagrams from Wayne Indicator	107
Indicator Diagrams from Wells Gas Engine	66
Indicator Testing	97
Indicator, Crosby	99, 100
Indicator, Simplex	108
Indicator, Tabor	101—103
Indicator, Wayne	105, 106

J
Junker's Calorimeter	119—121

K
Kilmarnock Gas Engine	49, 51
Koerting-Lieckfeldt Gas Engine	95

L
Lanchester Self-starter	72

M
Moscrop Recorder Diagram	45

O

	PAGE
Oil Engines (see Vaporizers).	
Otto Early Gas Engine	9

P

Pipettes for Gas Analysis	128—131
Priestman Oil Engine	216—218

S

Samuelson Spray Maker	222
Self-starter, Clerk	75
Self-starter, Clerk-Lanchester	76
Self-starter, Green	73
Self-starter, Lanchester	72
Simplex Carburator	213
Simplex Indicator	108
Spiel Oil Engine	210—212
Stockport Gas Engine	38—44

T

Tabor Indicator	101—103
Tangye's Gas Engine	55
Tangye's Oil Engine	236
Tangye's Self-starter	56
Trusty Oil Engine	228, 229

V

Vaporiser, Britannia	232
Vaporiser, Capitaine	224
Vaporiser, Campbell	231
Vaporiser, Crossley	226
Vaporiser, Fielding	237
Vaporiser, Griffin Sprayer	221
Vaporiser, Hornsby	223
Vaporiser, Priestman	217, 218
Vaporiser, Samuelson Sprayer	222
Vaporiser, Spiel Sprayer	211
Vaporiser, Tangye	236
Vaporiser, Trusty	228, 229
Vaporiser, Wells	227

W

Wayne Indicator	105, 106
Weak Spring Indicator Diagram	34
Wells Premier Gas Engine	66
Wells Oil Engine	227

INDEX TO SUBJECT MATTER.

A

	PAGE
Abel Oil Tester	207
Absorption of Gases	126
Acme Gas Engine	81
Air, Composition of	139
Air Proportions in Explosive Mixtures	190
Air Pulsation in Gas-engine Rooms	10
Air, Weight of	139
Amsler's Planimeter	150
Analysis of Coal Gas	126, 135, 189
Analysis of Dowson Gas	182
Analysis of Petroleum	242
Appendices, Gas-engine Trial Results	203
Appendices, Products of Combustion Experiments	209
Atkinson's Differential Engine	19
Atkinson's Cycle Engine	22
Averager for Indicator Diagrams, Coffin's	149
Averager for Indicator Diagrams, Goodman's	146

B

Barber's Patent Gas Engine	2
Farnard's Patent Gas Engine	5
Barnett's Patent Gas Engine	3
Barsanti and Mattenci's Engine	3
Beau de Rochas Cycle	5
Bearings, Pressures on	70
Belt Drives	18
Benz Gas Engine	88
Brayton's Oil Engine	211
Britannia Oil Engine	232
Brown's Engine	2

C

Calorific Value Calculations	120, 245
Calorimeter, Junker's	117
Campbell Oil Engine	231
Capitaine Gas Engine	92
Capitaine Oil Engine	234
Carbon-dioxide, Weight of	140
Carbon-monoxide, Ignition Temperature of	196
Carbon, Weight of	140
Carbon, Calorific Value of	140
Charon Gas Engine	87
Circulating Tanks, Arrangement of	17
Clerk's Self-starter	75
Clerk-Lanchester Self-starter	76
Clayton and Shuttleworth's Igniter	280
Coal-gas Constituents	126, 140
Coal Gas, Analyses and other Data	135, 138, 130, 139

INDEX.

	PAGE
Coffin Averager	149
Combustion Chamber, Size of	167
Comparative Efficiencies of Engines with different Dimensions, but having the same Compression	204
Compounding Gas Engines	6
Compression, Amount of	85
Connecting Rods	174
Consumption of Gas by Engines	22, 24, 50, 54, 71, 61, 155
Consumption of Oil by Engines	247
Crank Shafts	168
Crosby Indicator	99
Crossley Gas Engine	27
Crossley Oil Engine	225
Cycles of Gas Engines	25, 26, 46
Cycle Engine, Atkinson's	22
Cylinder Proportions	163—165

D

Daimler Oil Engine	240
Daimler Gas Engine	91
Day Gas Engine	77
Differential Gas Engine	19
Dougill Governor	79
Dowson Gas Analyses	138, 182
Dowson Gas, Air Required for Combustion of	182
Dowson Gas Plant	179
Dynamometer, Absorption	93

E

Economy, Effects of Governor on	246
Effects of Products of Combustion	183—198
Efficiencies of Gas Engines	158, 204
Electric Igniter	186
Engine-room for Gas Engine	7
Engines, Gas (see Gas Engines).	
Engine Trials, Analysis of Gas	123—138
Engine Trials, Calculations for Reports	139—158
Engine Trials, Calorimetry	117
Engine Trials, Gas Measurement	117
Engine Trials, Indicating	96, 109, 144
Engine Trials, Reducing Gear	109, 114
Engine Trials, Water-jacket Measurements	115
Exhaust Pipe for Gas Engine	14
Exhaust, Temperature of	124
Explosive Mixtures, Proportions	190

F

Flashing Point	206
Flywheels, Sizes of	37, 171
Fielding's Gas Engine	58
Fielding's Oil Engine	236
Forward Gas Engine	68
Friction Brake	93
Frost in Water Jackets	89

G

Gas Analysis	126, 138, 182
Gas Bags on Mains	13
Gas, Temperature of Exhaust	124, 151 156
Gas, Exhaust, Loss of Heat	157
Gas Measurements on Trials	117
Gas Producer	176, 183
Gas Engine, Atkinson's Cycle	22
Gas Engine, Atkinson's Differential	19
Gas Engine, Barber's	2
Gas Engine, Barnard's	5

INDEX.

	PAGE
Gas Engine, Barnett's	3
Gas Engine, Barsanti	3
Gas Engine, Beau de Rochas	5
Gas Engine, Benz	89
Gas Engine, Brown's	2
Gas Engine, Capitaine	92
Gas Engine, Charon	87
Gas Engine, Crossley	27
Gas Engine, Daimler	91
Gas Engine, Day	77
Gas Engine, Design of	159
Gas Engine, Dougill	79
Gas Engine, Efficiency of	160
Gas Engine, Fielding	58
Gas Engine, Forward	68
Gas Engine, Griffin	46, 53, 82
Gas Engine, Kilmarnock	47
Gas Engine, Koerting-Lieckfeldt	89
Gas Engine, Lalbin	88
Gas Engine, Lebon	2
Gas Engine, Lenoir	87
Gas Engine, Norris	84, 85
Gas Engine, Niel	88
Gas Engine, Otto	8, 27
Gas Engine, Palatine	79
Gas Engine, Premier	61
Gas Engine, Robey	84
Gas Engine, Simplex	86
Gas Engine, Stockport	36, 37
Gas Engine Trials with Coal Gas	203
Gas Engine Trials with Dowson Gas	203
Gas Engine, Tangye	58
Gas Engine, Weights of	37
Goodman Averager	146
Governor, Dougill	79, 80
Governor, Stockport	43, 44
Governing Oil Engines	246
Grashoff's Formula	152
Griffin Gas Engine	46, 53, 82
Green's Self-starter	74
Grover's Indicator Gear	110—113

H

Heat Account of Gas Engine	158
Hempel's Gas Apparatus	126
History of the Gas Engine	1—7
Hornsby-Akroyd Oil Engine	223
Horse Power, Brake	12, 96, 92
Horse Power, Nominal	12
Horse Powers, Weights, and Overall Dimensions of Gas Engines	37
Hydrogen, Calorific Value	140
Hydrogen, Ignition Temperature	196
Hydrogen, Weight of	140

I

Igniter, Electric	186
Ignition Temperatures of Coal-gas Constituents	196
Ignition Tubes, Crossley	30—32
Ignition Tubes, Stockport	39—41
Indicator Diagrams, Averagers for	146—149
Indicator Diagrams, Calculations on	144
Indicator Diagrams, Dougill Governor	81
Indicator Diagrams, Light Loads	60
Indicator Diagrams, Mean Pressures of Oil Engines	247
Indicator Diagrams, Premier Gas Engine	66
Indicator Diagrams, Starting	57
Indicator Diagrams, Wayne Indicator	107
Indicator Diagrams, Weak-Spring	34

INDEX.

	PAGE
Indicators, Crosby	99
Indicators, Reducing Gears	100
Indicators, Simplex	108
Indicators, Tabor	101
Indicators, Testing Springs	97
Indicators, Wayne	104

J

Jacket Water, Measuring Quantity of	16, 115
Jacket Water Temperatures	116
Junker's Calorimeter	117

K

Kilmarnock Engine	47
Koerting-Lieckfeldt Engine	89

L

Lalbin Engine	88
Lanchester Starter	72
Langen Engine	7
Lead on Gas Valve	163
Lebon Engine	2
Lenoir Gas Engine	4, 87
Lenoir Oil Engine	210

M

Marsh Gas, Calorific Value	140
Marsh Gas, Determination of	135—138
Marsh Gas, Ignition Temperature	196
Marsh Gas, Weight of	140
Mean Pressures in Oil Engines	247
Mechanical Efficiencies of Gas Engines	30, 71, 156
Methods of Governing Oil Engines	247
Million	5
Moscrop Recorder Diagram	45

N

Niel's Engine	88
Nitrogen, Weight of	140
Norris Engine	84, 85

O

Oil, Analysis of	242
Oil, Boiling Points	209, 247
Oil, Calorific Value of	244
Oil, Colour of	209
Oil Engine, Brayton	211
Oil Engine, Britannia	232
Oil Engine, Campbell	231
Oil Engine, Capitaine	234
Oil Engine, Clayton and Shuttleworth's	239
Oil Engine, Consumption of Oil	247
Oil Engine, Crossley	225
Oil Engine, Daimler	240
Oil Engines, Dimensions and Consumptions of	247
Oil Engine, Economy Affected by Governor	246
Oil Engine, Fielding	247
Oil Engine, Governing	247
Oil Engine, Hornsby	228
Oil Engine, Lenoir	210
Oil Engine, Mean Pressures of Indicated Diagram	247
Oil Engine, Priestman	215
Oil Engine, Samuelson	220

	PAGE
Oil Engine, Simplex	213
Oil Engine, Spiel	211
Oil Engine, Tangye	236
Oil Engine, Testing	241
Oil Engine, Trusty	228
Oil Engine, Wells	226
Oil, Flashing Point	206
Oil, Legal Restrictions in Using	206
Oil, Products of, by Distillation	206
Oil, Specific Gravity of	209, 210, 247
Olefines, Calorific Value	146
Olefines, Ignition Temperature of	186
Olefines, Weight of	140
Otto Gas Engine	9
Otto and Langen Engine	3–7

P

Palatine Gas Engine	79
Petroleum, Constituents and Data	205, 208
Petroleum, Discovery of	205
Petroleum, Distillation of	204
Phosphorus, Casting of	132
Pinkney's Self-starter	56
Pipettes for Gas Analysis	128
Piston Pin Sizes	175
Piston Speeds	70, 161
Planimeter, Amsler's	150
Premier Gas Engine	61
Priestman Oil Engine	215
Priestman Oil Engine Trials	219, 220
Producer Gas	176
Products of Combustion	183
Products, Effects on Time of Explosion	192, 199
Proportions of Explosive Mixture	190

R

Reducing Gear for Indicators	109, 113
Revolutions, Counting	123
Robey Gas Engine	84
Rope Drive	50

S

Samuelson's Oil Engine	220
Scavenging, Advantages of	184
Scavenging, Crossley Engine	33
Scavenging, Premier	64, 65, 67
Self-starter, Clerk	75
Self-starter, Clerk-Lanchester	76
Self-starter, Crossley	32
Self-starter, Fielding	61
Self-starter, Green	73, 74
Self-starter, Stockport	39, 42
Self-starter, Tangye	54, 56
Silencers	14
Simplex Gas Engine	86
Simplex Oil Engine	213
Simplex Indicator	108
Steam v. Gas	2
Stockport Gas Engine	36, 37
Stratification	28
Street's Patent	2
Specific Gravity of Oils	208
Specific Heat by Grashoff's Formula	153
Spiel Oil Engine	211

INDEX.

T

	PAGE
Tabor Indicator	101
Tandem Engines	51, 52
Tangye's Gas Engine	53
Tangye's Oil Engine	226
Temperature of Jacket Water	116
Temperature of Ignition of Carbon-monoxide	196
Temperature of Ignition of Hydrogen	196
Temperature of Ignition of Marsh Gas	196
Temperature of Ignition of Olefines	196
Temperature of Explosions	151, 196
Temperature of Exhaust	124
Testing Gas Engines	12, 114, 203
Testing Indicators	97
Testing Oil Engines	241
Time of Explosions	163
Time Recorder	187
Timing Valve Adjustment	40
Trials of Gas Engines	92, 114, 203
Trials, Calorimeter for	117
Trials, Counting Revolutions	123
Trials, Gas Measurements	117
Trials, Jacket-water Measurement	115
Trials, Sampling Gas	123
Trials, Temperature of Exhaust	124
Trusty Oil Engine	228
Two-cycle Engines	46, 83

U

Unit of Heat	120

V

Vaporisers, Classification of	245
Vaporiser, Britannia	232
Vaporiser, Campbell	231
Vaporiser, Capitaine	234
Vaporiser, Crossley	235
Vaporiser, Fielding	237
Vaporiser, Hornsby	223
Vaporiser, Priestman	215
Vaporiser, Samuelson	220
Vaporiser, Simplex	213
Vaporiser, Spiel	261
Vaporiser, Tangye	226
Vaporiser, Trusty	228
Vaporiser, Wells	226
Velocity Through Valves	70, 168
Vibration of Gas Engines	10

W

Water Jackets	15
Water Jackets, Quantity of Water for	16
Water Jackets, General Arrangement	17
Water Formed by Combustion	245
Wayne Indicator	104
Weak-Spring Diagram	34
Wells Gas Engine	61
Wells Oil Engine	226

Printed by JOHN HEYWOOD, Excelsior Works, Manchester.

THE "CAMPBELL" GAS ENGINE

(OTTO CYCLE).

We have recently re-designed all our GAS ENGINES, and can now offer an Engine which CANNOT BE EQUALLED by any other maker.

SELF STARTERS FITTED.

SOLE MAKERS:

THE CAMPBELL GAS ENGINE CO.

LIMITED,

HALIFAX, ENGLAND.

THE "Campbell" Oil Engine.

We are the largest makers of Oil Engines in the World.   All sizes and types from 1 to 50 brake horse-power.

SOLE MAKERS:

THE CAMPBELL GAS ENGINE CO. LTD.,

Halifax, ENGLAND.

Published simultaneously in London and Manchester.

EVERY FRIDAY, PRICE TWOPENCE.

THE BEST WEEKLY JOURNAL

OF

MECHANICAL AND MOTIVE POWER ENGINEERING

WRITTEN BY PRACTICAL ENGINEERS FOR PRACTICAL ENGINEERS.

The Journal has a large staff of Contributors, of special experience in every branch of Engineering to which it is devoted, so that its readers are kept fully informed with respect to the latest improvements and most modern practice in Steam and Gas Engines, Hydraulic Engineering, Electrical Engineering, Boiler Making, Machine Tools, &c.

SUBSCRIPTION 10s. PER ANNUM

(Including Free Copy of Pocket-Book).

POST FREE TO ALL PARTS OF THE WORLD.

Foreign Remittances by International Money Order.

THE TECHNICAL PUBLISHING CO. LIMITED,

31, WHITWORTH STREET, MANCHESTER,

ENGLAND.

SEND POST CARD FOR SAMPLE COPY.

THE TECHNICAL PUBLISHING CO.'S PUBLICATIONS.
Post Free to any Part of the World.

MECHANICAL ENGINEERING MATERIALS. By EDWARD C. R. MARKS, Assoc.M.Inst.C.E., M.I.M.E. Crown 8vo, 1s. 6d., post free.

PRACTICAL NOTES ON THE CONSTRUCTION OF CRANES AND LIFTING MACHINERY. By EDWARD C. R. MARKS, Assoc.M.Inst.C.E., M.I.M.E. Crown 8vo, cloth, lettered, 2s. 6d., post free.

INJECTORS: THEIR THEORY, CONSTRUCTION AND WORKING. By W. W. F. PULLEN, Wh.Sc. Cr. 8vo, cloth, 3s. 6d., post free.

THE CENTRIFUGAL PUMP, TURBINES AND WATER MOTORS. By CHAS. H. INNES, M.A. Crown 8vo, 3s. 6d., post free.

THE NAVAL ENGINEER AND THE COMMAND OF THE SEA. By FRANCIS G. BURTON. Cr. 8vo, cloth, price 2s. 6d. net, post free.

MODERN GAS AND OIL ENGINES. Profusely illustrated. By FREDERICK GROVER, Assoc.M.Inst.C.E. Second edition, Crown 8vo, cloth, price 4s. 6d. net, post free.

THE INDICATOR AND ITS DIAGRAMS: WITH CHAPTERS ON ENGINE AND BOILER TESTING. By CHARLES DAY, Wh.Sc. Second Edition, crown 8vo, cloth, price 4s. 6d. net, post free.

PROBLEMS IN MACHINE DESIGN. For the use of Students, Draughtsmen, &c. By CHAS. H. INNES, M.A. Crown 8vo, cloth, price 3s. 6d. net, post free.

THE APPLICATION OF GRAPHIC METHODS TO THE DESIGN OF STRUCTURES. Profusely illustrated. By W. W. F. PULLEN, Wh.Sc., &c. Crown 8vo, cloth, price 6s. net, post free.

ENGINEERING ESTIMATES AND COST ACCOUNTS. By F. G. BURTON. Crown 8vo, cloth, price 3s. net, post free.

OPENING BRIDGES. By G. WILSON, M.Sc. Cr. 8vo, 2s. net, post free.

GRAPHIC METHODS OF ENGINE DESIGN. By A. H. BARKER, B.A., B.Sc., Wh.Sc., author of "Graphical Calculus," &c. Crown 8vo, cloth, price 3s. 6d. net, post free.

HEAT AND HEAT ENGINES. A Treatise on Thermo-dynamics as Practically Applied to Heat Motors. By W. C. POPPLEWELL, M.Sc. Crown 8vo, cloth, price 6s. net, post free.

MARINE ENGINEERS: THEIR QUALIFICATIONS AND DUTIES. By E. G. CONSTANTINE, Assoc.M.Inst.C.E., &c. Crown 8vo, cloth, price 5s. net, post free.

THE A B C of the DIFFERENTIAL CALCULUS. By W. D. WANSBROUGH. Crown 8vo, cloth, price 3s. net, post free.

THE MANUFACTURE OF IRON AND STEEL TUBES. By EDWARD C. R. MARKS. Crown 8vo, cloth, price 5s., post free.

TURNING LATHES. A Manual for Technical Schools and Apprentices. Edited by J. LUKIN, B.A. Demy 8vo, cloth, price 3s., post free.

SCREWS AND SCREW-MAKING. Including an account of the origin of the Whitworth's, Swiss, British Association, and American Threads, &c.; with 95 Illustrations. Demy 8vo, cloth, price 3s. post free.

THE TECHNICAL PUBLISHING CO. LIMITED,
31, Whitworth Street, Manchester, England;
JOHN HEYWOOD, London and Manchester; and all Booksellers.

www.ingramcontent.com/pod-product-compliance
Lightning Source LLC
Chambersburg PA
CBHW032139230426
43672CB00011B/2394